Typographic Legality

Edinburgh Studies in Law, Justice and the Visual
Series Editors:
Peter Goodrich, Director of Law and Humanities, Benjamin N. Cardozo School of Law, New York
Desmond Manderson, Director of the Centre for Law Arts and the Humanities, Australian National University

With an editorial board comprising leading figures in interdisciplinary approaches to visual culture, this series grapples with the burgeoning fields of optical representation, depictive practices and aesthetic critiques of law. Moving beyond narrowly textual resources, *Law, Justice and the Visual* explores the ocular, plastic, and artistic, breaking new ground in expanding the sense and sensibility of the juridical. The series warmly invites innovative scholarly contributions on topics as precise as the typography of law, and as broad as the history of images of *Justitia* or theories of retinal justice. Working with both renowned and emerging scholars from around the world, we seek to apprehend the imaginal of law, its visual discourses, and the technologies and theories that subtend the social appearances and political performances of justice, both throughout history and in our contemporary world.

Titles in the series include:

Lady Justice: An Anatomy of Allegory
Valérie Hayaert

Typographic Legality: The Source and Transmission of the Common Law
Thomas Giddens

Visit the Edinburgh Studies in Law, Justice and the Visual website at https://edinburghuniversitypress.com/series-edinburgh-studies-in-law-justice-and-the-visual

Typographic Legality

The Source and Transmission of the Common Law

Thomas Giddens

EDINBURGH
University Press

Edinburgh University Press is one of the leading university presses in the UK. Publishing new research in the arts and humanities, EUP connects people and ideas to inspire creative thinking, open new perspectives and shape the world we live in. For more information, visit www.edinburghuniversitypress.com.

Grateful acknowledgement is made to the sources listed in the List of Illustrations for permission to reproduce material previously published elsewhere. Every effort has been made to trace the copyright holders, but if any have been inadvertently overlooked, the publisher will be pleased to make the necessary arrangements at the first opportunity.

Edinburgh University Press Ltd
13 Infirmary Street, Edinburgh EH1 1LT

Typeset in Warnock
by Biblichor Ltd, Scotland
Printed and bound in the UK using 100% renewable electricity by
CPI Group (UK) Ltd

A CIP record for this book is available from the British Library

ISBN 978 1 3995 1543 6 (hardback)
ISBN 978 1 3995 1545 0 (webready PDF)
ISBN 978 1 3995 1546 7 (epub)

EU Authorised Representative:
Easy Access System Europe
Mustamäe tee 50, 10621 Tallinn, Estonia
gpsr.requests@easproject.com

FSC
www.fsc.org
MIX
Paper | Supporting responsible forestry
FSC® C013604

This book is printed using paper from
well-managed forests, recycling and
other controlled sources

'We must obey the forms'

Frank Herbert, *Dune* (London: New English Library, 1985), 562

Contents

Illustrations

Figures

Tables

Acknowledgements

This book bears my name as its author, but its generation was not a manifestation of my autonomous will and intellect – quite the opposite. It emerged over a number of years of collegial and communal thought, conversation, and support, and without the wider networks of care that characterize the critical and cultural legal research community it would not have taken form. I suppose I must take some responsibility for it, but it is radically conditioned by the input and feedback from those around me, and any intellectual content it might be taken to signify is primarily a product of the reader's own interpretive imagination. This book is a function, too, of the personal networks of care that continue to provide the undeserved support that enable me to function as an ostensibly capable adult in our strange and complex contemporary milieu, without which I would likely have given up and gone to live in a cave somewhere many years ago.

Of the critical and collegial supporters, Peter Goodrich has been an enduring source and font of critical cheerleading over the years, including with respect to various iterations, early drafts, and adjacent papers in the development of this book. Alongside Desmond Manderson, their joint editorial guidance in bringing this work to its final form has been incisive, inspiring, and invaluable. Particular thanks, both critical and amicable, to Andreas Philippopoulos-Mihalopoulos and Kieran Tranter for their generosity, energy, and care in reading and commenting on a full draft of this work. Without them it would be much impoverished. A number of friends and colleagues also read earlier drafts of individual chapters and provided supportive comments. For such critical kindness, I extend thanks to Valérie Hayaert, Robert Herian, Daniel Matthews, Ashley Pearson, Laura Peterson, Roshan de Silva-Wijeyeratne, Dominic

Smith, and Ian Williams. Apologies if I have forgotten anyone, and to those whom I have not listed. To reduce the wider pools and oceans of collegiality that buoy up this work to a list of names would be both futile and denigrating to the bonds of community, so I will not attempt it, but know that without such communities of critique and care, works such as this – not to mention other works of much higher calibre and import – would not be possible.

On a more mundane level, I am bound to acknowledge the previous publication of Chapter 2, which appeared as Thomas Giddens, 'A Roman Face on an English Body: The Typography of Plowden's *Commentaries*', *Law and Humanities* 18, no. 1 (2024): 48–72. It is reproduced here with permission, edited and updated to integrate it into the book's argument and analysis.

On a personal level, I will pick out only one name: Helen. Far from launching ships, this Helen is the beacon and lighthouse that continues to guide me to safe harbours in the storms of life.

A Note on the Form of the Text

This book is a study of the typography of the common law, of its expression as visual text. Any study of the typographic form of text, requiring as it does a refocusing on the material image and techniques of writing, must account for its own material images. Accordingly, upon departure into the body text of this volume, the intrepid reader should note the typeface in which it is set: Warnock Pro (see Figure P.1 for a sample).

Warnock Pro

A quick x-ray job to map
the King's civilized law font

Figure P.1: Warnock Pro sample, complete with topical pangram. Image credit: Thomas Giddens (reproduced with permission).

Warnock Pro was designed by Robert Slimbach for Adobe Systems Inc, the company perhaps most famous in legal contexts for PDFs. Released in 2000, Warnock Pro was commissioned by the son of John Warnock, the co-founder of Adobe, in honour of his father's 'visionary spirit' that reshaped desktop publishing and document transfer the world over.[1] The history of Adobe Systems is one of the technological reform of print, implementing tools for typographic and document design that embraced emerging digital systems but remained integrated with printed output.[2] Adobe's development, guided by the visionary spirit of Warnock, expresses a detailed and proficient care for the appearance of letters and the techniques of this appearance, and marks a pivotal shift in the history of typographic print. The techniques developed by Adobe, such as the use of mathematical curves to model lettershapes to be made visible in display systems,[3] encapsulate a central feature of both typography and law: the manner in which the ideational becomes material, practical, and usable. Typography, like law, is a question of the relationship between the abstract and the specific, and in the development of Adobe this question is navigated and rationalized within a context of digital technologies, social change, and capitalist enterprise.

In terms of its design heritage, Warnock Pro is 'eclectic'. It has angular serifs, giving the text 'a chiseled appearance' and somewhat chunky or rugged feel, especially at smaller sizes.[4] This style avoids the smooth bracketed supports of classical renaissance faces, and is associated with the lesser-known twentieth-century Mediterranean calligraphic styles of 'Latine' typography, designed in resistance to the supposedly neutral modernism of Swiss typography.[5] The lettershapes themselves are of classical roman form, following the pattern now so familiar to western readers so as not to disrupt the reading experience – but with modernist refinements to produce what is known as a 'transitional' style somewhere between the calligraphic style of humanist letters, whose shapes derive from the movement of an imagined writer's hand,[6] and a rationalized geometric order of mathematical forms.[7] In its particular blend, Warnock Pro strikes 'a balance between innovation and restraint', and between being 'logical' and 'organic', while providing 'clarity and visual tension' in its crisp details[8] produced through the precise digital consolidation of Slimbach's hand-drawn writing experiments.[9] Its sprawling family of lettersets are intended to function well across the variable rigours of today's blended digital and print environments, displaying with clean readability on screen while being robust enough in its detailed design features to remain functional even in 'less than ideal' print conditions.[10] The eclectic blend of Warnock Pro's style, and its applicability across a range of digital and print contexts, aims to reflect both the character of John Warnock and the general project of Adobe Systems. As Slimbach says, it has 'a progressive and slightly technical feel, but with warmth and humanity', looking both to the past and the future.[11]

To use Warnock Pro to set a work of critical legal theory that engages the material manifestation of the common law is in part already to express the work's central thesis: that the invisible wants to appear, but is always frustrated in that desire by the necessary images required to enter the social and material world. The eclectic heritage expressed in Warnock Pro's forms also mirrors the potted history this book encounters in its common law context, its resistance to embracing a supposedly neutral modern law, and its somewhat askant perspective. In counterpoint to this, the capitalist context of Warnock Pro's development as a commercially licensed group of letterforms, and the near-global spread of Adobe's influence on print and publishing practices, provocatively embeds in this book – itself produced within a commercially conditioned context – certain capitalist and imperial qualities shared by the common law, thereby resonating with another of the book's major themes.

While readers can form their own judgement as to the chunky robustness of the current text, the fields of letterforms they navigate as they wander through this book are not disconnected or necessarily at odds with the imagined content those letterforms might stage. Indeed, although typography is often discounted or pushed aside as mere decoration, as poet and typographer Robert Bringhurst observes, to study typography is not to indulge some frivolous distraction, but to study 'the relationships between type designs and the rest of human activity – politics, philosophy, the arts, and the history of ideas.'[12] Further to Bringhurst's list, typography also intervenes – as this book hopes to make apparent – in longstanding and emerging discourses central to questions of the common law's authoritative sources and technologies of transmission.

Notes

1. *Warnock Pro: A Multi-Faceted OpenType Family* (Adobe Systems Incorporated, 2000), 7.
2. See, for their own account of the history of Adobe, John E. Warnock and Charles Geschke, 'Founding and Growing Adobe Systems, Inc', *IEEE Annals of the History of Computing* 41, no. 3 (2019): 24–34.
3. See Warnock and Geschke, 'Founding', 28. This process is discussed in detail in Chapter 5.
4. *Warnock Pro*, 8. For details on the adjustments within Warnock Pro when used in different point sizes, see *Warnock Pro*, 10–11.
5. *Warnock Pro*, 8. On 'Latine' style, see Luc Devroye, 'La Graphie Latine' (https://luc.devroye.org/fonts-72111.html, accessed 20 June 2025). On the modernism of Swiss typography, which sought to derive letters from rational principles

rather than mere tradition, see Robin Kinross, *Modern Typography: An Essay in Critical History* (Éditions B42, 2019), 103–19.

6. See Robert Bringhurst, *The Elements of Typographic Style* (Hartley and Marks, 2002), 123.
7. See Bringhurst, *Elements,* 132.
8. *Warnock Pro,* 8.
9. *Warnock Pro,* 9.
10. *Warnock Pro,* 7.
11. *Warnock Pro,* 8.
12. Bringhurst, *Elements,* 122.

Introduction: 'font' as source and transmission

Contrary to law's general character, the sensory encounter with its sources is specific, material, and unique. The feel and smell of a law report retrieved from the library stacks; the texture of the paper, the yellowing or freshness of the pages; the residue of the type. The arrangement of the stacked and bound pages, of the visual forms that adorn them and the style and feel of their lettering. The heft of the report as an object, the sounds of paper on paper. Even digital reports have a unique ness, conditioned by the particular computer system by which a subject accesses and displays them, and the settings and preferences used. These things are specific to the held volume, the displayed text, and across the archive of the common law they are plural – each encounter distinct. Each text, whether print or digital, is a thing in itself, a material artefact encountered by a reading subject. And it is in such encounters, from this bare matter, that legal meaning is crafted.

Typographic legality describes the material expression of law as visual text. Instead of attending to the conceptual structures of law, knowledge, and reason that are traditionally the focus of legal study, to engage typographic legality requires attention to be refocused on the visual matter of the common law's texts, on the encounter with the page. Such a refocusing requires the undoing of a long-entrenched cultural conditioning to ignore a text's material conditions and form during the reading process, a conditioning particularly evident in the common law tradition where modern lawyers invariably read for what is not on the page.[1] The focus of the legal reader tends not to be on the peritextual elements of binding and margin, the smell and texture of paper or the flicker of the screen, the visual and material techniques by which a law report appears as a printed or displayed object. The common lawyer 'reads' a report not for its features as an artefact of print culture, nor as an expressive material register within a heritage of communications technologies and textual governance. Instead, they read for its words as indexes of an ostensibly rational structure of knowledge and principle, not found on the page itself but imagined or constructed from it in the reading process, conditioned by its unacknowledged materiality.

Meanwhile, reading for what is on the page – whether paper, digital, or otherwise – means accounting for the contingency and heritage of the visual forms arrayed before the reading subject and the techniques by which they appear. When common lawyers read for what is not on the page – for legal reason and authority – the material basis of this reading is not incidental or meaningless. It is by means of the techniques of the page that any imagined or ideational 'content' is constructed or accessed: the material text stages its immaterial content, and the two are unavoidably entangled. For common lawyers, the primary typographic materials of the common law's archive of decision (law reports and court transcripts) are the dominant tools by which legal principle and obligation are constructed in the imagination. While pressed into the background of the common law's typographic address, the visual matter of a judicial text nevertheless carries the baggage of its accumulated associations and possible meanings into both the lawyers' interpretive practice and – more profoundly – the institution's jurisdictional claim to authority. It is precisely by means of typography, as the central element in the aesthetic features that make up a material law report, that the common law first becomes visible and tangible. It is thus by means of typography, as a jurisdictional technology, that the common law performatively claims its authority and is able to have governmental effects in the material and social world.

Typographic legality describes and enables critique of this radical theatre of power. By attending to the visual text as a primary expression of authority, as the study in this book aims to do, a window is opened to the complex play of forces and influences at work in the common law's media technologies and that become encoded and expressed in the very form and matter by which the common law appears.

On the meanings of 'font'

The project of this book is to stage an introductory encounter with the typographic dimensions of common law texts. To frame this encounter, the concept of 'font' is centrally important. Font is a term commonly associated with the typography of a written document. When using a word processor, for example, a writer-user may select their preferred font from a list of available styles: Times New Roman, Calibri, Comic Sans, to name but a few.[2] Font, however, is a term that encompasses not only the visual style of letterforms, but also the more general idea of a source or origin. According to the Oxford English Dictionary (OED), 'font' has two sets of meanings:

font, *n.1*

1. 'A receptacle in a church for the water used in baptism'
2. 'A spring, fountain, source . . . a source or origin providing a constant or abundant supply of something'
3. 'A receptacle or basin for holy water, esp. at a church entrance'
4. 'The reservoir for oil in an oil lamp'

font, *n.2*

1. 'Cast iron'; 'The action or process of casting or founding'; 'a crucible or foundry'
2. 'a set of [cast metal] type of a particular size, weight, and style (such as roman, italic, bold, etc.), forming part of a type family'; 'a [digital] typeface or type family (such as Times, Helvetica, etc.)'[3]

Font is both origin (*n.1*, from Latin *fons* or *font*), and foundry (*n.2*, from Latin *fondre* or *fundere*).[4] These two lines of meaning map onto questions of 'source' (as origin) and 'transmission' (as the crafting of meaningful or remediating artefacts)[5] that map onto enduring questions in common law understanding.

In the history of legal thought, 'the first question to be posed of the law is that of its origins.'[6] This question leads, ultimately, to the mythology of a 'sacred mouth that speaks the law and in turn of a speech that embodies or incarnates the holy will.'[7] Figuratively, the distinction between mouth and speech – between the origin of law that precedes the text, and the archived text as the material source of legal meaning and truth that remains available – maps onto the distinction between the two meanings of 'font': as source and transmission. Such a connection may, on its face, seem merely fortuitous for a study that purports to engage with the typographic forms of the common law. Yet there are meaningful analytical connections to be examined between the 'font' of common law texts, understood as their techniques of visual form and arrangement that are rarely seen to be significant, and the 'font' of the common law itself, understood in terms of its status as an authoritative source that has animated centuries of jurisprudential thought.

When engaging with common law sources, Peter Goodrich warns against ignoring 'the imagery in which the law is clothed . . . in favour of some notion of its rational content'.[8] One effect of such a warning, if taken seriously, is to shift attention from the ideational or conceptual structure of principle and obligation to the appearance and manifestation of legal texts as material and cultural artefacts. Refocusing attention in this way, common law texts are seen to have both authoritative and typographic dimensions, both 'content' and 'form', with the typographic aspects demanding a methodological attunement in order to be read.[9] Common law texts both house or transmit the law, and are materialized as words printed on paper or displayed on screen. The texts of judgments, merely because they are taken to have authoritative dimensions, are not immune from the effects of their typographic form, and this form is not simply self-evident but requires analytical engagement with appropriate tools – namely those of typographic discourse and design (while this text seeks to make these aspects clear for the reader as its analysis unfolds, Appendix 1 provides an introductory overview of typographic anatomy and terminology and further reading). Legal analysis, however, tends to be concerned exclusively with the authoritative, and at best relegates the typographic (if it is recognized at all) to being only a question of practical legibility.[10] The question of what is at stake in the typography of the law in general, or of the common law specifically, is one that is rarely asked, and (beyond legibility) even more rarely answered.

The common law's letterforms and typographic designs are often dismissed as neutral containers for law's authoritative substance or its presumed 'content', or as practical tools for legal communication.[11] Yet, as Bland notes in general, typography is 'the point of confluence where the constructions of meaning' take place.[12] Printed form has also had a number of practical effects in the evolution of the common law, including in the development of precedent and the consolidation of the identity of the legal profession by facilitating its movement away from the supposed vagaries of oral tradition.[13] Not only is legal substance contingent upon and potentially interchangeable with its written sources and the material forms of type that constitute them, but common law letterforms themselves play a significant visual role in the articulation of legal meaning and authority beyond mere legibility. The significance of typographic form for the material distribution of state authority is so much the case that Louis XIV commissioned a font of his own, a bespoke set of roman letterforms – the *romain du roi* – exclusively for official use.[14]

The common law is also caught between two sets of authorizing narratives: one concerned with a flowing source to be drawn upon to authorize judgments, the other with the concrete and stabilized transmission of those judgments as authorized pronouncements. The authority of decision is generally understood to be found in the precedent origins of the common law which judicial decisions embody and from which they are derived,[15] or in the processes of reasoning that construct a particular ideational form of judgment taken to be authoritative.[16] A question of source is embodied in these claims: legal authority is found in, and invoked from, its source that flows from time immemorial, the divine, the sovereign, or the objective structures of reason. Resonances of these can be seen in the various references in the OED's rendering of font *n.1* (*fons*), which invoke metaphors of liquidity to indicate sources in the divine (the holder of baptismal or holy water), the secular (the oil lamp as a light of reason), and the generic idea of a source (the fountain or spring).

Alternatively, common law authority is found in its transmission: in the set, written, or otherwise concrete correctness of official processes and their resulting records. Resonances of this are found in the forging practices and outputs described by font *n.2* (*fundere*) that invoke not metaphors of the fluid, but of the setting or freezing of liquid into solid form. The specifically typographic forms of legal decisions – as law reports and court transcripts, which are drawn upon as 'sources' in future processes of legal founding – manifest centrally in the OED's meaning of font *n.2(2),* as letterforms cast in metal[17] or digital data. This meaning of 'font' points to the textual appearance of court transcripts and law reports, the letterforms utilized in the visual or material recording and dissemination of the law: to the literal 'setting out' of principles and doctrine.[18] If the common law is forged in the crucible of the judicial process, what is cast in the sense of a practically citable source is the typeset letters of a transcript or law report, whose face is made visible when the forms of the font are pressed onto the page in the printing process or displayed on screen. The interpretive, rational, and rhetorical processes of decision-making result not only in an (authoritative) decision, but also a (typographic) record or remediation of that decision as the trace left by the cast forms of the font.

Reading for font thus enables a dual concern with both the unformed 'content' and the formed 'matter' of legal texts, as typographic artefacts that stage or enable access to law's rational content or its imagined or absent source. And this duality is what is encompassed by the term 'typographic legality', which describes the material expression of law as text. Entering this book's study through the framing of 'font' foregrounds its jurisprudence to be one concerned not only with the question of the source of common law authority, nor just with the 'content' of legal reasoning, nor merely the procedures of judgment as part of the tradition's authorizing practices – but with the entangled material-discursive artefacts or cultural techniques of the common law: the frozen transmission of its flowing source of authority.

This can be emblematized in the historical practice of using wax seals as symbols of authority. As Dorsett and McVeigh note, a 'seal was an impression made into melted red wax . . . [and functioned as] a mode of authorisation.'[19] Encoded in this is a material performance of authority in terms of font, as a theatrical play of source and transmission. The seal is set wax: the frozen shape of the seal replaces its preceding formless form. The authority that the seal expresses is crystallized, made certain, as the wax is melted and fused into the form of the seal. As a material performance, it stages its own derivation from a formless and potential power that exists prior to its solid appearance, and that it cancels and replaces as it is set.[20] As in the forge, where molten metal as the formless source is set into pieces of type used to stage the presence of the common law, the wax seal is a technique of jurisdiction that stages evidence of an authorized presence. Typography follows the same theatrical trajectory and performance: the common law's formless form is staged as present by the typographic shapes left behind on the page by the forged forms of the font.

In terms of the visual technologies of text, the advent specifically of typography – rather than the broader and older practice of writing in general – similarly embodies the setting of power in matter. Ancient writing practices did not include typographic techniques, such as spaces between words or standardized visual punctuation systems. Instead, written text flowed as a continuous string of hand-written letters as a *scriptio continua* which demanded expertise on the part of the reader to decipher as a score for oral reading.[21] Punctuation existed only as bespoke notation to assist inexperienced readers in their oral performance of the text.[22] Only later did word spacing and a 'complex of graphic conventions'[23] emerge to stabilize the grammatical form of written text as it moved towards being 'an independent manifestation of language' in its own right.[24] Eventually, such conventions became further stabilized in their evolution into the typographic forms of the printing press,[25] forged in the crucible of the type foundry. From its source in the ancient flow of continuous script, as much as from molten metal, was set a structured and increasingly standardized visual form that, in certain contexts, is taken to transmit the common law's authorized presence.

Recognizing the 'font' of the law raises explicit questions of the authorized presence of the law in text. The decision and its record are not preexisting or objective 'sources' to be cited and deployed in argument, but are the outputs of legal craft whose forged quality is paradoxically denied. Louis XIV's *romain du roi*, for example, was the king's font, and was by royal decree forbidden from counterfeit:[26] although printed letters at the time were forged from metal, forged letters were forbidden. The source of legitimate authority in the sovereign could not be forged in unsanctioned letters, but only in those that were not forged – but that existed somehow as pre-existing manifestations of sovereign will. This is a proscription that moves between different understandings of the term 'font', indicating that the signs of common law texts carry with them the question of their official quality as genuine rather than counterfeit copies of the law, or of the suppressed nature of their origin in a foundry or process of crafting. To speak of legal craft is thus to foreground the contingency of law and its claim to authority:

> The language of craft and crafting has always had an uneasy relationship to law. It clearly relates to the practice or activity of the making and shaping of objects of various kinds. When we talk of craft in law, the language of craft might be viewed in terms of the creation and figuration of (giving form or shape to) lawful relations . . . in the institutional version of lawful relations the figuration work of technologies points to the ways in which persons, places and events are bound to the body of law.[27]

It is by means of the crafted forms of judgments that lawful relations are established and administered, and that communities are bound to law. It appears, as the epigraph to this volume asserts, that one 'must obey the forms.'[28] Yet in attending to these forms, as this study hopefully shows, it is evident that the legal encounter involves a contingent jurisdictional performance of authority that, in the craft of its form of address, seeks to bind a presumed audience of subjects to the common law's institutional presence.

To study the font of the common law is not to indulge in the study of some irrelevant or frivolous aspect of documentary design, as if the medium were separate from the message or functioned only to somehow provide unmediated access to legal concepts, but to recognize the typographic aspects of common law authority. The medium of the common law, as Marshall McLuhan argues of media in general, 'is not a bodiless milieu but a *substance* for the transmission of force, power and energy.'[29] Where the broad geography of media shapes and conditions perception and knowledge ('categories of understanding . . . [are] structures imposed on the mind by the technological environment'),[30] typographic legality describes the entangled textual and discursive conditions of common law authority. The medium of the common law is its message: it is the expression of its authority. Framed in terms of font, the medium of the common law text expresses the divine or secular sources of legal authority as bound up with the material sources of the law itself: it is the theatre of conceptual and material processes by which those sources are produced and their presence circulated.

The common law springs forth from a trinity of fonts. From the font of authority (be it divine or secular, rational or customary), it is established through the font of the judicial process, to finally be recorded and stored via the technologies of typographic fonts. These records in turn become distributed as fonts of law, from or through which future decisions wrought within the foundry of the courts may draw authority, using them as resources to craft the law anew. To read the law is not simply to derive legal substance from the matter of the page, but to search for the source of law itself as an entangled instance of matter-discourse. In the early days of legal print, Edward Coke tellingly notes that, when the subject encounters the printed reports of common law decisions, these texts enable them to '*petere fontes*':[31] the legal reader must work with the typographic edifice of the law 'to seek out sources'.[32] The legal reader looks at and for the *fons* – the font – of the common law, as and through the written forms – the fonts (*fundere*) – of the archive.

This book's introductory study of common law typography embodies this impetus, but reads the font of the common law not merely as a means of constructing an imaginary order of principle and norm, as Coke prioritized, but as a cultural technology for the governance of society whose entangled materiality has meaningful baggage for which lawyers and jurisprudes should account. The matter of common law texts is not independent from its discourse; one cannot be thought without the other. There can be no speech without a mouth and, if law is to function, no mouth without manifested speech. In this study, the entangled relationship between source and transmission is understood primarily as one of staging: authoritative legal discourse is staged by, and is thus entangled with, the material images of its typography.[33] And, moreover, the style, details, and histories of meaning attached to these material images matter.

If the first question asked of the law is that of its origin, and while any origin is predominantly fictional, the idea of it invokes a concomitant question of actual transmission. If law comes from somewhere else, some practically inaccessible elsewhere, it needs to be relayed wherever it is to be witnessed or to have effects. The object of this study is to show how the origin of law is staged in the crafting of its material sources. It is in the typographic forms of the common law that the authority of law is performed, as a technology of jurisdiction, as a cultural technique, as an aesthetic practice. This performance is understood not as a representative endeavour to make present something pre-established, but as an expression of legality in its own right. Law does not come from somewhere else – it is in encountering the very matter and form of the common law's texts that legality is found, and that the myth of its absent and authorizing origin is crafted. As an introductory device, 'font' facilitates engagement with what is at stake in common law typography, moving across the visual matter of common law texts as a source or relay of meanings, and as a conceptual register for the general tensions between the source and transmission, the origin and relay, of the common law and its legitimate authority.

A map of the work

This book has five substantive chapters, the first of which provides the groundwork for the case studies undertaken in the following four. The overarching structure is historical: the analyses move from the first printed law report in the sixteenth century, via the industrial contexts of mass-produced law reports in the nineteenth century and the imperialism embedded in twentieth and twenty-first century court transcripts, to the vanishing faces of the common law's digital archive. Underpinning these case studies is a concern with typographic appearance as a theatre of the archive that stages the common law's authority as a technology of jurisdiction. The five chapters move through subsequent processes of typographic appearance. After setting the stage for the law's appearance in Chapter 1, 'Staging the law', the potted history moves through printing, copying, delivering, and finally displaying the law. Chapter 1 articulates the underpinning structure through which common law typography is understood, after which the law emerges in print, is duplicated on a mass scale in the press, arrives with its presumed audience of distributed subjects and binds them in an imperial community, before being remediated in the digital archive for display on screen. Across its trajectory, what the current text intends to stage for its presumed reader is an understanding of the complex interactions between the idea of the common law's source and the matter of its transmission, indicated by the term *Typographic Legality*.

Chapter 1, 'Staging the law: the theatre of the archive', engages the material distribution of law in text as a technique of jurisdiction that stages law's claim to its own authority. Jurisdiction is the moment law appears or is spoken as law. To attend to the common law's typography is to attend to its jurisdictional performance of veridiction by means of its archived materials and records. It is in or through the typographic matter consigned to the common law's archive that its lost source or origin is staged. The theatre of the archive is the play of sources that generates the authorized presence of the common law in text. Through the exemplary case studies undertaken in the following chapters, it is the manner in which the staging of the common law's authority takes place that is focused upon, demonstrating how the visual, material, and aesthetic qualities of the typeset texts of judgment complicate, augment, or reveal unacknowledged features of the institutional form of the common law.

Embarking on our case study journey, Chapter 2, 'Printing the law: A Roman face on an English body', examines the typographic details of the first modern printed law report: Plowden's *Commentaries*, first set in typographic images in 1571. While statutes had started to be printed earlier, this took place under a different authority: the licence to print statutes was granted independently from that to print common law reports and commentaries. Within this wider shift towards a printed law, and embedded in the wider contexts of printing history and conventions, Plowden renders the first printed judgment of the common law in a humanist, roman typeface. This appearance is understood through a complex of tensions the chapter encodes as 'romanizing'. The romanizing of the law in Plowden challenges the traditional model of common law authority as deriving from time immemorial by not only codifying the unwritten law in text, in a manner akin to Roman law, but by doing so using a humanist roman font that embeds the values of scholarly citizenship associated with the renaissance into this primordial performance of common law authority. At the same time, as a report on a law or a decision from elsewhere, Plowden's text remains at a distance from the law it instantiates and preserves its unwritten quality and customary source of authority. It is a roman face – codified, readable – on an unwritten body of English principle that supports it – accessible only through the cloistered proficiency of the legal profession.

This chapter thus shows that, in this opening imprint, the typographic dimension of the common law meaningfully connects with and contributes to enduring questions about the authority and status of the common law's written texts.

Next, we jump to the industrial wake of the Enlightenment. The printing press, so new when Plowden appeared, is now widespread and steam-powered, churning out huge amounts of text and, in the context of the common law, smothering the unwritten law in a mass of typography. In this context, Chapter 3, 'Copying the law: the romance of empire', examines the process of standardization that led to the establishment of Incorporated Council of Law Reporting (ICLR) in England and Wales. Preoccupied with the question of authentic encounters with the common law, this project resulted in a single, authorized set of law reports that replaced the divergent and variable market of judicial texts that had emerged by the turn of the nineteenth century. Examining the typographic quality of this project, however, as the mass production of material images of a text, reveals it to be a failure. In each strike of the press, a unique media object is produced, repeatedly undercutting the authorized quality of the ICLR's aspiration to have a single authentic report of each case by duplicating each report across the British Empire. At the colonial frontier, where there are too many laws, the case of *Cooper v Stuart* asserts that the common law is the only law available. Yet in its romantic typography is expressed the romantic media problem of authentic encounter in a context of technologized reproduction, and in the uniqueness of each of its copies it undercuts its own claim to unitary authority. From the industrial quest for natural resources from beyond the frontier in *Cooper*'s substance of claim, to the industrial edifice of steam-powered printing presses, to the medial display of a statuesque text in a romantic font, to the colonial suppression of pluralism, to the ICLR's failed standardization of common law sources, all of which is encoded in the infamous typographic artefact 'practically unoccupied' – judicial typography is again seen to have important legal interactions beyond its legibility.

Chapter 4, 'Delivering the law: all roads lead to Times New Roman', looks at contemporary court transcripts as the primary typographic moment that modern judgments are delivered to the legal and wider community – and are indubitably delivered dressed in 12 point, Times

New Roman. Typography is always a question of rhetoric and use: one must design the appropriate form for each particular text. In many ways, Times New Roman is a perfect font for the common law: it invokes the tradition of typographic design as a historical pastiche, while rationalizing letterforms and aspiring to the spread and inculcation of modern civilization, all crafted within a material heritage of imperial capitalism. As a rationalist, patriarchal, imperial, and capitalist typeface, it resonates powerfully with dominant features of the common law tradition. No wonder, then, that the Court of Appeal (in the case of *Baigent v Random House*), the Supreme Court (in reverting their transcripts to Times New Roman), and the wider conventions of court transcripts in England and Wales, all adhere to a clear normative convention that the words of judgment appear first and foremost – before remediation via law reports or online databases – in 12 point, Times New Roman.

Chapter 5, 'Displaying the law: apparitions on the screen', turns to consider what is probably the most dominant way that common law texts are encountered in the current context: digital typography. In online databases such as WestLaw and Lexis, in web pages, or in downloaded Word documents and PDFs – this is how the common law increasingly appears and is encountered by its anticipated subjects. In such a medial environment, the specific form of a text becomes mutable, changeable, radically contingent on the operating system, software, and font data available, and on a particular user's hardware set-up and preferences. It is thus to the underlying material conditions of appearance that this chapter attends, examining the structure of font files and the processes of display, whereby font data is mathematically modelled before being reduced to contingent material appearance in the very moment of display. Digital display, however, requires the constant refreshing of the screen – the constant vanishing and redrawing of the staged presence of the common law. The common law's digital texts are thus read as vanishing signs, fleeting apparitions on the screen that, read as a jurisdictional performance, constitute a rapidly repeated gesture to the absent or invisible source the common law's typographic appearance seeks to make manifest.

Ultimately, as becomes most apparent in Chapter 5, what this book's study of typographic legality enables the reader to witness is the common law's impossible desire to appear unfettered by the contingency of a medium. In the constant repetitions of textual appearance, whose speed is increasing from the slowness of the handpress to the refresh rate of a computer display, is expressed a performative desire not only that the law appear, and appear in a particular visual and material manner, complete with meaningful baggage authorized by its deployment in the archive of precedential decision, but also that it disappear and permit the law's formless form to proceed unhindered. An impossible dream that is constantly overwritten by the material images of the common law's typography.

Typographic legality thus expresses the law's frustrated desire to manifest authority. Attending to the distributed matter of the common law's appearance, a performance is witnessed. Not a performance of substantive argument, of principle and doctrine, or of good reasons why the common law should be taken to be authoritative. But a performance of the way in which law is spoken in images – as jurisdiction, as a staging of authority. A staging that repeatedly seeks to make the invisible authority of law present, by a plurality of means across a plurality of times, in each instance necessarily rendering it contingent and fallible as mere crafted matter. In the diverse theatrical instances of the archive, where the play of transmissions seeks to manifest the common law's authorizing source, the meaningful baggage of the common law's typographic forms rides along with the ideational meanings of the law upon which legal readers tend to place their exclusive attention. As the study in this book seeks to demonstrate, these forms are not incidental: the typography of the common law carries untold meanings into its reading, study, and practice.

To read the law critically requires us to care not only for the interpretive possibilities of the common law, but also for its entanglement with its forms of appearance and the wider meanings and forces that study of those forms enables us to recognize as present in law. As we navigate the archive, with its vast network of inherited forms, its exclusive language and techniques, it matters what form the law takes. Typographic legality comes complete with its own meanings, its own hidden ideologies, unspoken assumptions, and unconscious influences. The heritage of any typographic device, by which focus is placed on the rational order of modern law, is unavoidably embedded in its form of address to its presumed subject. The quality of the community a text enables us to imagine is conditioned not only by the ideational discourse it is taken to stage, but also by the quality of its performance that is crafted not as a neutral container of meaning, not as a transparent tool for the seamless transmission of its source – but as contingent and entangled matter that is a core element in the affective techniques of power.

Notes

1. Peter Goodrich, *Judicial Uses of Images: Vision in Decision* (Oxford University Press, 2023), 128.
2. Technically, 'font' (or, more traditionally, 'fount') refers to the cast pieces of type, while 'face' or 'typeface' refers to the appearance or shape of the letterforms, e.g. on a page. In digital usage, these become conflated as the distinction between the 'font' file (which contains the data that can enable the display of a given set of lettershapes) and the 'face' used in a particular document seems to break down: users commonly select a 'font' in their word processor, for example, but technically are selecting the underlying 'font' data which then conditions the apparent 'face' of their specific document. Practices and technologies of digital typography are engaged in more detail in Chapter 5.
3. Definitions from the Oxford English Dictionary.
4. While less detailed, the *Chambers Dictionary of Etymology* concurs with these two lines of meaning: as 1. 'fountain, spring' (*fons*) and 2. 'casting' (*fondre*).
5. Tracing its etymologies, font *n.1* derives from the Latin *font* or *fons*, meaning spring, well, or source, and from the French *funt* or *font*, referring to the religious font as a source of holy water, while font *n.2* derives from the Latin *fondre* or *fundere*, meaning melt or fuse. In the first sense (*n.1*), 'font' encapsulates both natural and manufactured sources. In the second sense (*n.2*), 'font' refers to the processes and locations of casting metal, to the cast metal itself, and also to the casting of metallic letterforms in the process of mechanical print, the formed letters themselves, and digital versions of these processes and forms. In these divergent etymologies we find our two notions: first, the concept of an origin from which something might emerge or flow (*n.1*), and second, an understanding of the material production or rendering of an object or form (*n.2*); 'font' refers both to an origin and to a process of manifestation, to both 'source' and 'transmission'.
6. Peter Goodrich, *Languages of Law: From Logics of Memory to Nomadic Masks* (Weidenfeld and Nicolson, 1990), 270.
7. Goodrich, *Languages of Law*, 271.
8. Goodrich, *Languages of Law*, 271.
9. On the methodological attunement demanded by attending to law as an encounter with cultural artefacts, see Thomas Giddens et al., 'Cultural Legal Studies: Methodologies of Reflexive Attunement', in *The Routledge Handbook of Cultural Legal Studies*, ed. Karen Crawley et al. (Routledge, 2024).
10. Matthew Butterick provides the leading guide on appropriate and effective typographic practice for those working in law: see Matthew Butterick, *Typography for Lawyers*, 2nd ed. (2018), https://typographyforlawyers.com/. See,

more pithily, Athelstane Aamodt, 'Legal Typeface: The Letter of the Law', *New Law Journal* 166, no. 7703 (2016): 22. The other way law engages with typography, of course, is as an object of regulation: see Benjamin Goh, 'Two Ways of Looking at a Printed Book', *Modern Law Review* 85, no. 3 (2022): 697–725.

11. See, for example, Derek H. Kiernan-Johnson, 'Telling Through Type: Typography and Narrative in Legal Briefs', *Journal of the Association of Legal Writing Directors* 7 (2010): 87–122. Peter Goodrich goes as far as detecting 'an unease' with any consideration of visual form in legal argumentation: see Peter Goodrich, 'The Emblem Book and Common Law', in *The Oxford Handbook of English Law and Literature, 1500–1700*, ed. Lorna Hutson (Oxford University Press, 2017), 144–45.
12. Mark Bland, 'The Appearance of the Text in Early Modern England', *Text* 11 (1998): 127.
13. See Richard J. Ross, 'The Commoning of the Common Law: The Renaissance Debate over Printing English Law, 1520–1640', *University of Pennsylvania Law Review* 146, no. 2 (1998): 325–26. For a general evaluation of the effects of the printing press on legal culture, see David Harvey, *The Law Emprynted and Englysshed: The Printing Press as an Agent of Change in Law and Legal Culture 1475–1642* (Hart, 2017).
14. See Stanley Morison, *Type Designs of the Past and Present* (The Fleuron, 1926), 33–36.
15. The genealogy of decision from 'time immemorial' is the traditional myth of common law authority. See, for example, Shaunnagh Dorsett, '"Since Time Immemorial": A Story of Common Law Jurisdiction, Native Title and the Case of Tanistry', *Melbourne University Law Review* 26 (2002): 32–59. Another common source is in the divine: see, for an exemplary genealogy of legal images from an ultimate divine source, Peter Goodrich, 'Specters of Law: Why the History of the Legal Spectacle Has Not Been Written', *UC Irvine Law Review* 1 (2011): 773–812.
16. Extended formalism is a key example, in which particular procedures of rational deliberation and construction are taken to authorize a judge's decision, independently from its content as derived from a traditional or divine source. See, for example, Neil MacCormick, *Rhetoric and the Rule of Law: A Theory of Legal Reasoning* (Oxford University Press, 2005).
17. Letterforms are not cast in iron, as the OED might imply, but more commonly an alloy of tin, copper, antimony, and other metals. For a detailed account of the technicalities of early type, see Harry Carter, *A View of Early Typography up to about 1600* (Hyphen Press, 2002), 5–22. For a fuller contextual discussion of the development of type technologies in Europe, see Lucien Febvre and Henri-Jean Martin, *The Coming of the Book* (Verso, 1997), 45–76. As they note, even by the eighteenth century type foundries were still experimenting with different alloys to find the most suitable mix: Febvre and Martin, *Coming of the Book*, 58.
18. The common phrase 'set out', as in e.g. 'setting out the principle' or 'setting out the regulatory framework', is itself a typographic term, evoking what Rachel Stenner calls the 'typographic imaginary'. This literary device uses the language

of print technologies (including, e.g. the spatial arrangement or 'setting' of words) as resources within a text's reflection on its own media status. See Rachel Stenner, *The Typographic Imaginary in Early Modern English Literature* (Routledge, 2019). For more on the topographic imaginary of legal judgment, see Thomas Giddens, 'Sentences Matter: Law and the Typographic Imaginary', *CounterText* 11, no 1 (2025): 94–113.

19. Shaunnagh Dorsett and Shaun McVeigh, *Jurisdiction* (Routledge, 2012), 34.
20. See Cornelia Vismann, 'Cancels: On the Making of Law in Chanceries', *Law and Critique* 7, no. 2 (1996): 131–52. We engage this more fully in Chapter 5.
21. See M. B. Parkes, *Pause and Effect: An Introduction to the History of Punctuation in the West* (Routledge, 2016), 9–12.
22. Parkes, *Pause and Effect*, 12–13.
23. Parkes, *Pause and Effect*, 23.
24. Parkes, *Pause and Effect*, 24. On the critical divorce of spoken 'language' from typographic 'text', note Ellen Lupton, 'A Post-Mortem on Deconstruction?', in *Texts on Type: Critical Writings on Typography*, ed. Steven Heller and Philip B. Meggs (Allworth, 2001), 46.
25. See Parkes, *Pause and Effect*, 50–61.
26. Morison, *Type Designs*, 36.
27. Dorsett and McVeigh, *Jurisdiction*, 56.
28. Frank Herbert, *Dune* (New English Library, 1985), 562.
29. Michael MacDonald, 'Empire and Communication: The Media Wars of Marshall McLuhan', *Media, Culture and Society* 28, no 4 (2006): 508.
30. MacDonald, 'Empire and Communication', 508.
31. Coke, quoted in Richard Helgerson, *Forms of Nationhood: The Elizabethan Writing of England* (University of Chicago Press, 1992), 83–84.
32. This is Helgerson's translation: see Helgerson, *Forms of Nationhood*, 84.
33. On the new materialist entanglements of judicial typography, see Giddens, 'Sentences Matter'.

Chapter 1

Staging the law: the theatre of the archive

Introduction

The interpretation of legal texts typically involves a literal reading for conceptual content. When lawyers read, the typography of the text and its attendant heritage, meanings, ideologies, and techniques, are not accounted for. The typographic style and meanings of the legal page – alongside the broader material aesthetics of paper and binding – are suppressed, ignored, or overlooked. While such aspects are presumed to be irrelevant to the substance of legal meaning imagined to be transmitted by the words and letters, it is precisely by means of typographic images that the making of legal meaning is made possible. The typographic page is a dominant material technique by which the idea of law is performed as present, yet it remains in the background of legal study and perception. If we take the point that the 'immateriality of law is greatly exaggerated',[1] while lawyers tend to read for the abstract or conceptual structures or 'content' of legal texts it is evident this content nevertheless remains contingent on the bare materiality of the page that stages the presumed existence of law and its authoritative presence. Accordingly, the study in this book shifts focus from the ideational content of the law to its material pages, and its typographic forms in particular, as central features of these pages. Addressing the explicitly visual quality of the written common law radically shifts the quality of legal reading, engaging typographic legality as the material expression of law as visual text. This opening chapter refocuses attention on the matter of the legal page – on typographic legality – and constructs an understanding of it as a technique of jurisdiction.

Refocusing on the common law's typographic form, we are no longer seeking only to account for reasonable or divergent interpretations of the law's rational 'content', structure, or imaginary, or their potential effects. Instead, the study of typographic legality seeks to encounter the specific materiality of law's articulation as a practice of power, its aesthetic appearance, visual heritage, techniques of meaning-making, and claim to authority – as performed on the very pages of the primary sources of the common law. While a similar exercise could be undertaken in relation to statute law, with its particular histories and jurisdictional claims, the scope of this book's analysis remains focused specifically on texts of judgment as central to the material unfolding and practice of the common law. In doing so, it reconfigures common law jurisprudence to include what is typically left in the background and ignored or overlooked as irrelevant to legal understanding and judgment. Through the study of typographic legality in the common law context, this book seeks to demonstrate that such background features are, in fact, of real importance for the study and practice of the common law.

Traversing the dual meanings of 'font', as both origin and foundry, looking at the page as a visual artefact reveals that the source of the common law is not self-evidently present, but must be staged by the contingent medium of its transmission that unavoidably comes with its own particular baggage. The printed texts of law reports are not sources, but material relays of a lost or mythical source for a legal tradition that grounds its authority in its genealogy from time immemorial. It is in the theatre of the archive that the mythical 'source' of the common law is staged, and staged in particular by the typographic techniques and style that constitute the pages of the common law's records of decision. Attending to these images encounters the material encoding of a range of forces and ideological tensions that have shaped, and continue to shape, the common law's expression.

The analysis of this chapter unfolds across five sections. The first section ('Reading judicial typography') highlights the backgrounded quality of typographic legality and reorients legal reading towards the visual dimension of the common law archive. A framework is then developed for reading judicial typography within the broad jurisdictional practices by which law stages its authoritative presence ('Staging authority'). This performative staging is then extended to encompass the continuum of legal expressions that includes both the media of the institution and the device of the legal person, such that the legal subject, entangled with legal media, is both the audience and the performer of legal authority ('Performance and community'). From here, the register of cultural techniques is added, and typography recognized as a technique of legal media as much as a technique of 'speaking law' as jurisdiction ('Typographic techniques'). The final section ('Staging the source') then turns explicitly to the archive, as the repository of traces that, through its predominantly typographic techniques, stages the presence of the common law's lost origin. The movement of this chapter sets the groundwork for the subsequent chapters of this book's study, which substantiate the concept of typographic legality through analysis of particular examples from the media history of the common law.

Reading judicial typography

Typographic legality does not attract much critical attention. As Dorsett and McVeigh note, we 'do not treat material representations as having legal significance'.[2] Studies exist of the wider staging or aesthetic envelope that surrounds the primary texts of law,[3] and others of the literary or poetic quality of the content of legal texts,[4] but the visual form of the texts themselves are generally not attended to in detail as typographic artefacts. Peter Goodrich's recent examination of visual images found in the archive of judicial decisions[5] comes close, however, and is worthy of some extended consideration. But despite potentially engaging some aspects of typographic legality, Goodrich does not engage with the design, heritage, meanings, layout, and so forth, of the common law's typographic forms per se, relying heavily on a seemingly naturalized distinction between figurative and typographic images commonly found in western law.

Goodrich's work argues that judicial images reveal an unconscious ground of decision, uncontrolled by the conscious techniques of law's linear reason that lacks proficiency in the use and interpretation of the visual.[6] While judicial images signal the organization of the conceptual or imagined forms of judgment, which lawyers might read from the surfaces of the common law's pages and screens, they do not merely reveal rational content, but unlock latent desires that spin out beyond a court's reasoned arguments. These unconscious desires are the unspoken ground of decision, yet remain insufficiently examined or understood and thus, says Goodrich, have free reign and unaccountable influence. Unless controlled by proficiency – the 'methods of curation, critical analysis, and careful viewing' demanded by the image and its expansion of potential meanings[7] – the image 'introduces and opens legal reason . . . to the danger of unacknowledged affect, the desires, moods, [and] untutored reflections' of judicial fantasy.[8] But written text is also a visual phenomenon, and so Goodrich's study remains incomplete: the typographic images found in judgments should also be understood, if we follow his method, to reveal these unconscious features of common law decisions. Common law typography requires proficient study to account for its otherwise uncontrolled effects.

But we should not be too dismissive. Goodrich does recognize the visuality of the text as part of a general observation that visuality permeates legal practice and study. His concept of 'retinal justice' begins from an 'acknowledgment that the visual has always been present [in law], that the word is a visible sign, the text an aesthetic and haptic material form' and thus part of law's material expression, which extends across the lawscape, beyond the pages of law reports.[9] Words are material-discursive phenomena that collapse the cartesian split between the mind or the conceptual on the one hand, and the body or material on the other.[10] Concept and form are inseparably entangled: 'Matter is not the pregiven or the other of signification or discursive practices. Matter is always involved in meaning-making (and unmaking).'[11] Indeed, the media landscape in general provides the non-linear and constantly fluctuating conditions for meaningful encounters,[12] a non-linearity also found in the specific medium of a page of typographic images that only in a particular style of encounter is interpretively arranged into the conceptual structure of language. Despite such primal entanglement, however, Goodrich's study attends not to acknowledged typographic images as a non-linear or matter-discursive visual form, but to instances of maps, diagrams, emojis, and photographs that are inserted into the always already visual field of judicial texts. On the one hand, the visual nature of written text is acknowledged, but while undertaking full examination of the images of judgment, Goodrich's preferred genre of images omits and overlooks the typographic medium, prioritizing instead those figures presumed to be outside the 'linear discursive abstractions'[13] of printed words.

This focus is symptomatic of wider conventions and assumptions within modern legal understanding in relation to law's typographic form and the supposed distinction between 'text' and 'image'. Following traditional assumptions within the legal discipline, Goodrich's understanding of the page knowingly conflates textual appearance with conceptual content in a way that excludes text's visuality from critical perception, inhabiting a seemingly naturalized distinction between typographic and other figures. When Goodrich seeks to distinguish the realms of reason and image, for instance – of the rationally discursive that, in law, takes priority over the material and the imaginal – he notes law's explicit distinction between the 'written document' and 'the image', highlighting the tendency for images to be 'subject to print methodology' as their meanings are ignored in favour of rational discourse.[14] Such a distinction is, for Goodrich, characteristic of a tradition of legal understanding that is a product of a sedimented method that suppresses the matter of the text:

> It is not that such sensory facets are lacking in the scriptural forms of written reason, but rather that they are not generally viewed or apprehended as such. The words are signs . . . but the juristic propensity, from the glossators [of the twelfth to thirteenth century] onwards, has been to read rather than to view.[15]

Despite his own study focusing on the more obvious images found in judgments, the association between the textual and the rational of law is one that Goodrich's general thesis undoes. 'The lawyer', Goodrich explains, 'reads with incredible intensity for the insensible, for what isn't on the page'.[16] In printed law, it is the material hermeneutic form that enables the constructions of 'insensible' legal meaning. But the material texts of the common law are not passive; they are hybrid material-conceptual objects out of which lawyers and judges build their reasoning and decisions,[17] and – as Andrew Zurcher puts it – that come to act as material substitutes for 'illegible states of mind'.[18] The staging of intellectual content by the page is a general feature of the technologies of writing,[19] and such a method embraces the cartesian split between 'matter' and 'meaning' that recognizing typography's material staging of discourse collapses. Observing the legal page, the lawyer tends to see not the entangled presence of matter-discourse, but suppresses the typographic forms as merely incidental to the representation of what is sought: the conceptual structures of linear reason and the architecture of principle. This suppression results, as we see in Goodrich, in an on-going surprise at finding the visual within law – when from a wider perspective that recognizes and engages the necessary medial quality of all communications the visual is always already everywhere. Typography, in law's preoccupation with rational content, remains distinct from other kinds of image that, by their insertion, have the paradoxical effect of foregrounding the material and visual form of legal transmission in general, thereby – for Goodrich, at least – opening analysis to unconscious judicial desire. Yet we need not attend to inserted non-typographic images to recognize that text is already visual: typographic legality approaches the written law from a media perspective that already foregrounds the broadly visual and material quality of communication in general.

Law's preoccupation with rational content at the expense of typographic form can be seen more starkly in other examples where the visual presentation of legal texts is consciously discussed. In such examples, the concern is almost exclusively with practical readability: 'bad' typographic practices hinder the operation of documents that need to be read efficiently by lawyers and judges.[20] It remains the decision of a judge or the content of a statutory section that is legally significant, not the size, shape, and arrangement of the characters used to record or communicate it whose features are presumed only to impact on the effective transmission of legal meaning. When we see and interpret written words, the assumption goes, we should be seeking out their legal content, with their appearance being largely irrelevant.

This assumption, as Lyotard claims, is not exclusive to law: we are educationally and culturally conditioned to ignore visual form in favour of intellectual content,[21] such that the reader 'does not see what she or he reads, striving instead to hear the meaning of what the absent speaker – the author of the text – "meant to say"'.[22] The distinction between the content of a written document and the image of its type is imposed post hoc, although it is a distinction heavily sedimented by convention and cultural association. As Lyotard puts it: 'the graphic ceases to present itself as something to be seen and . . . [is only] recognized by its place in a system', such that figural space is replaced with 'informational space'.[23] To undo law's sedimented practices of reading for the invisible thus requires work. For Lyotard, 'the mind used to language' struggles to see the visual text as having any meaning that is not that of the abstract discourse it stages or transmits.[24] Hence typography is judicially understood as something 'on which nothing turns'.[25] Yet if 'the eye [is] to give in to form', and 'become receptive to the energy stored therein', says Lyotard, the alphabetic conditioning of the modern subject must be undone.[26]

The concern for content over the form of discourse runs deep. While fundamentally concerned with the visual dimensions of textual form and letter design, the tension between text's visual appearance and its ideational content can even be seen in typographic discourse. In typography, this tension manifests itself between the idea of the textual form as a transparent container and as an active and overt resource for meaning making. Beatrice Warde's 1930 speech to the British Typographers Guild, entitled 'The Crystal Goblet, or Printing Should be Invisible', gives a classic articulation of text's ideal transparency, and many typographers share the dream of a typeface that enables efficient communication free from visual disturbance.[27] It is often the practical aim of typographic design to maximize the ease with which readers can suppress a text's visual appearance – as the use of Warnock Pro to set the current text seeks to do: its careful blend of conservative tradition and rational innovation is well suited to the unfolding of original yet well-grounded academic arguments.[28] Yet others claim that typography should not 'be judged simply by its ability to render itself invisible', recognizing instead that it is capable of encoding multifarious meanings.[29]

Regardless of whether one follows the impetus towards transparency or embraces a text's visuality, the way words appear is unavoidably meaningful: 'Type matters because it is always rhetorical, including when it tries to be invisible'.[30] In order to fade into the background, font choice and layout must complement the dominant meanings in a text or its contextual conventions so as not to jar with readerly content or highlight its materiality and distract readers from the intellectual digesting of content. And the desire for invisibility is more generally a rhetorical choice in itself. It is a particular effect or atmosphere that the typographic style and arrangement of a document seeks to generate, actively shifting the typography into the background of the readerly experience.[31]

Rejecting any distinction between 'dead' letters and 'living' images,[32] foregrounding typography encounters the common law's texts as part of the general 'mattering' of the law.[33] The visual matter of text is in and of the lifeworld, not some dead remnant; it is always already alive with entanglements that escape and diverge from those of the symbolic order of discourse imagined as somehow separate from the static or 'dead' type that stages it. There is no written judgment – no written text – that is not also already an image. If we take the core of Goodrich's argument seriously, printed letters – radically indistinct from any 'inserted' images – also express the 'rhizomatic plenitude'[34] of meanings and unconscious associations of the visual. Letterforms operate as symptoms of a juridical unconscious, clues that reveal the desire that animates judgment and norm while disrupting its supposedly linear logic. Law's 'stability . . . is broken up by the apparent disorder of the unconscious associations of imaginal transmission'[35] – and this imaginal transmission includes its typography.

But the significance of typographic legality is not just in providing possible access to unspoken desires that animate judicial decisions. The typographic articulation of the common law, its extensive practice of encoding the rational legal order as embodied in judicial decision via the technologies of the page, is a more general feature of the institution of western law. What it reveals is not merely the desire of a particular judge or decision, but its operation as a central site of the legal institution's rhetorical appearance. As a core device by which the common law is made available to legal readers of all kinds, typography is the dominant method by which the legal order is staged. As both typographic and legal, typographic legality denotes the visual and material practices of legal speech – of jurisdiction, as the material articulation or staged presence of legal authority. And staged in a particular style, with particular lines of heritage and meaning that its style encodes or opens up to, and that can be interrogated through analysis of its letterforms – as the studies in this book hope to demonstrate.

Staging authority

Typographic legality is a technology of jurisdiction. Jurisdiction is 'derived from the Latin *ius dicere* – literally to speak the law',[36] and typography is a technique by which the institution speaks the law in text. It is a primary institutional means by which we are given legal form.[37] Reading judicial typography, rather than merely the abstract or conceptual 'content' of the law, means encountering a core rhetorical site within the modern legal institution where authority is expressed or made visible. Jurisdiction, as a general category, describes the grounding practices of veridiction in which law's material inscriptions both manifest and claim themselves as law. As Peter Rush puts it, jurisdiction is the 'site or space of enunciation' that refers 'first and foremost to the power and authority to speak in the name of law', upon which any articulation of legal substance is contingent.[38] Yet there is no location from which legal jurisdiction can be spoken – and concomitantly no position from which other jurisdictions can be heard or recognized:[39] the common law is 'suspended' by its jurisdictional practices,[40] self-verifying and unassailable.

On a material level, jurisdiction describes the manner in which law generates its own appearance. For Bradin Cormack, jurisdiction is both 'the order power takes and the topographical expression of that order'.[41] The existence and effects of the common law are contingent upon the techniques of jurisdiction that enunciate it and make it visible. Without such techniques, law has no technological substrate through or in which to manifest itself or be 'spoken'; it remains immaterial and thus unable to enter the minds of subjects or gain governmental purchase in social and communal life. It is 'the expressive register of the law', as Daniel Matthews puts it,[42] distinguishing between *ius* as a broader normative or juridical order and *lex* as the 'written and substantive law': jurisdiction is the 'speaking of *ius*', converting unwritten norms into positive legality in written form.[43] Jurisdiction, in short, 'makes the unwritten . . . visible'.[44] By doing so, however, it also moves in the opposite direction, feeding positive rules back into a wider structure of normativity: by enabling the encounter with legal meaning, jurisdiction naturalizes mere rules into norms.[45]

The manner in which jurisdiction renders the law visible is performative of its authority. Jurisdiction is 'the complex scene of the law's own making.'[46] It is in its moment of visual appearance that law grants itself the quality of law,[47] that it 'constitutes (its own) legal authority.'[48] Yet it is not mere technical competence, nor bare force – the foundation of legal appearance stages both the existence of the law that appears and its authoritative quality as law, thereby enabling the transmission of legal content and effects. Jurisdiction is 'the law speaking itself into existence'[49] and 'manifests law as performative through speech': it is a '*staging* of authority'[50] rather than a brute assertion of power or presumptive command. In her study of law as performance, Julie Stone Peters demonstrates that staging is a dominant means by which law is enacted: 'law's aesthetic power is essential to its force.'[51] The performative quality of law's power is evidenced in legal practices and training at least since ancient Greece.[52] For Peters, the coercive practices of state law are contingent on their successful performance – it is all about delivery. Matthews, too, examines how the might of the sovereign is displayed through performative practices, from mapmaking to carefully choreographed royal events.[53] Sovereignty, Matthews tells us, not only 'stages and performs its claims to plenary power with drama and ceremony',[54] but also in the everyday affects usually unseen in the background of social life.[55] Indeed, within the history of western political thought, the maintenance of a civil order can be seen to rely in large part on the management of the population's sensory perceptions, generating the appearance of a power to which the population in general remains obedient.[56]

The typographic expression of law performs its claim to authority, in part, by staging an absent or invisible source or origin. As Goodrich reads Legendre, it is the immaterial quality of law that operates most powerfully to bind the subject to the western institution.[57] But this absent form and source requires a material staging to enable its imaginative reception within the interior of the subject. As Victoria Ridler notes: 'when the judge . . . passes down a sentence, they not only presuppose the power to do so, but the power exercised is always derivative from . . . a mythical referent external to law that provides it with legitimacy.'[58] The author of the law is always absent, has no 'body or voice to perform itself',[59] and only manifests itself insofar as the expressive register of jurisdictional performance claims legal authority through its delivery. The practice of 'jurisdiction inaugurates law', providing for law 'its own source of authority.'[60] Yet, in terms of its textual form, writing 'is not the place of law, but gives access to the place of law' as a jurisdictional technology, as a 'stabilizing sign'[61] that provides formal expression to an authority located elsewhere.[62] The performance of jurisdiction – law's speech – covers up and gives form to the otherwise formless authority of legality, setting the fluidity of judgment in matter. For Ridler, this is not a representative act, but a 'creative paradox' at the heart of jurisdictional expression in which law's authorizing referent is created only in the expressive act of reference itself.[63] The staging of jurisdiction is performed, says Ridler, by 'actors who give the law its voice', deferring to an absent force as the source of the law they speak,[64] yet paradoxically creating that referent in the act of referring to it. Jurisdiction is a performance that is 'productive of legal authority' and takes place 'at the limits' where 'law reflects on (and asserts) its own powers'.[65]

The performance of jurisdiction is oriented towards the legal subject – a subject presumed by law to exist and to be under law's authority.[66] The theatre of power requires an audience whose senses and perceptions the aesthetics of state power seek to cultivate and manage,[67] and while law structurally assumes an audience of subjects exists (an audience explicitly recognized, as we will see below, in the regulated display of vehicle registration marks), the success of the performance is not left to be contingent on the supplication of actual individuals. As Ridler explains, the force of a legal performance 'is not derived from individual acceptance [of an obligation to obey], but rather a context of shared social understanding' that certain performances have particular effects.[68] What matters is not subjective acceptance of law's performative claim to authority, but that individuals recognize themselves as being addressed in general:

> It is not that the legal 'subject' must consider herself bound to 'law' nor even accept that the address is in fact lawful, but it is to recognise herself as addressed by a form of speech which presupposes her subjectivity.[69]

Jurisdiction is thus both the appearance of law and its audience, its specific visible forms and their generalized scope of action and affect. While the techniques of jurisdiction focus on the appearance or image of law as a form of 'speaking' or performance, they also simultaneously produce a space of witness: a juristic auditorium is implied by authority's staging. This auditorium is generally implied rather than explicit, embedded in the form of address that, for Ridler, constitutes law's authoritative veridiction. Jurisdiction is 'a legal performance in which the addressee of law's speech is presupposed as subject to it'.[70] But when placed upon the motor vehicles of legal subjects, the space of witness for the textual apparatus of law becomes more explicitly recognized.

The staging of legal authority in typographic form – that is, typographic legality – is a performance that not only occurs on the textual pages of the common law's primary documents that are the focus of this book. Although seemingly distinct from the typographic form of common law reporting, as a practice of typographic legality vehicle registration marks also seek to make legal authority present and thereby effect social governance through the techniques of visualized text. Registration marks are ostensibly different from the texts of judgments, but are nevertheless part of a wider set of jurisdictional techniques (textual and non-textual) that articulate state power and governmental effects.[71] Registration marks label vehicles with precisely determined visual forms that serve a plethora of governmental activities linked with the control and use of motor vehicles, from taxation and ownership to criminal investigation and enforcement. Registration marks, as specific instances of governmental control, thus facilitate a wide range of regulatory activity; they are an instance of jurisdictional appearance, manifesting legal power in the mobile contexts of everyday communal life. They are also distinctly typographic, and – in the United Kingdom at least – closely regulated for their visual dimensions and availability for viewing. The regulations surrounding the display of registration marks require not simply that marks are affixed and legible, but that they adhere to a specific typographic style, proportion, and arrangement (the nameless 'prescribed font', for example, is reproduced in Figure 1.1). Constructed and attached to the material forms of registration marks' typography, moreover, is an imaginary space of witness that moves with the vehicle, a mobile theatre within which registration marks – as jurisdictional expressions of governmental authority – must, on fear of criminal sanction, remain visible.[72] The affixing of registration marks to motor vehicles thus provides an example of explicit regulatory acknowledgement of the constitution of a presumed audience or space of witness for jurisdictional images.

Figure 1.1: The 'prescribed font' for motor vehicle registration marks in the United Kingdom. Reproduced from the Road Vehicles (Display of Registration Marks) Regulations 2001, Schedule 4, Part 1.

Within the state's broad institutional theatre, registration marks are a peculiar example of a highly detailed concern with typographic appearance and witness as a technique of governance. They are, however, only one small part of the larger drama of legal power that unfolds across the material forms of the modern state, forms that include things like court architecture[73] and dress,[74] but also – as this book's study demonstrates – the commonly overlooked minutiae of the typographic appearance of the common law's records and reports. Typographic legality recognizes simultaneously that jurisdiction refers to the speaking of law (that is, *juris dictio*), and that typography refers to the encoding of language in visual images. In this context, understanding jurisdiction as a predominantly performative technique for veridiction results in a concern for the manner in which the visual encoding of legal speech functions as part of jurisdiction's staging of authority, encompassing its audience of presumed subjects.

Performance and community

The question of staging authority and its concomitant audience, however, goes further than the presumed presence of a witnessing subject. In the practices of jurisdiction, of law's multifarious expressions of which judicial typography is a central part, the material performances of authority unfold toward the maintenance of community. Adam Gearey, for example, recognizes the communal quality of legal performance in his study of the poetics of practical reason, which develops a re-reading of the jurisprudence of Joseph Raz. As he explains, for Raz:

> Rule-following is conscious and rational. It is the articulation of those standards that are held in common. We could say, then, that it is the point at which the individual becomes conscious of [their] belonging to a community of shared values. It is the quilting point that stitches the individual into the social fabric.[75]

For Raz, following rules is the articulation of common standards. Despite the seeming abstraction of law's practical rationality, its authority rests not on its rational basis per se, but on its expression through individual conduct: the behaviour of legal beings that is always expressive of their identity and values, of reasons for and against action.[76] The binding force of modern law, on this understanding, is contingent on the harmonized connection between law's practical reason and the communal life of the subject.[77]

In terms of jurisdiction, the work of Edward Mussawir reformulates law not as a representation of some transcendental abstract reason, as if rules represent an underlying rational order or authorizing norm, but as the multifarious forms in which law 'becomes something acted.'[78] Concerned with jurisdiction as a technique in the articulation of legal power, Mussawir reorients jurisprudence towards law's expressive forms.[79] Jurisprudence is about turning 'law and rights toward the matter of their invention and expression' in order to develop 'creative resources for making-do within [law's] medium.'[80] Mussawir preserves a core distinction between 'representation' and 'expression': the project of jurisprudence, he argues, 'is concerned not so much with the [representation of] subjects and objects of legal knowledge but with law's medium, technology, performance and articulation.'[81]

Reoriented in this way, the performance of jurisdiction encompasses the legal subject itself as part of the media of jurisdictional expression, breaking down any division between the 'stage' and the 'audience' as such. The 'legal subject' is neither an abstract conception nor a living individual, but mediated through the category of the legal person as the aesthetic expression – the dramatization – of authenticated legal identity.[82] The person is a legal device, a specific bit of institutional media that exists on a continuum with other legal media, such as court architecture, judicial dress, and common law typography. And it is a device, moreover, through which rights become manifest. The legal person is a particular means by which the 'subject' takes form as a concrete unfolding and traversing of privileges and obligations as part of lawful community. Like other technologies of jurisdiction, the person functions to shape lawful relations.[83] The person is not an immaterial category applied to a living individual, as if the category of 'person' seeks to *represent* the individual-as-subject within the abstraction of legal structures, but is 'a device invented in law to make a certain set of rights liveable in and through a definite role', and unfolds in its specificity with no abstract or transcendental dimension.[84] As a jurisdictional device, the person thus enables the articulation of legal authority in its moment of performance. Like the legal text, the technical features of the legal person function as part of the continuum of 'jurisdictional devices' that *express* legality,[85] dramatizing 'the value and existence of rights'[86] as part of the vast staging of legal authority. Indeed, as part of the large-scale theatrical production of modern western politics, the person is part of the performance of modern institutional power, functioning as an emblem that inserts the living being into the structures of governance both as a process of rendering visible and governable, and as an expression of the powerful qualities of the performance itself.[87]

With Gearey's reading of Raz, legal authority is expressed by the conduct of legal subjects, and remains authoritative only insofar as this conduct is in line with an expressive performance of communal values and norms. Where the expression of legal authority diverges from the values of the community, that law becomes self-authorized – an imposed demand for conduct rather than an authoritative expression of communal norms – and thus enforceable only as a matter of convention.[88] To behave in a law-abiding manner yet outside the normative framework of communal values may be expressive of law's authority, but what is expressed in such cases is arbitrary. Insofar as it deviates from the shared, rational values of community members, the law's 'authority' is only found in the fact of its enforcement, in line with 'the basic positivist article of faith: the law is the law,' and is thus 'essentially the language of . . . an elite of rule applicants whose practice provides the test for the nature of law.'[89] If law is to generate obligations for it to be obeyed as a form of legitimate authority, legal expressions must seek to connect themselves to the rational commons of community members.[90]

Yet successful legal persuasion does not rest on rational argumentation alone, as Raz's concern with the alignment of reasons for action might suggest – emotions and feelings wield the greater power.[91] The harmonizing work of establishing legitimate authority is accordingly effected through poetics, through the rhetorical or performative quality of power's institutional expression that manages the population's sensory experience[92] and ultimately stages its own authoritative presence: that is, its jurisdictional theatre. For Pierre Legendre, the staging of institutional images is the radical appearance of legal forms that establishes what is available to perception.[93] Thus, as Peters elaborates, legal authority cannot function without theatricality. As well as being present to the senses in general, it must also 'showcase justice, visibly represent its own force and dignity, induce deterrent awe in the populace, produce docile legal subjects . . . [and] promise catharsis and closure.'[94] The theatre of the law makes 'the greatest evils perceptible to the senses,'[95] for example, as part of the generation of catharsis. Jurisdictional staging carries or invokes an affective dimension. Put more generally, there is an aesthetic dimension to the staging of sovereign authority, running 'parallel to legal and political reason'[96] that is typically understood as divorced from its matter of expression.

Emotions and the affective harmonization of rhetor and spectator is a significant dimension to the staging of authority: we are persuaded 'not only because they [legal performances] vividly signify the emotions of the scene but also because they produce similar emotions in the audience'[97] – what Peters calls 'affective transfer' or 'emotional mimesis.'[98] Such emotional techniques[99] are part of what enables institutional images to generate harmonization effects in legal subjects, not only via the persuasive power of an argument in court, but, in Gearey's reading of Raz, in the authorization of legal expressions as something worthy of being obeyed within a communal order.[100] Mussawir, too, demonstrates that the authority of law 'is composed of more than its reasons, logics and outcomes', although his concerns are not with emotions but with 'the instrumental or technical envelope that mediates its force and authority in the social terrain'.[101] Justice is not represented in the positive forms of law, but is expressed as, or is done through or in, the very moment of legal performance – of jurisdiction, in its broadest understanding.

Justice is not to do with 'the authority of what is said', as if judgment or legal rule merely represented or signalled an abstract reason, but instead 'concerns the staged authority of saying it' – law's delivery generates a 'fundamental affect' within its expressive theatre.[102] Justice is produced, as Legendre holds, in the 'procedural dramatization' of the tripartite structure of judgment that relies on the judge occupying the space of the 'third' party that mediates between the others.[103] For Mussawir, such 'dramatizations of judgment' are part of the formal practices of jurisdiction,[104] and it is the marker of the success of such performances that they harmonize with the emotional and rational commons of the actors that occupy the space of the institution's presumed audience: the community of legal subjects.

Legal authority is dramatized in the lawful performance of communal actors as much as the technical forms of institutional practice and media. These aspects are on a continuum of legal expression that, taken together, make up what we might term a jurisdictional theatre. A theatre with an audience of implied subjects that are entangled with the articulation of law's authority as both its witnesses and performers: witnesses of law's medial expression, and performers who express legal authority themselves through their conduct. The law is not 'out there', represented through its forms so as to be applied and have impact upon individuals 'here' – rather, law's authority is generated through a continuum of expression, found only in the matter of its unfolding. The linear reason typically prioritized by modern lawyers (as seen in Raz's focus on the rational commons) sits as one dimension of legality alongside a large-scale material production that is performative of legal authority. The jurisdictional staging of authority is radically prior to the modern rational order of legal thought this staging enables, encompassing the conduct of legal actors and their props. The jurisdictional techniques and media of legality extend unbroken from the conduct of the person, to the architectural stylings and ritual dress of courts and trials, to the under-examined details of typographic design by which the recorded decisions taken to embody the common law are expressed.

Typographic techniques

Legal authority, founded in its jurisdictional performance, is contingent not just on a broad idea of performativity, but on the specifically technological quality of the media by which it is enabled. Jurisdiction, as an activity or practice, inaugurates law as legally meaningful speech through particular devices and techniques.[105] Jurisdiction is not an abstract concept, but a technological process that speaks legal authority in images.[106] Not simple static images, however, but a set of apparitional techniques central to the 'staging and performance of law' and its authority by means of visual matter.[107] Framed more generally, jurisdiction is 'the matter of law's expression.'[108] And modern legality's technologies of expression are the cultural techniques of legal power. On one level, law's cultural techniques are the simple requirement that law needs a medial form to function, that rights and obligations must be expressed in materialized language if they are to exist in any practical sense. There is 'no right without words,' Cornelia Vismann tells us; 'to have a certain right implies the right . . . to have a language, in which they [rights] can be articulated.'[109] But the technologies that materially render the law, even understood on a pragmatic basis, extend beyond the overt example of language to include mechanisms by which that language can be uttered, disputed, settled, and take effect, including – as we have seen – through the conduct of persons. The category of law's cultural techniques thus encompasses the multifarious technologies or material practices by which institutional legality is made present, legal meaning transferred, and ideologies given purchase in the material world.

These techniques of appearance are also the practices of jurisdiction. In Dorsett and McVeigh, jurisdictional processes are understood with a particular focus on their technological quality: the staging of authority requires a specific set of techniques by which law is promulgated and maintains its operations. It is the technical or medial features of law that instantiate jurisdiction as the radical staging of authority: jurisdiction 'is the practice of pronouncing the law', and to exercise it is 'to bring law into existence . . . *in a certain way and by certain means*.'[110] Jurisdiction thus 'gives us the form and shape of law,'[111] instantiating the idea or invisible idiom of law in matter. Just as there is no right without a concomitant language, 'there is no talk of law without speech – and there is no consideration of lawful speech without [jurisdictional] form.'[112] In a broad sense, then, cultural and jurisdictional technologies of law coincide.

Dorsett and McVeigh highlight the jurisdictional significance of the common law's textual techniques: legal writing, of which law reporting is a core example, 'both inaugurates law . . . and gives shape to law.'[113] Even taking account of the ritual paraphernalia that surround its records of decision, or the fact that legal writing goes beyond law reporting to encompass many different kinds of documents and practices outside of the judicial record (writs, contracts, titles, charters, to note but a few),[114] the common law is still largely materialized as the visual matter of its primary sources: the texts and documents that constitute the record of judicial decision. Jurisdiction takes place in multiple sites, but to a large extent it takes place in the linguistic practices of legal power as enacted by the typographic techniques instantiated in the common law's records of decision. More than incidental images that can reveal the unconscious desire of a judgment, judicial typography is a central practice that expresses legal authority as a collection of visual artefacts, 'mattering' the law as words and sentences in the visual space of the page.[115]

Courts, judgments, the protocols of files and filing – indeed, the whole set of administrative techniques and technologies of state bureaucracy – all work to stage law's legitimate presence as an authorized practice of governance. And, in the state context at least, these elements are joined up by the modern rationalized organization of the state's corporate activity, and thereby carry 'the sovereignty of the entire state.'[116] From each material object that is embedded in the structures of administration, from each 'module, the whole of the state emerges.'[117] In this way, the specific typographic practices of recording and disseminating legal judgments signal or enable interrogation of the state in general. Each medial element in the vast system of the legal armature encodes the articulation of state power. The particular letters of judicial texts, and the techniques involved in their reproduction or display, are part and parcel of law's authorizing performance.

The particular techniques of legal language are also central for Ridler, in her claim that law's 'very expression' constitutes its authoritative status and enables the subjectification of individuals, unfolding the technologies of jurisdiction as material speech always already addressed to a (presumed) subject.[118] For Mussawir, in turn, the expressive form of the text 'supervises and manages the "space" of interpretation.'[119] The materialized text, the common law's manifestation as typographically constituted documents, as visual pages, is a technique for the articulation of power within the auditorium of jurisdictional performance, establishing as it manifests legal authority for an anticipated subject that is constructed in advance by the techniques of the expression itself. The anticipated subject is then supervised by the text as law's meanings – rights, obligations, personhood – are constructed, with these meanings becoming liveable by the subject as they continue the jurisdictional performance.

Law's media technologies, however, are not neutral or transparent. Law is contingent on them, but they do not enable radically autonomous action or the free exercise of governmental power. For Vismann, cultural techniques are the *sine qua non* of communication and governance. As she explains:

> The opposite of cultural techniques . . . [is] a world where techniques do not exist at all, a notion which cannot even be mentioned without using yet another cultural technique: the act of naming, which allows things to be used and studied in the first place.[120]

Without cultural techniques, without media technologies that provide the means by which otherwise imperceptible things are perceived, no knowledge can be shared, no meaning can be constructed, and no governmental effects can unfold. The media by which power is articulated conditions, limits, and shapes what is possible and how that power can function. 'Tools prescribe their own usage,' Vismann tells us.[121] Law's textual language, in particular, filters and limits the exercise of sovereign power.[122] Accordingly, we must distinguish between the autonomous conduct supposed by the logic of hierarchical sovereignty and the structure of the modern, rational subject on one side, and the material features of cultural techniques that operate to determine 'the field of action' on another.[123]

A focus on cultural techniques shifts understandings of law from the fountain to the foundry: from a concern with law's source to questions of law's transmission. Acknowledging the medial quality of cultural techniques not only highlights the crafted nature of jurisdictional practices, as particular techniques for the manifesting of lawful relations,[124] but also disempowers the centralized model of sovereign authority and undermines the assumptions of the autonomous subject, such that 'things' become 'invested with agency.'[125] Modern legality 'holds that things and media are strictly passive.'[126] Yet by recognizing the conditioning effects of things and media in the context of legal power, we can reformulate understanding of modern sovereignty as an abstract hierarchy or source of authority. The promulgation of authority is not contingent on particular (immaterial) practices of reasoning – as an unwritten source – but ultimately on the material techniques of transmission.

The common law's typographic objects function as a central device in the staging or relaying of its authority, shaping the scope and quality of its effects.[127] While the complex material elements of courtrooms and processes enable the theatrical staging of the abstract world of law[128] and the impartiality of judgment,[129] replaying the events under judgment within law's linguistic and conceptual order[130] and facilitating the vicarious participation of subjects in this order via the player of the lawyer,[131] amongst other things,[132] the cultural technologies of law function beyond the heightened crucible of the trial. Indeed, the modern state in general can be seen through its technological processes and forms – of which courts and judicial process are but a part, alongside others, including judicial typography. In the context of the common law's printed judgments, far outside or long after the court has completed its procedures, it is the materialized text that stages the presence of law – a technology of jurisdiction that takes place as a typographic performance. The design of, and aesthetic encounter with, the common law's letterforms and page layouts are jurisdictional techniques; they are the ways and means by which law is staged as present and assumes its audience.

Staging the source

For typographic legality, the archive is a central technology of transmission. It is in the archive that we find the record of judicial decisions made in the past, encoded in typographic form, and it is from out of the archive that legal practice and study seeks to (re)construct the law for the present and future. The archive, arguably, is where we find the common law's 'sources' – the documents of decision and the concomitant interpretations of law they are taken to embody.[133] The concept of the archive can, of course, be understood beyond only typographic documents, to encompass almost any kind of trace repository.[134] But despite this, the dominant conceptions of the archive within mainstream legal study and practice concerned with the primary legal documents of the common law remain preoccupied with the typographic image on the page, albeit only as a marker for a structure of legal reason or normative value.[135] A preoccupation that, warranted by both its dominance and its backgrounding, the study staged in this book both shares and seeks to disrupt by bringing it to the foreground for critical scrutiny.

Despite its preoccupation with typographic forms, legal study and practice has given little attention to typographic form itself or how it interacts with and conditions law's rational order, its imaginary structure of principles and doctrine. Work on technologies of jurisdiction and law's cultural techniques, however, help prioritize the material contingency of legal power. Vismann's work in particular refocuses attention on the techniques, while not of type design and practice specifically, of filing and documents. Her major work *Files*, for instance, traces the emergence of the modern state, not as a political centralization of dominant force, but as a particular emerging set of material practices for securing and promulgating governmental influence.[136] It is through filing techniques that law takes form and unfolds in the particular manner familiar to western legal scholars and practitioners.

> [L]aw and files mutually determine each other. A given recording technology entails specific forms and instances of the law. A new way of binding or of writing things down, a change in the way data are collected, affects the legal framework.[137]

Studying the media of legality shifts the histories of western law and jurisdiction away from stories of the centralization of power and the movement from oral to written tradition, to an elaboration of the structure and function of law as administrative techniques. Legal forms are 'not subject to the logic of speech', as a simple encoding of oral history, but instead derive from the practices of written record keeping.[138] Yet this history – like the disregard of typographic legality more generally – is one not often told within legal study. Within the jurisdictional theatre of power, law tends not to be critically reflexive about its own material contingency.[139]

A core site of typographic legality's jurisdictional theatre can thus be found in the archive. The connection between law and the archive is intimate, to the extent that, as Renisa Mawani claims, 'law is the archive', as evidenced by the 'citational and organizational structure of command' that grounds legal authority in the practices of the archive itself.[140] Like Vismann, who holds the articulation of state authority to be contingent on documentary matter, for Mawani the 'force and command' of law is 'grounded in a proliferation and profusion of documents and documentation'.[141] By making (typographic) matter available for recall and reference, the techniques of the archive are 'a mode of articulation and a form of governance'.[142] Conceiving simply of law as a structure of normative value or as authority, in either case 'distinct from files and documents' per se, erodes key connections between legal power and the overlapping of history, command, and archive in state practices.[143]

The archive is both constituted by its documents and by the techniques by which those documents are included or excluded in the archive, and rendered visible or invisible in their recall. As Derrida famously articulates, the archive emerges in the process of forgetting, as things are consigned to a repository in a process of 'gathering together' traces under an ordering principle, from which to be later recalled.[144] Under the violence of the archive's organizing principle, there is a policing function at work as to what is made available to history and thus the construction of knowledge in the future: the archive 'underwrites what counts as history in the first place'.[145] Historical knowledge in general, as grounded in the archive as a collection of authentic historical evidence, is thus understood as a construction produced out of what is available in the archive, which is itself a constructed consignment of traces with no access to the 'original' events that left them behind.[146] For law, there is further gatekeeping in terms of what can be legitimately recalled and by what techniques, which for the common law relies on the practices of precedent as a means of authorizing statements in the present. In referring to what came before, and in policing what can be referred to, 'law cultivates its meanings and asserts its authorities while at the same time concealing and sanctioning its material, originary, and ongoing violence.'[147] Such practices embody a legal order's normative conventions of how authority is reproduced.[148] More critically, it is by virtue of the technologies of the archive that 'the preservation and destruction by which law generates the veracity of its own legality' is expressed.[149]

The western desire to recover original moments is embedded in the technology of the archive,[150] yet for the common law the process of recall entails an unrequited quest for its lost original that – if it ever existed – cannot be remembered or called up, but only mediated through the traces available within the matter of the archive.[151] The legal source, the ultimate origin of the common law located in time immemorial,[152] can categorically only be found via the evidence left to us in the recorded history of decisions that embody that law. Yet it is a source that cannot be found in that history, which as a system of cultural *memory* is structurally unable to extend back to time *immemorial*, and as an archive contains only evidence of the law – its recalled traces – not the law itself. The techniques of precedent function to bind persons, things, and lawful relations into the established body of law within the common law's jurisdictional performance.[153] Precedent is the means by which law, as an archival technology (as 'recall, translation, and reinterpretation' over time), 'continues to maintain the relevance of its own history to the present and future,'[154] connecting current and future forms of life and relation to what can be called up from the material record.

Typographic legality both stages law's lost origin and undermines the existence of that origin. In the context of judicial typography, it operates as a material trace consigned to the common law archive, staging the myth of the common law's ultimate source, lost to the mists of time. But, despite being lost, the desire for the recovery of the common law's source is always present in the structure and technique of the archive itself – of the technologies of its transmission. Playing into the dual meanings of the word 'font' explored in the introduction, the theatre of the archive straddles both source and transmission: as a crafted or forged transmission, the typographic form of the material law stages the existence of a precedent and ultimate source or origin. The common law's typographic font (*fundere*) conditions the visible face that stages the existence of the common law's originary font (*fons*). The materialized text, as a technique of jurisdiction, seeks to authorize legal statements, as we saw above, through reference to a precedent author or origin – but cannot make that original source present. The origin of law – in the sovereign, in the divine, in the democratic adoption of a legal system, in the founding moment of violent imposition – 'remains deeply buried' beneath the documents of the archive.[155] The theatre of the common law archive is a play of traces that generates legal authority. At least since the advent of printed reporting – which we explore in the next chapter – this is a particularly typographic production that, through the cultural technologies of printed text as a practice of jurisdiction, stages the authoritative existence and presence of legal power.

Conclusion

Although typically placed in the background, the typography of the common law's primary documents is a fundamental aspect of the theatre of jurisdiction. Jurisdiction is the radical speech of law, its founding practice of veridiction by which it appears and claims its own authority through a staging that authorizes its presence through derivation from some precedent source. As the primary record of legal speech, the typographic manifestation of the common law archive is a quintessential jurisdictional practice that participates in the theatrical staging of legal power. The manner in which this performance unfolds, then, is of particular concern for understandings of common law practice and authority. The remainder of this book undertakes to study examples of the common law's typographic legality at key moments in its media history. In these studies, as we will see, the staging of authority takes on variable valences as the typographic form of the common law's matter attaches unacknowledged meanings, ideological heritage, and political resonances to its supposedly conceptual or rational content.

Notes

1. Dorsett and McVeigh, *Jurisdiction*, 5.
2. Dorsett and McVeigh, *Jurisdiction*, 5.
3. See, notably, Desmond Manderson, *Songs without Music: Aesthetic Dimensions of Law and Justice* (University of California Press, 2000); Linda Mulcahy, *Legal Architecture: Justice, Due Process and the Place of Law* (London: Routledge, 2011); Illan Wall and Daniel Matthews, 'Sovereignty and the Persistence of the Aesthetic', *Modern Law Review* 87, no 6 (2024): 1393–421.
4. See, for example, Martha C. Nussbaum, *Poetic Justice: The Literary Imagination in Public Life* (Beacon Press, 1995); Peter Goodrich, *Advanced Introduction to Law and Literature* (Edward Elgar, 2021).
5. Goodrich, *Judicial Uses*.
6. See Goodrich, *Judicial Uses*.
7. Goodrich, *Judicial Uses*, 238.
8. Goodrich, *Judicial Uses*, 237–38.
9. Goodrich, *Judicial Uses*, 201. On the expanse of the lawscape, see Andreas Philippopoulos-Mihalopoulos, *Spatial Justice: Body, Lawscape, Atmosphere* (Routledge, 2014).
10. See Daniela Gandorfer, *Matterphorics: On the Laws of Theory* (Duke University Press, forthcoming).
11. Karen Barad and Daniela Gandorfer, 'Political Desirings: Yearnings for Mattering (,) Differently', *Theory and Event* 24, no. 1 (2021): 29.
12. MacDonald, 'Empire and Communication', 507–9.
13. Goodrich, *Judicial Uses*, 196.
14. Goodrich, *Judicial Uses*, 18.
15. Goodrich, *Judicial Uses*, 128. For more general analysis of the changes in manuscript practices and technologies in this period that came to prioritize the rational order of discourse over the matter of the page, see Ivan Illich, *In the Vineyard of the Text: A Commentary of Hugh's* Didascalicon (University of Chicago Press, 1993).
16. Goodrich, *Judicial Uses*, 128.
17. Andrew Zurcher, 'Spenser, Plowden, and the Hypallactic Instrument', in *The Oxford Handbook of Law and Literature, 1500–1700*, ed. Lorna Hutson (Oxford University Press, 2017), 655. See also John Bell, 'Sources of Law', *The Cambridge Law Journal* 77, no. 1 (2018): 40–71.
18. Zurcher, 'Spenser', 657.
19. This arguably results in the psycho-social evolution of the modern subject's rational interiority: see, for example, Walter J. Ong, *Orality and Literacy: The Technologizing of the Word* (Routledge, 1988). We will examine this in more detail in Chapter 4.
20. Suzanne Suarez Hurley, 'Advancing the Legal Profession with Typography', *The Florida Bar Journal* 86, no. 9 (2012): 53–57; see also Aamodt, 'Legal Typeface'. On this point, it is worth noting the burgeoning 'legal design' movement,

which seeks to improve legal practice and access to justice via principles of clear, efficient communication and document design: see 'Legal Design WTF?', Legal Geek, 2018, http://legalgeek.co/learn/legal-design-wtf.

21. Jean-François Lyotard, *Discourse, Figure* (University of Minnesota Press, 2010), 211–12.
22. Lyotard, *Discourse, Figure*, 211.
23. Lyotard, *Discourse, Figure*, 208.
24. Lyotard, *Discourse, Figure*, 212.
25. *Baigent v Random House* [2007] EWCA Civ 247 at [3]. We will examine this exemplary judicial slip more fully in Chapter 4.
26. Lyotard, *Discourse, Figure*, 212.
27. See Christopher Scott Wyatt, 'On Type and Typographic Anatomy', in *Type Matters: The Rhetoricity of Letterforms*, ed. Christopher Scott Wyatt and Dànielle Nicole DeVoss (Parlour Press, 2018), 6–8.
28. The reader can judge the relative originality or well-groundedness of this book's argument, but for more details on Warnock Pro, see the Preface.
29. Frank Serafini and Jennifer Clausen, 'Typography as Semiotic Resource', *Journal of Visual Literacy* 31, no 2 (2012): 5–7.
30. Wyatt, 'Typographic Anatomy', 28.
31. On the generation of an atmosphere that backgrounds particular aspects of legality, see Illan rua Wall, 'The Ordinary Affects of Law', *Law, Culture and the Humanities* 19, no. 2 (2019): 191–209.
32. 'The dead letters of the reports are a rather covert, distanced and . . . occluded manner of recording . . . [while] the image, to borrow from St Augustine, gives life': Goodrich, *Judicial Uses*, 249–50. See also Ong, *Orality and Literacy*, 80.
33. See Giddens, 'Sentences Matter'.
34. Goodrich, *Judicial Uses*, 76.
35. Goodrich, *Judicial Uses*, 211–12.
36. Dorsett and McVeigh, *Jurisdiction*, 4.
37. The 'technologies of jurisdiction give us the form of law': Dorsett and McVeigh, *Jurisdiction*, 54.
38. Peter Rush, 'An Altered Jurisdiction: Corporeal Traces of Law', *Griffith Law Review* 6 (1997): 150.
39. See Rush, 'Altered Jurisdiction'. He is particularly concerned with the recognition of indigenous jurisdictions on the landmass now known in the west as Australia.
40. Rush, 'Altered Jurisdiction', 147.
41. Bradin Cormack, *A Power to Do Justice: Justice, Jurisdiction, English Literature, and the Rise of Common Law, 1509–1625* (University of Chicago Press, 2008), 14.
42. Daniel Matthews, 'From Jurisdiction to Juriswriting: At the Expressive Limits of the Law', *Law, Culture and the Humanities* 13, no. 3 (2017): 427.
43. Matthews, 'Juriswriting', 430. See also Peter Goodrich, 'Visive Powers: Colours, Trees and Genres of Jurisdiction', *Law and Humanities* 2 (2008): 215–21.
44. Matthews, 'Juriswriting', 430.
45. See Cormack, *A Power to Do Justice*, 10.
46. Cormack, *A Power to Do Justice*, 23.

47. Rush, 'Altered Jurisdiction', 149.
48. Victoria L. Ridler, 'The Exercise of Jurisdiction and the Absent Author of Law's Speech', *Law and Literature* 31, no. 1 (2019): 72.
49. Ridler, 'Exercise of Jurisdiction', 75.
50. Austin Sarat, 'Editorial', *Law, Culture and the Humanities* 9, no. 2 (2013): 205. Emphasis added.
51. Julie Stone Peters, *Law as Performance: Theatricality, Spectatorship, and the Making of Law in Ancient, Medieval, and Early Modern Europe* (Oxford University Press, 2022), 5.
52. See, generally, Peters, *Law as Performance*.
53. Daniel Matthews, 'The Aesthetics of Sovereignty', in *The Routledge Handbook of Cultural Legal Studies*, ed. Karen Crawley et al. (Routledge, 2024).
54. Matthews, 'The Aesthetics of Sovereignty', 100.
55. Matthews, 'The Aesthetics of Sovereignty', 100–103. See also Wall, 'Ordinary Affects'. For more general discussion of the role of aesthetic in the western tradition of political thought, see Wall and Matthews, 'Sovereignty'.
56. See Wall and Matthews, 'Sovereignty'.
57. See Goodrich, *Languages of Law*, 260–96.
58. Ridler, 'Exercise of Jurisdiction', 83.
59. Ridler, 'Exercise of Jurisdiction', 86.
60. Dorsett and McVeigh, *Jurisdiction*, 11.
61. Cormack, *A Power to Do Justice*, 84.
62. Cormack, *A Power to Do Justice*, 73.
63. Ridler, 'Exercise of Jurisdiction', 83.
64. Ridler, 'Exercise of Jurisdiction', 72.
65. Ridler, 'Exercise of Jurisdiction', 75.
66. Ridler, 'Exercise of Jurisdiction'.
67. As Wall and Matthews put it, 'sovereignty has a necessary relation to aesthetic devices, modes and themes which are ultimately concerned with the cultivation and management of the body's senses': Wall and Matthews, 'Sovereignty', 1421.
68. Ridler, 'Exercise of Jurisdiction', 78.
69. Ridler, 'Exercise of Jurisdiction', 82.
70. Ridler, 'Exercise of Jurisdiction', 72.
71. Olivia Barr, for example, highlights the role of roads in jurisdictional expansion of the British Empire: see Olivia Barr, 'A Jurisprudential Tale of a Road, an Office, and a Triangle', *Law and Literature* 27 (2015): 199–216. See also, for fuller analysis of the typographic governance afforded through vehicle registration practices, Thomas Giddens, 'Keeping up Textual Appearances: The UK Road Vehicles (Display of Registration Marks) Regulations 2001', *Law, Technology and Humans*, 2020.
72. On the regulatory construction of this 'relevant area', see Giddens, 'Textual Appearances', 97–100.
73. See, for example, Linda Mulcahy, 'Architects of Justice: The Politics of Courtroom Design', *Social and Legal Studies* 16, no. 3 (2007): 383–403; Mulcahy, *Legal Architecture*.

74. See, for example, Peter Goodrich, 'The Example of Undressing: Obnubilations on the Empty Space of the Rule', *Law and Literature* 30, no. 3 (2018): 409–22; Gary Watt, *Dress, Law and Naked Truth: A Cultural Study of Fashion and Form* (London: Bloomsbury, 2013).
75. Adam Gearey, 'The Poetics of Practical Reason: Joseph Raz and Philip Larkin', *Law and Literature* 19, no 3 (2007): 380.
76. Gearey, 'Poetics of Practical Reason', 380–81.
77. Gearey, 'Poetics of Practical Reason', 381.
78. Edward Mussawir, *Jurisdiction in Deleuze: The Expression and Representation of Law* (Routledge, 2011), 116.
79. Mussawir, *Jurisdiction in Deleuze*, 7–8.
80. Mussawir, *Jurisdiction in Deleuze*, 7.
81. Mussawir, *Jurisdiction in Deleuze*, 10–11.
82. Mussawir, *Jurisdiction in Deleuze*, 26.
83. As Dorsett and McVeigh argue, lawful relations 'are shaped by the technologies of jurisdiction': Dorsett and McVeigh, *Jurisdiction*, 55.
84. Mussawir, *Jurisdiction in Deleuze*, 24–25.
85. Mussawir, *Jurisdiction in Deleuze*, 109.
86. Mussawir, *Jurisdiction in Deleuze*, 48.
87. See Peter Goodrich, 'The Theatre of Emblems: On the Optical Apparatus and the Investiture of Persons', *Law, Culture and the Humanities* 8 (2012): 47–67.
88. Gearey, 'Poetics of Practical Reason', 381–82.
89. Gearey, 'Poetics of Practical Reason', 382.
90. Gearey, 'Poetics of Practical Reason', 384.
91. See Peters, *Law as Performance*, 70.
92. See Wall and Matthews, 'Sovereignty'.
93. See Pierre Legendre, *God in the Mirror: A Study of the Institution of Images (Lessons III)*, trans. P. G. Young (Routledge, 2019).
94. Peters, *Law as Performance*, 8–9. In the classical context, affective performance enabled spectators to 'exhaust their dangerous emotions . . . to feel their feelings and then purge them [in the theatre] rather than to act on them', thereby producing 'obedient subjects'. See Peters, *Law as Performance*, 51. On the production of catharsis in general, see Peters, *Law as Performance*, 49–51.
95. Peters, *Law as Performance*, 55.
96. Wall and Matthews, 'Sovereignty', 1416.
97. Peters, *Law as Performance*, 48.
98. Peters, *Law as Performance*, 49.
99. Peters notes the advanced proficiency with emotional awareness and control needed to master one's feelings and align them with another's in an act of persuasion: 'the ability simultaneously to access another's emotional truth while mastering it is, for Cicero and Quintilian, a model for the kind of highly skilled empathetic identification that is essential to doing justice': Peters, *Law as Performance*, 60. More recent study has also engaged the necessity for emotional competence in judicial work: see, for example, Terry A. Maroney, 'The Persistent Cultural Script of Judicial Dispassion', *California Law Review* 99 (2011a): 629–81. For an introduction to emotions as in tension with legal

reason, see Thomas Giddens, *Judgment: New Trajectories in Law* (Routledge, 2022), 29–33.

100. Wall and Matthews also discuss the generation of habitual obedience, among the generation of other kinds of affective outcomes (e.g. awe and majesty) in state theatre: see Wall and Matthews, 'Sovereignty', 1410–13.
101. Mussawir, *Jurisdiction in Deleuze*, 138.
102. Mussawir, *Jurisdiction in Deleuze*, 125.
103. Mussawir, *Jurisdiction in Deleuze*, 128. See also Legendre, *God in the Mirror*.
104. Mussawir, *Jurisdiction in Deleuze*, 128.
105. Dorsett and McVeigh, *Jurisdiction*, 14–15.
106. Rush, 'Altered Jurisdiction', 150.
107. Dorsett and McVeigh, *Jurisdiction*, 12–14. Quotation at 13.
108. Mussawir, *Jurisdiction in Deleuze*, 160.
109. Cornelia Vismann, 'Derrida, Philosopher of the Law', *German Law Journal* 6, no. 1 (2005): 6. See also, on the practice of law as the establishment not only of particular outcomes but also of a language for resolving disputes and imagining the communal order, James Boyd White, 'Law as Rhetoric, Rhetoric as Law: The Arts of Cultural and Communal Life', *The University of Chicago Law Review* 52, no. 3 (1985): 684–702.
110. Dorsett and McVeigh, *Jurisdiction*, 4–5. Emphasis added.
111. Dorsett and McVeigh, *Jurisdiction*, 5.
112. Dorsett and McVeigh, *Jurisdiction*, 6.
113. Dorsett and McVeigh, *Jurisdiction*, 15.
114. For more on the role of writing in legal transmission in this broader context, see Dorsett and McVeigh, *Jurisdiction*, 59–62. And, for detailed studies of a range of different documentary forms and contexts in law, see Katherine Biber et al., eds., *Law's Documents: Authority, Materiality, Aesthetics* (Routledge, 2022).
115. For fuller articulation of the 'mattering' of law in typographic form, see Giddens, 'Sentences Matter'.
116. Cornelia Vismann, *Files: Law and Media Technology*, trans. Geoffrey Winthrop-Young (Stanford University Press, 2008), 110.
117. Vismann, *Files*, 133.
118. Ridler, 'Exercise of Jurisdiction', 83.
119. Mussawir, *Jurisdiction in Deleuze*, 147.
120. Cornelia Vismann, 'Cultural Techniques and Sovereignty', *Theory, Culture and Society* 30, no. 6 (2013): 88–89.
121. Vismann, 'Cultural Techniques and Sovereignty', 83.
122. See Ino Augsberg, 'Reading Law: On Law as a Textual Phenomenon', *Law and Literature* 22, no. 3 (2010): 26.
123. Vismann, 'Cultural Techniques and Sovereignty', 84.
124. See Dorsett and McVeigh, *Jurisdiction*, 56.
125. Vismann, 'Cultural Techniques and Sovereignty', 86.
126. Vismann, 'Cultural Techniques and Sovereignty', 86–87.
127. As Biber, Luker and Vaughan explain, 'an examination of the properties and features of the document enables us to come to some understanding of how legal

authority becomes embedded within – and enforced through – documentation' as a practice of authority: Katherine Biber et al., 'Law's Documents: Authority, Materiality, Aesthetics', in *Law's Documents: Authority, Materiality, Aesthetics*, ed. Katherine Biber et al. (Routledge, 2022), 9.

128. Cornelia Vismann, 'Tele-Tribunals: Anatomy of a Medium', trans. Sara Ogger, *Grey Room* 10 (January 2003): 5–21.
129. In the courtroom, the humble table, Vismann observes, 'is what allows for the judge to be installed in the position of neutrality at the head of the administration of justice' and thus to function as 'a higher third party' to which litigants refer their cases for resolution from the other side of the divide': Vismann, 'Cultural Techniques and Sovereignty', 312.
130. Cornelia Vismann, '*"Rejouer Les Crimes"* – Theater vs. Video', *Law and Literature* 11, no. 2 (1999): 161–77.
131. See Cornelia Vismann, 'Three Versions of a Defendant's Final Statement to the Court', *Law and Literature* 23, no 3 (2011): 297–308.
132. Other work on the arrangements of court environments has indicated the way architectural and layout decisions encode the politics of legal rights and power in identifiable ways: see, for exemplary analysis, Mulcahy, 'Architects of Justice'.
133. For lawyers, it is conventional interpretations that are invoked in the citing of material sources in law, both in terms of what counts as a source, and of what the legal meaning of a source might be: see Bell, 'Sources of Law'.
134. On the broad interconnectivity of legal and other kinds of archive, understood through the concept of the 'multiframe', see Thomas Giddens, 'Multiframe Fever: Comics as Archive', *Studies in Comics* 14, no 2 (2023): 263–79.
135. As Bell puts it: 'Texts are understood within the legal community as part of a network of rules and values . . . we identify the material source . . . but actually the justification we are offering relies on the normative source, the rule derived from that collective decision or process' by which the material source was produced: Bell, 'Sources of Law', 44.
136. Vismann, *Files*.
137. Vismann, *Files*, xiii.
138. See Vismann, *Files*, 4.
139. As Vismann observes, 'the law remains silent about its records': Vismann, *Files*, 13.
140. Renisa Mawani, 'Law's Archive', *Annual Review of Law and Social Science* 8 (2012): 340.
141. Mawani, 'Law's Archive', 358.
142. Mawani, 'Law's Archive', 339.
143. Mawani, 'Law's Archive', 351.
144. See Jacques Derrida, 'Archive Fever: A Freudian Impression', *Diacritics* 25, no. 2 (1995): 10.
145. Mawani, 'Law's Archive', 356.
146. See Carolyn Steedman, *Dust* (Manchester University Press, 2001).
147. Mawani, 'Law's Archive', 341.
148. See Bell, 'Sources of Law'.
149. Mawani, 'Law's Archive', 341.

150. See Steedman, *Dust*, 1–12. See also Derrida, 'Archive Fever'.
151. On the recall of law's lost original in the archive, see Hayley Gibson, 'Reopening the Archive: From Hypomnesis to the Ontology of Law', in *Law and Philosophical Theory: Critical Intersections*, ed. Thanos Zartaloudis (Rowman and Littlefield, 2018).
152. See, for example, Dorsett, 'Since Time Immemorial'.
153. Dorsett and McVeigh, *Jurisdiction*, 67–71.
154. Mawani, 'Law's Archive', 354.
155. Mawani, 'Law's Archive', 359. On the ultimately violent foundations of western law, see, famously, Jacques Derrida, 'Force of Law: The "Mystical Foundation of Authority"', *Cardozo Law Review* 11 (1990): 920–1045.

Chapter 2

Printing the law: a Roman face on an English body

Introduction

The early printing of common law decisions in roman type embeds the continental practices of Roman law and renaissance humanism into the English tradition.[1] While representational aspects of authority tend to be seen as 'incidental to modern forms of law',[2] typeface – often seen in itself to be merely incidental, passive, or decorative – has particular and identifiable effects on the meanings available in printed texts,[3] analysis of which opens to the broad set of forces and ideological heritage that typography expresses. Like other affective or 'decorative' qualities of the legal institution, the typographic dimension of law usually sits in the background where its meanings and significations tend to be overlooked or discounted. This is in line with more general tendencies, under which 'we commonly . . . suppress the connections between format and design and the history of their meanings' in textual reading practices.[4] But, perhaps by being overlooked, law's typographic dimension has smuggled Roman traditions into the English common law in its earliest printed expression.

The forms of printed text are not merely transparent 'containers' of meaning, but have latent significations worthy of critical elaboration within the study of the common law tradition. In particular, the heritage of the roman fonts used to represent the written language of early common law decisions connects these texts with renaissance humanism and Romanist codification. To elaborate this heritage and its common law meanings, the current chapter presents a study of the typographic form of a key early common law text: Plowden's *Commentaries*. This text was first published in the sixteenth century following the introduction of the printing press to England, and this chapter traces the continental inheritance of its roman letterforms. In doing so, Plowden's typographic appearance becomes a visual and material expression of on-going tensions around the codification and study of the English common law within (arguably) the first modern printed law report. This chapter thus shows the radical way in which the traditions of Roman law and renaissance humanism were typographically embedded into an English common law tradition that was (and generally remains) resistant to both. As a staging of authority out of the archive, the first printed law report is thus seen to invoke earlier sources of authorization: in both the rational civilizing practices of codification and scholarly humanism, and the oral process of judgment it seeks to transmit within the common law's immemorial tradition.

This chapter proceeds in four main sections. The first ('Writing the unwritten') recounts the debates around printing the common law, a practice that emerged at a time when printing statutory law was already becoming conventional. These debates centred largely on the propriety of making the common law – as a practice characterized by judgment and cloistered expertise – visible and accessible to the general population, and encompassed resistance to these efforts that sought to maintain the authority of the legal profession and protect the English tradition from continental influences. These were debates within which print, and printed form, played significant roles. This context set out, the second section ('Analysing Plowden's typeface') stages a close analysis of the typographic form of Plowden's *Commentaries*, a text that is considered to be one of, if not the, first 'modern' law report in terms of form and method. Printed initially in 1571 by Richard Tottel – the printer who held the first patent to 'officially' print common law texts[5] – Plowden's text participates in a complex process of what this chapter terms 'romanizing' the common law. The chapter subsequently reads the details and heritage of these typographic forms within the contested contexts of renaissance humanism ('Roman font's humanist heritage') and the influence of Roman legal method on the English common law tradition ('Romanizing the law'), ultimately demonstrating how these tensions are encoded in the visual design of the letterforms used by

Tottel to imprint the *Commentaries*. From the very first moments of printed common law reporting, despite being an uncodified and unwritten law that was grounded in the authority of a tradition descending since time immemorial, the common law's transmission was infused with the Latinist ideals upon which it was substantively dependent but to which it was politically opposed.

Writing the unwritten

The common law tradition is one of an ultimately unwritten law, yet common law study and practice is replete with written sources. If the common law is unwritten, in the sense that it is uncodified, why and how is it dependent on legal texts? If it is unwritten in the more general sense of being grounded in cloistered expertise and practices of judgment outside or before the text itself, how does the common law appear as communicative media? In either case, the question is what systems of inscription (broadly understood) are used to reveal the common law's principles? There are many practices surrounding the revelation of the law, beyond the seeming ubiquity of textual writing. Beyond text, the law may be revealed through the visual images of legal emblems,[6] or manifested in architectural forms,[7] or judicial dress,[8] or – if one is radical enough – in space itself.[9] Such appearances are important for a broad understanding of the modern legal institution, but the written or typographic law remains a central or dominant form that also requires attention. Words, and the appearance of the letters used to build them – of alphabets and the shape of literal figures – are neither merely transparent containers of legal meaning, nor naturally occurring or predetermined forms or conventions.[10] In the case of mechanically reproduced typographic figures – that is, the western alphabetic system of printed inscription by means of which the English common law is typically recorded – their evolution took place initially under the impetus and requirements of the technologies of print, an evolution that moved from the manuscript culture of handwritten documents to the increasingly standardized forms of printed type.

Prior to print, legal information circulated primarily via manuscripts, oral culture at the Inns of Court, and the shared expertise of legal professionals. Legal understanding was based on convention and the erudition of those steeped in the practices of the vocation, anchored to and supported by a rich professional culture of manuscript production and use.[11] In terms of the common law, the year books are arguably the most prominent example of early written texts produced by the legal profession, but even these were only sporadically printed and were not 'reports' in a modern sense. The function of the year books was not to record authoritative judgments;[12] they were akin to technical manuals on the 'occult science' of pleading,[13] and required a high degree of proficiency to understand and apply.[14] Lawyers 'required special skills to make sense of what was on the page', de facto excluding lay readers from this socially privileged profession.[15]

Early legal print focused on royal proclamations and statutes, as expressions of sovereign authority that required official promulgation, codified and distributed as written law for the public good.[16] Official sanction was given to the King's Printer for this activity, and only later was a separate royal patent granted for the printing of common law reports and statutory abridgements[17] that operated alongside the manuscripts of professional legal culture. The authority to print statute was treated separately from that to print the common law, with law reports only regulated later and falling under the category of commentary and reporting understood to be distinct from statutory law's quality as codified royal decree. The conventions and emerging practices of statutory printing are important for typographic legality in a general sense,[18] but are distinct from the specifically common law sources that this book's study focuses upon – both practically and jurisdictionally. The printing of statutes has a different relationship with royal authority than does that of common law texts, which, as we will see across this chapter, encounters more complexity in terms of expressing or constraining sovereign power.

While the question of printing the common law was distinct from that of printing statute, some common themes do exist. The concern was not simply the potential benefits of consistent and accessible legal sources that may be familiar to modern lawyers, and that in the common law context rendered print instrumental in the development of precedent.[19] Print was also seen to be dangerous: it risked reproducing errors in the original, amplifying those created in the printing process overseen by individuals without lawyerly expertise, or granting too much influence to the printer as a kind of de facto lawmaker in how doctrinal texts were presented for interpretation,[20] as well as enabling the general public to access law's mysteries without sufficient training or authority to do so. There were concerns related to statutory printing that readers without sufficient understanding would become more litigious, leading to social division.[21] In legal print generally, it was feared that unwarranted access to it would invite its abuse.[22] William Hudson, writing after legal print was already underway,[23] argued that the legal system 'should present to the multitude . . . a surface layer of commands while reserving to professionals the deeper stratum of fictions and judgments.'[24] This is particularly the case in relation to the unwritten common law, which rested more centrally on the professional expertise and juridical erudition than the royal declarations of statute. The occult science of establishing the common law should only be handled by those suitably adept in this complex and powerful art. But even the wide promulgation of bare rule or principle, without their establishing reasons and debates, presents interpretive opportunities to those insufficiently versed in the accepted conventions of reading such law.[25]

In its most general terms, this problem is that of the governmental principle of *arcana imperii*, which dictates that subjects should not 'wade in all the deepest mysteries that belong to the persons or state of kings.'[26] Within the general context of the mysterious nature of governmental practice, common lawyers are connected with 'magicians,'[27] 'alchemists,'[28] guilds, and other early modern specialists unwilling to reveal their secrets. To publish the common law was an affront to both the crown and the professional expertise of lawyers; it should thus remain safely hidden within the halls of the profession, a safety facilitated by the limited circulation of the manuscript format and the common law's bespoke languages.[29] Yet the material promulgation of the common law does not automatically undo the occlusion of *arcana imperii*, since even printed appearances still require appropriate expertise to decode – as the culture surrounding manuscript proficiency demonstrates. Put more generally:

> Those who rule do so by specialized means, by virtue of their knowledge of the *arcana imperii*, the hieroglyphics of power, and that message requires

> expression of an absent and invisible source in a temporal and visible, though elliptical and properly speaking involuted, form.[30]

The signs and symbols of the common law do not give direct access to it, whether handwritten or clearly printed, but cover it up by dressing it in words and pictures in a theatrical sleight of hand that keeps the source of legal authority hidden, absent, inaccessible – and thus powerful. However, the largely unwritten quality of the common law – based as it is on erudition and expertise – does not mean it lacks structure or particularity, but merely that it remains contingent upon the material, upon written forms that enable the circulation and establishment of its supposedly immaterial structure:[31] the figure is the 'costume' that discourse requires 'to enter the social and juridical stage'.[32] As Andrew Zurchner explains:

> Despite its vaunted status as a *lex non scripta*, the English common law in practice came by the sixteenth century to rely on a body of texts after which lawyers and judges ordered their thinking and judgements [sic] . . . [Moreover], expositors and judges . . . tended to view legal texts as permeated by a *sensus* beyond the texts' mere words . . . [that] was essential to the true construction and working of the common law.[33]

More precisely, then, the common law is not simply invisible and thus unknowable: it involves instead the 'substitution of some evident and material thing for the illegible state of mind',[34] for the cognitive geography of legal principle,[35] the meanings and effects of which are controlled not only by the text itself, but by a limited few with the requisite erudition to do so – and who thereby maintain power.

While it may be impossible to fully display law's raw and unmediated source,[36] or the principles that constitute or underpin its immaterial structure,[37] the other side of the publication debate was nevertheless characterized by an impulse to permit public access to the common law. Initially associated with law printer John Rastell,[38] this position favoured wide dissemination of the law as part of a humanist educational movement aimed at increasing virtue through classical scholarship.[39] To reveal the law in the vernacular enhanced the subject's capacity to know and understand the limits of their conduct and the freedoms of community members. Downplaying any reformist tendencies, Rastell promoted knowledge of the law as enhancing the order and peacefulness of society,[40] as shoring up royal power rather than undoing its theatrics – at least, insofar as the common law was seen to descend from the crown rather than constrain it.[41] The humanist position favoured the recourse to rational or scholarly principle-building, and revealed the historical contingency and disciplinary connections of legal knowledge and professional expertise.[42] Accordingly, it did not resonate with the common law's practical focus, and contradicted its traditional model of authority and the exclusive erudition of its practitioners.[43] A shift from manuscript to print also appeared to set solid what should remain a fluid flow of common law expertise, fixing in an apparently static form the legal knowledge constituted by the professional culture of the Inns of Court.[44] Printing the law would not only undo law's rhetorical power, permitting the masses to enter the sacred space of legal reasoning, but also distract from its ability to function as a practical system of adjudication and expert judgment, and undo the mythic source of the common law's authority found in its timeless English heritage and supposedly isolated from continental influences.[45]

Analysing Plowden's typeface

Amid these tensions over common law printing emerged *Les Commentaries, ou les Reports de Edmunde Plowden.* Initially circulating as manuscript, it was first printed in 1571 by Richard Tottel, and was distinct in providing for each case: a record of pleadings; the various arguments of counsel and judges; and, the ultimate judgment given by the court.[46] Prior to Plowden, the year books represented the main – if not only – printed forms approaching reports (although only some were printed), and, as noted above, these did not focus on reporting legal decisions, but instead the practice of pleading.[47] Plowden, meanwhile, omitted the procedural pleadings and inconclusive debates of the year books, and focused on providing a record of decisions on substantive points of law[48] – that is, a materially accessible record of the common law, as embodied in judicial decision. Plowden's text is thus the first 'modern' law report, demonstrating the core methods and formal elements that would become conventional. As J. H. Baker puts it, 'Plowden represents the beginning of modern law reporting.'[49]

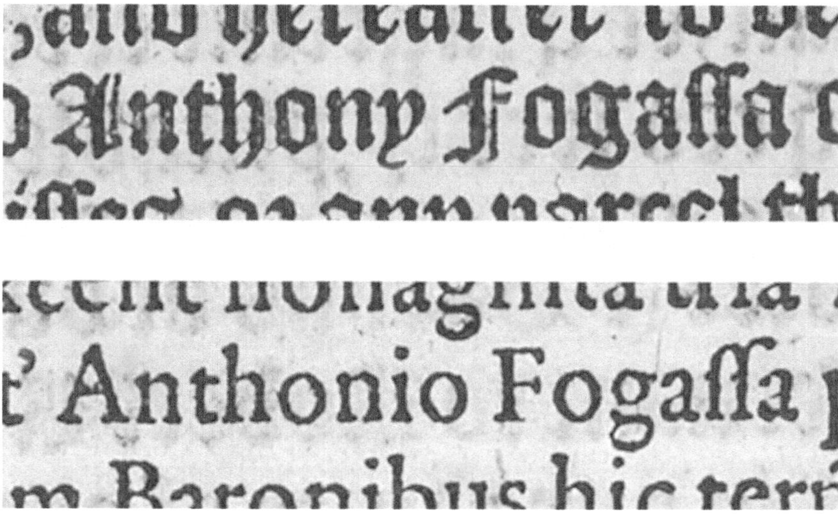

Figure 2.1: Examples of text in 'blackletter' (Anthony Fogassa) and 'roman' (Anthonio Fogassa), sampled from fol 21 of Plowden. Image kindly provided by the University of Aberdeen, Museums and Special Collections (licenced under CC By 4.0: https://creativecommons.org/licenses/by/4.0/).

While the term 'blackletter law' is commonly used to denote a certain traditional conservatism of legal textuality, focused on the internal doctrinalism of the law, Plowden is set in a variety of letterforms – not just blackletter. Tottel's printing typographically demarcates the arguments of counsel in traditional blackletter, the court record in roman (not usually accessible at the time, even to practising lawyers), and the reporter's commentary in italics (see Figure 2.1 for examples of 'blackletter' and 'roman'). In even a basic sense, then, its typography has authoritative functions, delineating 'law' from other genres of discourse present within its corpus. On this level, Baker merely notes the use of 'a different type' for the commentary.[50] An exemplary page can be seen in Figure 2.2. The text at the top of the page is set in a characteristically angular blackletter face, while the lower portion of the page is set in the thinner roman – perhaps more familiar to the eyes of readers today – and recounts the decision made by the court. However, there is more sophistication evident.[51] Plowden's text reproduces the Latin record of the court's judgment,[52] with the key arguments of council presented as 'blackletter law' in the specialist vernacular of Law French, alongside Plowden's own italic commentary (also in Law French).[53] As glimpsed in Figure 2.2, where the record is in Latin it is invariably set in roman type

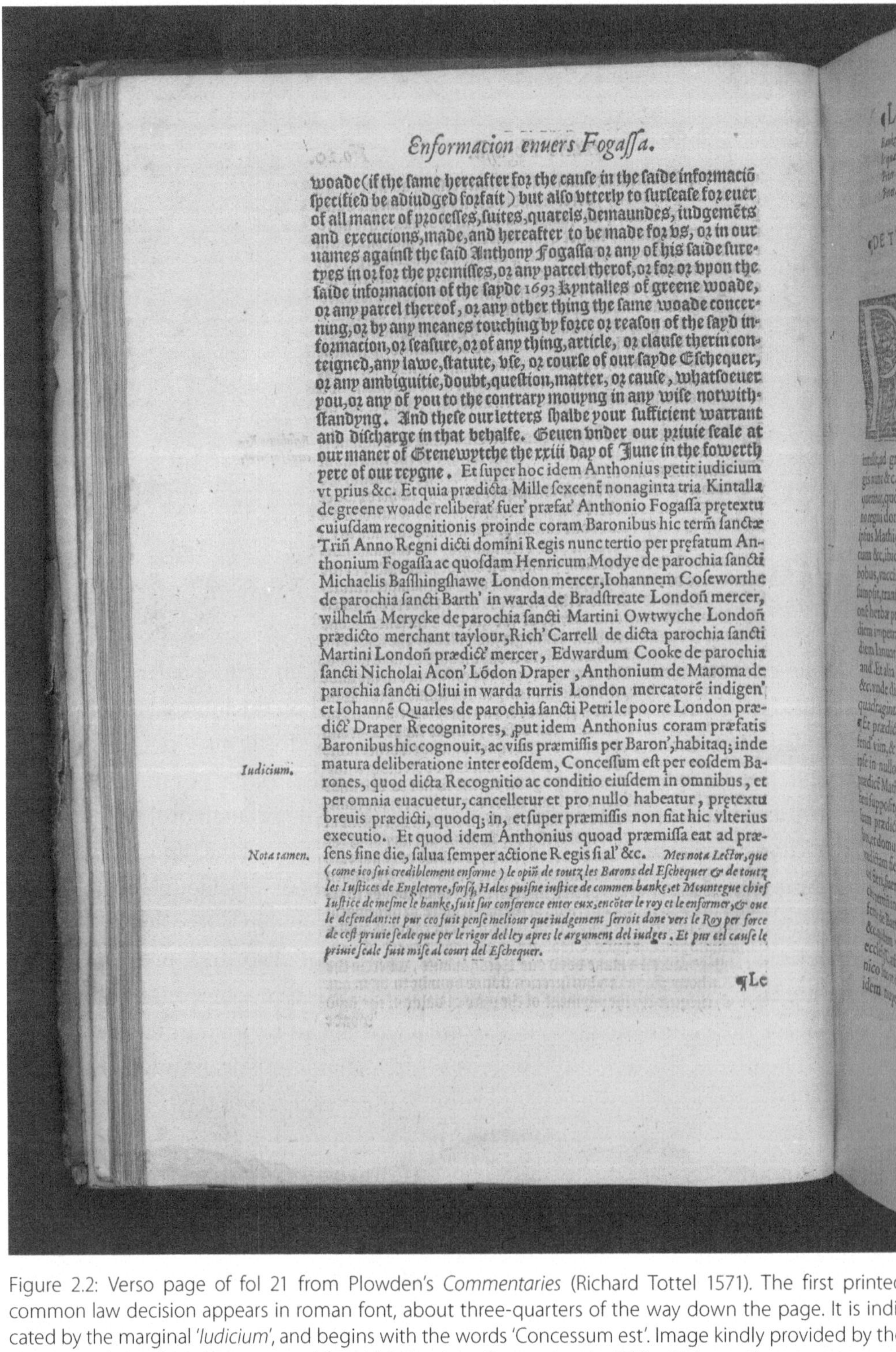

Enformacion enuers Fogassa.

woade (if the same hereafter for the cause in the saide informaciō specified be adiudged forfait) but also vtterly to surcease for euer of all maner of processes, suites, quarels, demaundes, iudgemēts and execucions, made, and hereafter to be made for vs, or in our names against the said Anthony Fogassa or any of his saide suretyes in or for the premisses, or any parcel therof, or for or vpon the saide informacion of the sayde 1693 Kyntalles of greene woade, or any parcel thereof, or any other thing the same woade concerning, or by any meanes touching by force or reason of the sayd information, or seasure, or of any thing, article, or clause therin conteigned, any lawe, statute, vse, or course of our sayde Eschequer, or any ambiguitie, doubt, question, matter, or cause, whatsoeuer you, or any of you to the contrary mouyng in any wise notwithstandyng. And these our letters shalbe your sufficient warrant and discharge in that behalfe. Geuen vnder our priuie seale at our maner of Grenewytche the xxiii day of June in the fowerth yere of our reygne. Et super hoc idem Anthonius petit iudicium vt prius &c. Et quia prædicta Mille sexcent̄ nonaginta tria Kintalla de greene woade reliberat' fuer' præfat' Anthonio Fogassa prętextu cuiusdam recognitionis proinde coram Baronibus hic term̄ sanctæ Triñ Anno Regni dicti domini Regis nunc tertio per pręfatum Anthonium Fogassa ac quosdam Henricum Modye de parochia sancti Michaelis Basshingshawe London mercer, Iohannem Coseworthe de parochia sancti Barth' in warda de Bradstreate Londoñ mercer, wilhelm̄ Merycke de parochia sancti Martini Owtwyche Londoñ prædicto merchant taylour, Rich' Carrell de dicta parochia sancti Martini Londoñ prædict' mercer, Edwardum Cooke de parochia sancti Nicholai Acon' Lōdon Draper, Anthonium de Maroma de parochia sancti Oliui in warda turris London mercatorē indigen', et Iohannē Quarles de parochia sancti Petri le poore London prædict' Draper Recognitores, ꝑut idem Anthonius coram præfatis Baronibus hic cognouit, ac visis præmissis per Baron', habitaq; inde

Iudicium. matura deliberatione inter eosdem, Concessum est per eosdem Barones, quod dicta Recognitio ac conditio eiusdem in omnibus, et per omnia euacuetur, cancelletur et pro nullo habeatur, prętextu breuis prædicti, quodq; in, et super præmissis non fiat hic vlterius executio. Et quod idem Anthonius quoad præmissa eat ad præ-

Nota tamen. sens sine die, salua semper actione Regis si al' &c. *Mes nota Lector, que (come ico fui crediblement enforme) le opiñ de toutz les Barons del Eschequer & de toutz les Iustices de Engleterre, forsq; Hales puisne iustice de commen banke, et Mountegue chief Iustice de mesme le banke, fuit sur conference enter eux, encōter le roy et le enformer, & oue le defendant: et pur ceo fuit pense meliour que iudgement serroit done vers le Roy per force de cest priuie seale que per le rigor del ley apres le argument del iudges. Et pur cel cause le priuie seale fuit mise al court del Eschequer.*

¶Le

Figure 2.2: Verso page of fol 21 from Plowden's *Commentaries* (Richard Tottel 1571). The first printed common law decision appears in roman font, about three-quarters of the way down the page. It is indicated by the marginal '*Iudicium*', and begins with the words 'Concessum est'. Image kindly provided by the University of Aberdeen, Museums and Special Collections (licenced under CC By 4.0: https://creativecommons.org/licenses/by/4.0/).

(with vernacular text in blackletter); indeed, even when used within the Law French pleadings, which are otherwise set in the more traditional blackletter, the manual arrangement painstakingly sets Latin terminol ogy in roman. The marginal notes are in a smaller roman, and Plowden's concluding commentary (evident at the bottom of the page in Figure 2.2, as indicated by the marginal '*Notatamen*') is in italic.

Plowden's letterforms were influenced by wider trends in printing conventions across the sixteenth century: Latin was commonly set in roman, and the use of italic for Plowden's opinions, for instance, associates this text with the cursive hand lettering of Italian renaissance scripts, suggesting a contingent human origin to the opinions set in the text.[54] Thus, even if typeface is recognized to be more than a neutral device in the 'background' of the reading experience, on one level it may be tempting to dismiss Plowden's typography as simply reflecting contemporary conventions. Even the non-blackletter features of Plowden, it seems, are the product of convention and tradition. However, in their extensive study of the heritage of visual conventions in information transmission, Kostelnick and Hassett argue that any 'convention carries the rhetorical weight of the discourse community that sanctions it.'[55] By reproducing contemporary print conventions within a leading legal text, Plowden's typography not only encodes the histories of meaning and convention associated with the visual form of its letters, but embeds and sanctions them within the legal tradition of which it was – and has increasingly become – a leading artefact. The mere fact the use of a particular kind of face may be conventional does not reduce the meanings available in that face, and in fact – by virtue of its very conventionality – reveals the entrenched or hegemonic nature of the values represented by that convention.

Refocusing attention to these traditionally 'background' elements enables us to read the typographic dimension of Plowden as a discourse on 'romanizing' the common law. The term 'romanizing' is more than a legal-typographic pun: its wordplay evokes the question of 'Roman-style' legal codification in a sense that is meaningfully connected to the concerns of typography and the cultural heritage of roman letterforms.[56] 'Romanizing' is intended to have at least a dual sense: (i) as the codifying of law through a method akin to that of Roman law; and (ii) as the rendering of text in roman letterforms. These dimensions of 'romanizing' are interlinked in the common law context, operating at the intersection of the authoritative and the typographic – a nexus made explicit by a close analysis of Plowden's visual appearance within the wider printing and legal histories of which it is a part.

To unpack the 'romanizing' of the common law in Plowden, our analysis focuses on its first reported case: *Renyger v Fogassa*.[57] And, more specifically, the style in which the opening words of the stated judgment or decision in that case appear. This typographic artefact sits on the verso page of folio 21 (see Figure 2.2), indicated by a marginal note of *Iudicium* ('Judgment'):

> Concessum est per eosdem Barones, quod dicta Recognitio ac conditio eiusdem in omnibus, per omnia euacuetur, cancelletur et pro nullo habeatur, pretextu breuis praedicti, quodq ('it is granted by the same barons that the said recognizance and the condition thereof in and by every thing be made void, cancelled, and holden for none, by reason of the writ aforesaid'[58]).

As the first words of the first judgment in the first printed law report that represents, as Baker put it above, 'the beginning of modern law reporting',[59] this artefact is of significant importance for the intersection of typography and authority in the development of the common law. Figure 2.3 contains a more detailed image of the relevant lines as imprinted in roman type by Tottel in 1571.

Before we can trace its visual heritage, it is necessary to undertake a detailed analysis of the letters in order to identify the face used to set the *iudicium*. Type historian Harry Carter asserts that one can only know what type a text is printed in by knowing (i) its conventional

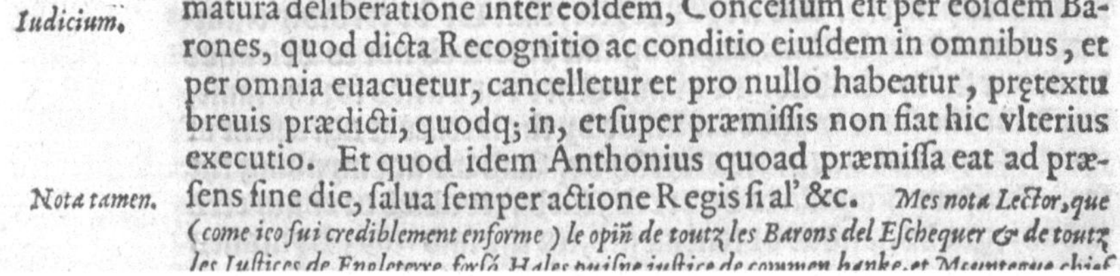
Baronibus hic cognouit, ac viſis præmiſſis per Baron',habitaq; inde
Iudicium. matura deliberatione inter eoſdem, Conceſſum eſt per eoſdem Ba-
rones, quod dicta Recognitio ac conditio eiuſdem in omnibus, et
per omnia euacuetur, cancelletur et pro nullo habeatur, prętextu
breuis prædicti, quodq; in, et ſuper præmiſſis non fiat hic vlterius
executio. Et quod idem Anthonius quoad præmiſſa eat ad præ-
Nota tamen. ſens ſine die, ſalua ſemper actione Regis ſi al' &c. *Mes nota Lector, que*
(come ico ſui crediblement enforme) le opiñ de toutz les Barons del Eſchequer & de toutz

Figure 2.3: Excerpt from Plowden's Commentaries (Richard Tottel 1571), fol 21, verso. Image kindly provided by the University of Aberdeen, Museums and Special Collections (licenced under CC By 4.0: https://creativecommons.org/licenses/by/4.0/).

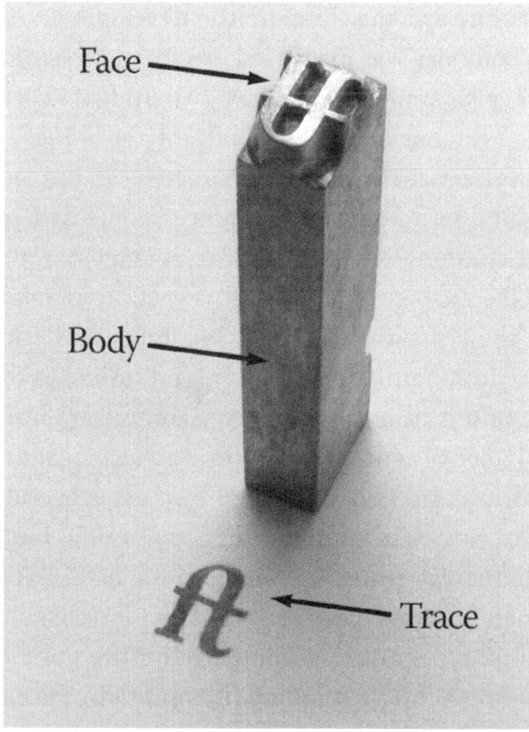

Figure 2.4: Example of a piece of metal type (a Garamond 'ft' ligature), showing its 'body' and 'face', and the trace it leaves on the page. Labels added by Thomas Giddens. Original image credit: Daniel Ulrich (CC BY-SA 3.0: https://creativecommons.org/licenses/by-sa/3.0/deed.en). Image source: https://commons.wikimedia.org/wiki/File:Garamond_type_ft ligature.jpg

style classification, (ii) its body-size, and (iii) the name of the person who cut the type.[60] These aspects are progressively harder to identify: we have already noted the type is roman in style, but what is its size, and who cut it? Once we have established all three of these elements, we will be in a position to analyse the history of meanings attached to the letterforms themselves, and thereby to properly substantiate the history and associations that the *iudicium*'s letters carry and their connotations within the common law tradition.

In print typography, the size of a text is determined largely by the 'body' of the font being used. The body refers to the piece of metal which carries the raised shape of a letter (see Figure 2.4),[61] and thus determines the blank space around a printed letter on the page. The body is usually the same across all letters for a particular font, which are arranged in a grid or frame for printing, and is a significant factor determining its line spacing.[62] Before the development of the modern 'point' system, body size was measured using a number of conventional labels, such as 'pica' and 'long primer', that roughly corresponded to commonly used dimensions.[63] The body of the *iudicium* is 'english' size:[64] Plowden's text measures approximately 95mm over 20 lines[65] (roughly 13 'point' in modern measurement). The first printed words of the modern common law thus appear as 'english roman': the style convention of the face is roman, and it is cast on an english body.

In terms of the typecutter, Frank Isaac notes that Tottel's printing house used predominantly 'post-Garamond' fonts, and increasingly so as the sixteenth century unfolded.[66] Claude Garamond worked in early to mid-sixteenth century Paris, producing elegant roman letterforms 'of uniform design distinguished by their graceful proportions and brilliance of cut'.[67] The influence of Garamond is large, and firmly allied with a humanist ethos.[68] Although in a 'post-Garamond' style, Plowden's roman font was more likely cut by Pierre Haultin – another leading humanist typecutter working around the same time.[69] There were very few punchcutters working in London in the early sixteenth century, but Haultin's nephew Jérôme did cast and sell type there using type matrices[70] created by his uncle Pierre in Paris. Carter thus claims that a London-printed text that initially looks like a Garamond is often actually a Haultin,[71] and it seems Plowden might fit this thesis.

According to Vervliet, Haultin's 'english roman' equates to approximately 92mm for 20 lines[72] – but these measurements can vary slightly between different examples and usages, and the 95mm of Plowden is within tolerance for the 'english' standard.[73] Vervliet's extensive study of Haultin's type specimens reveals key features of his english roman on the capitals R (and K), T, M, and P. Haultin tended to cut his Rs narrow, omitting the elongated tail as found on a Garamond (his Ks are similarly 'steep-tailed'), and his capital Ts with serifs above and below the crossbar, rather than only hanging below.[74] Perhaps most distinctive is Haultin's 'very particular treatment' of the upper serifs of the capital M, which Vervliet terms 'dog-eared'.[75] Other humanist typecutters, such as Garamond, tended to give their Ms top serifs with defined inner corners, while Haultin's are tilted slightly inward and curved, giving the impression of a canine ear. Along with the 'steep-tailed' R and a large-bowled[76] P, Vervliet notes the dog-eared M as a key letter in identifying Haultin's english roman.[77]

We can see a number of these distinctive features of Haultin's work in Plowden's letterforms. Figure 2.5 reproduces an example of Haultin's english roman, from a 1700 type specimen by printer Johannes Rolu. This particular cut was first seen in 1559 in Venice, but is also evident by at least 1566 in London in the work of printer John Day[78] (many printers commonly purchased from the same limited pool of available fonts).[79] This Rolu specimen shows examples of Haultin's 'dog-eared' M, steep-tailed R, double-serifed T crossbar, and large-bowled P (see extracted letters in Figure 2.5). Table 2.1 shows enlarged letters M, R, and P sampled from Fol 21 of Plowden, with T from Fol 1, placed alongside the same letters from the Rolu specimen and from various examples of Garamond. There is clear similarity of letter shape and design between Plowden and Haultin, notably with respect to these four key features.

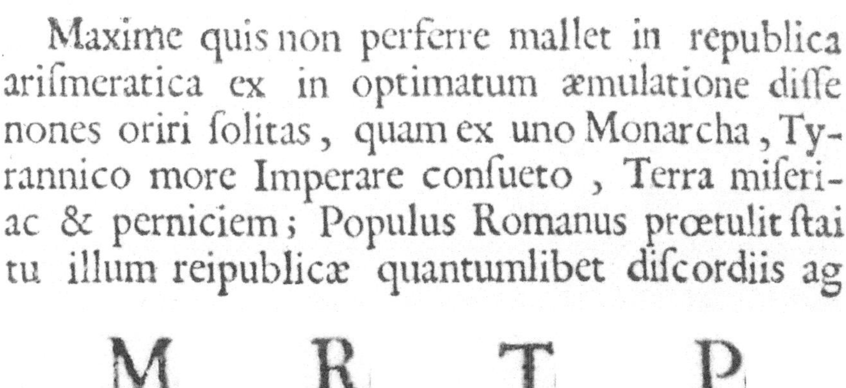
Maxime quis non perferre mallet in republica
ariſmeratica ex in optimatum æmulatione diſſe
nones oriri ſolitas, quam ex uno Monarcha, Ty-
rannico more Imperare conſueto , Terra miſeri-
ac & perniciem; Populus Romanus prœtulit ſtai
tu illum reipublicæ quantumlibet diſcordiis ag

M R T P

Figure 2.5: The Rolu specimen of Pierre Haultin's english roman type, from Dreyfus,[80] with details of key letters M, R, T and P. Image is in the public domain.

While this may not be a conclusive analysis, reading Plowden through existing historical evidence compiled by Carter and Vervliet suggests that Tottel's letters could have been of Haultin's design.[82] At the very least, Plowden's roman is a text in a 'post-Garamond' humanist style, as Isaac notes of Tottel's press generally. This humanist character is demonstrated

Haultin	Plowden	Garamond

From Rolu specimen ('Monarcha')	From fol 21 of Plowden ('Modeye')	From Plantin 1567 ('Mater')

From Rolu specimen ('Romanus')	From fol 21 of Plowden ('Recognitio')	From Plantin 1585 ('Romanae')

From Rolu specimen ('Terra')	From fol 1 of Plowden ('SANCTI')	From Plantin 1585 ('Theophrastum')

From Rolu specimen ('Populus')	From fol 21 of Plowden ('Petri')	From Plantin 1585 (first 'Plutum')

Table 2.1: Comparing Plowden's letters with Haultin and Garamond. The Plowden letters show more similarity to Haultin than Garamond: note the 'dog-eared' serifs on the M, the 'steep-tailed' R, the 'double-serifed' T, and the 'big-bowled' P, all of which are not reflected in the Garamond letters. The Haultin letters are the same as in Figure 2.5 and are in the public domain. The Garamond letters are reproduced from Dreyfus[81] under fair use. The letters from Plowden were taken from images kindly provided by the University of Aberdeen, Museums and Special Collections (licenced under CC By 4.0: https://creativecommons.org/licenses/by/4.0/).

further in Figure 2.6, which shows the opening words of the printed common law ('*Concessum est*') adhering to what Bringhurst calls a 'humanist axis'. Typographic 'axis' refers to the orientation of an imagined writer's 'hand and forearm', as evidenced by the variation in line width on the page, as if the letters were 'produced by a broadnib pen held in the right hand in a comfortable and relaxed writing position'.[83] With a humanist font, the 'thick strokes run NW/SE, [along] the axis of the [imagined] writer's hand and forearm',[84] connecting the letterforms to their human origin. The letters of '*Concessum est*' display their thick lines generally flowing from upper left ('NW') to bottom right ('SE'), with the thinner lines perpendicular to this, displaying a modest but clear variation in line width – matching the humanist lines produced by Bringhurst's imaginary pen. (Note that the capital C appears to be damaged, with its lower end bent down, out of line with the axis displayed in other capital Cs in Plowden.) The crossbar on the lowercase e does not fit this pattern, but – as Bringhurst also notes – from about 1500, the humanist style of e adopted a horizontal bar out of line with the 'natural' axis of the rest of the letters.[85]

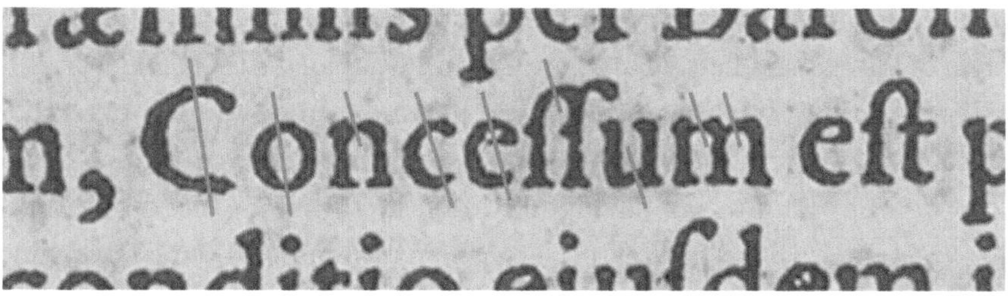

Figure 2.6: The humanist axis of the printed *iudicium* in *Renyger v Fogassa.* Mark-up produced by Thomas Giddens from an image kindly provided by the University of Aberdeen, Museums and Special Collections (licenced under CC By 4.0: https://creativecommons.org/licenses/by/4.0/).

The *iudicium* appears in a humanist 'english' sized 'roman' face, potentially cut by Pierre Haultin. Speculatively, the juxtaposition of the terms 'english' and 'roman' indicate something of the paradox or tension involved in the 'Roman-style' codification of the unwritten 'English' common law, to which 'romanizing' refers. As Figure 2.4 shows, the body of the type supports the visible face of the imprinted text, and thus remains unprinted and invisible to the reader. Plowden's 'english roman' can be read as indicating a visible face of Roman text with structure and support given by an invisible and unprinted (that is, unwritten) body of English principle. Given that the opening word of the *iudicium* is '*Concessum*', this might be pushed further: printed reports involve a 'concession' to materiality by the invisible and inaccessible authority of (English) law, granting visible form to the mysteries of the law in order to enable a practical decision to be taken (the imperfection of the opening C, if it attracts any meaning at all, might support this reading, with the 'perfection' of principle appearing in 'imperfect' form in the very first letter of the common law's typographic materiality). Such readings may appear superficial, coincidental, or strained, but fuller analysis of this typographic form can bring substance to at least some of these connections.

Roman font's humanist heritage

While it is arguably on one level mere coincidence that an 'english' size was used to print Plowden's *iudicium* in 'roman' text, there is a deeper significance at work in the material conventions of the type – beyond its name. The naming of roman font, in particular, is not a coincidence, but derives from the historical and geographic emergence of a particular style of letterform. Letters are contingent visual forms that reflect wider forces of influence and genealogies of meaning. In order to understand the arrangement of the opening moment of the printed common law in Plowden more fully, and having now identified them, we need to trace the meaningful heritage of the letterforms themselves, and how they encounter and thus encode wider tensions over the influence of (visible) Roman law on the (invisible) common law of England. Understanding the cultural and aesthetic influences that shaped Plowden's particular typographic appearance involves examining the heritage of roman letterforms, and of 'humanist' letters in particular, and how this history of meanings plays into the authoritative debates over printing the common law. To understand the significance of the deployment of (Haultin's) roman font in Plowden, we need to go back to the development of humanist script.

The usual origin cited for roman type is Nicolas Jenson, who in fifteenth-century Venice produced arguably the first full set of roman letterforms. The heritage of his typographic consolidation, however, lies in the scribal forms of the Italian renaissance. Humanist script evolved out of Carolingian letterforms, which were promulgated as one of the leading written forms of both the Roman Empire and the empire of Charlemagne, and eventually resulted in what is now known as roman type.[86] While the Carolingian form was replaced across most of Europe by angular gothic script (blackletter), it persisted in a 'relatively pure and graceful' form in Italian manuscripts,[87] characterized by the 'round and wide'[88] forms of the humanist hand. Ullman's analysis detects innovations in the handwriting practices of early humanist Coluccio Salutati. Ullman claims this was inspired by the comparably open legibility of the earlier Carolingian script he was reading, and the need for more legible script for humanists devoted to the benefits of scholarly study:[89] 'The humanists of the fourteenth century . . . read more, perhaps, than their predecessors, [and] preferred manuscripts in large, clear writing, . . . i.e. in the Carolingian script of the ninth to twelfth centuries.'[90] The prefer ence could also, however, have been due to a desire to 'add a sense of authority' to their texts by using 'visual reference to classical sources.'[91] Alternatively, these early experiments may have initially stemmed from replacing lost or damaged sections of text in a style intended to emulate the older script of the original.[92] In either case, Ullman's analysis of surviving manuscripts traces the development of the evident technical shifts in scribal handwriting in Italy across the fourteenth and into the fifteenth century, resulting in what De Robertis also observes as the 'instant success'[93] of a newly evolved Latin script based on the 'qualities of formal balance, sobriety, and legibility'[94] of the earlier Carolingian model.[95] These innovations eventually led to roman type, as writing developed 'almost imperceptibly into the printer's art,'[96] with the bifurcation of blackletter and roman styles of text becoming 'canonized in the fonts of typography.'[97]

The evolving forms of humanist script were preferred not only by humanists, but also by book collectors across Europe. Given this widespread preference, it was inevitably 'preferred by the early Italian printers.'[98] Scribes experimented in ways they hoped would improve their products, primarily by making them more legible, emulating older models of 'legibility' and 'cleanliness' in manuscript style,[99] and while some experiments did not succeed, 'others have persisted to this day' in typographic design.[100] As Bringhurst puts it, Roman type shares the 'sensuous and unhurried light and space' of Renaissance handwriting, and this typographic design itself has had lasting effects, serving 'as typographic benchmarks for five hundred years.'[101] Indeed, Bland notes that 'the arrival of roman as the primary face of composition in English books, and the changes that it brought, are still with us and . . . are never likely to be entirely displaced.'[102]

Jenson, then, did not create his roman type out of nothing. He took the 'rounder, lighter forms' of humanist script as his model,[103] just as blackletter typecutters derived letterforms from existing gothic script. In both cases, typecutters sought to emulate existing forms of handwriting in a regularized and legible manner for the printing press, adapting familiar textual forms to the technology of the press.[104] Febvre and Martin note how early printers 'took extreme care to produce exact imitations' of existing manuscripts.[105] The more cramped and less readable blackletter style, which was adopted by Gutenberg and others, was traditionally dominant in most of Europe as the most usual form of hand-written script. Despite both clearly being linked with the human hand,[106] however, blackletter and roman have different lines of heritage and different cultural associations: blackletter typically resonates with tradition and conservatism, and roman with the 'humanist' scholarship of the Italian renaissance and its civilizing ethos. The visual form of letters has a significant practical dimension, especially in a book or prose context where legibility and ease of reading are paramount concerns. Yet such practical questions have evident ideological significance in terms of their commitment to the openness or accessibility of a text, or the decorative traditions that might be maintained at the cost of legibility.[107]

The spread of roman letterforms was not immediate, and moved quicker in some textual contexts than others. Like the conventions of handwriting, blackletter was the dominant typographic form in most of Europe in the early days of print, and was gradually displaced in different kinds of texts at different times.[108] Blackletter was the first type to dominate England, with roman only being used to set Latin text, in line with sixteenth-century convention.[109] 'Despite the appearance of some well-printed books in roman or italic during the 1570s and 1580s, the [London] trade remained conservative in its typographic practices.'[110] In the sixteenth century, many printers would thus carry sets of both roman and blackletter types in various sizes, as well as italics, as the conventions of different texts demanded. Yet it was the conservative blackletter that 'remained the predominant English language typeface' until the late 1600s.[111] Blackletter was also heavily associated with Norman French, and thus endured in the texts of 'blackletter law' (as well as in, for example, Bibles) long after it had died out elsewhere.[112]

Roman typography thus carries various political and cultural connotations, regardless of any conscious choice or intent on the part of the printer, and these were heightened in a legal context. On the one hand, blackletter was familiar and traditional, visually similar to the hand-written texts of manuscript culture and strongly associated with the technical French used by common lawyers. Roman text, on the other hand, was Latin, connected with the linguistic and legal traditions of

Rome as much as the scholarly ethos of the renaissance. Indeed, the spread of roman fonts across Europe was symptomatic of a 'triumphant humanism [that] had imposed the use of roman type'.[113] And the connections of roman fonts with renaissance learning and Roman heritage have particular resonances for common lawyers that are intricately linked, as outlined above, with the debate over print itself.

Plowden's typographic details go to the heart of the concept of 'romanizing' the common law. While the specificity of Haultin may be questionable, the visual design of the roman letters in Plowden's text are nevertheless an expression of the humanist influences stemming from continental Europe. The loose 'school' of early Parisian typecutters that includes the likes of Garamond and Haultin exerted a lasting influence over type design, evolving the initial model founded by Jenson that in itself was modelled on the humanist handwritten script of the renaissance. A genealogy can be traced from the humanist ethos of the Italian renaissance, via the practical changes in handwriting in the humanists' scholarly endeavours that were seen to underpin good civilization, through the typographical encoding of this humanist script into printed letterforms by the likes of Jenson, to the development of more refined characters in the work of Garamond and his contemporaries.[114] As a staging of authority, Plowden's typographic expression reveals a general institutional desire for legal humanism. The intricate details of the roman text in which Plowden's first reported words of the common law appears are not mere decoration, technical happenstance, or design pretence – but represent the material expression of a pragmatic shift in writing technologies, heavily freighted with a humanist ethos that found civilizing value in scholarly study and rational principle-building, and resulted in the innovations in written form that became encoded in the typographic design of roman fonts.

Romanizing the law

Displaying the law in 'roman' form embeds the question of a 'Roman' method into Plowden as an artefact of both printing heritage and common law history – a Roman method connected both to the general humanism of the Italian renaissance and the specific practices of codification and scholarly glosses in Roman law. Plowden is not simply a marker of legal humanism, but is itself materially caught in the complex tensions over printing the common law – of 'writing' what is essentially 'unwritten.' Indeed, Plowden himself equivocated on the benefits of print, but resolved that a stabilized and thus authoritative version of his well-respected manuscript – with its production overseen by himself and the seemingly trustworthy Tottel[115] – was better than the alternative.[116]

Chronologically, Plowden is located between the progressive humanism associated with Rastell and the stronger Romanist codification associated with the later Francis Bacon. Where Plowden hesitates around printing his law reports, Bacon was directly inspired by the Roman model in his desire for a total codification of the common law in text.[117] Yet, despite this desire, Bacon remained firm in his commitment to the common law as an unwritten law, even though it seemed unavoidable that codification would radically alter the nature of common law authority. The structure of the Roman *Corpus Iuris* hung entirely on the word of the sovereign as the ultimate source of the law: 'Without a royal author,' according to Romanist logic, 'the law could not be written.'[118] While Plowden published his reports only because his manuscript was highly valued in the legal community, and suffered or risked error in its reproduction as a manuscript, Bacon's dream of a Roman-style code would render the common law the direct textual expression of sovereign authority – as a de facto written law, rather than remaining essentially unwritten.[119]

Edward Coke's counter-rendition of a printed common law, meanwhile, avoided such a fate. Coke was keen on print, and supported the publication of his *Reports* and later treatises. His general 'emphasis upon learning, understanding and a knowledge of the law . . . could only be resolved by a wide distribution of information, which print enabled.'[120] It was for the good of law students that an accurate text be widely available for study, and for the good of Coke's political position that the superiority of the common law to the crown be publicly set out.[121] Importantly for the current argument, Coke also challenged the inevitability of a Romanist code in the mere fact of common law print. The prefaces to Coke's *Reports* took the nascent and relatively passive practice of law reporting and recast it 'as an ideological weapon.'[122]

Judges, not the sovereign, author the law:[123] it 'embodies the wisdom of generations' of judicial acts.[124] The law may be the sovereign's, but 'only as the kingdom is his, by due and lawful inheritance; it is not his to make or to alter.'[125] Presented as reports – as evidence of an unwritten law ultimately decided somewhere other than within the text – Coke's typographic edifice represents the 'raw' material of legal decision, with such reports (like the older year books) requiring sophisticated expertise to understand and apply. One can only glean their insights through immersion in the textuality of their available form, through a diligent study[126] by which one might come to master the bespoke or artificial mode of reason that characterizes the occult science of the common law.[127]

Reports are indexes, evidence of a law elsewhere, accessible only with proficiency in the requisite methods. Coke's writing of the common law is emblematic of this structure, being – as Helgerson puts it – 'a writing against the written.'[128] Reporting decisions resolves questions of the source of law in a particular way, positioning its textual appearance – its transmission (*fundere*) – as a hermeneutic of the true and unwritten source (*fons*) it claims as its authorizing reference. For Coke, digests and abridgments resolve legal sources in the opposite direction, setting up ever more barriers that stop the law flowing from its judicial source to its reader.[129] This version of the common law, intimately connected with its expression through typographic artefacts, also increases the legitimacy of the law by divorcing it from the whims of a monarch: 'while written laws contain only the wisdom of one Prince, or Legislator, customary law by definition contains the wisdom and experience of generations of people who have tested and used it.'[130] The immemorial quality of the common law disarms any suggestion that it has an ultimate author in the sovereign, and retains for it a separate line of heritage – and thus an alternative source of authority and concomitant jurisdiction. One that provides the crown with limits through which its power may be exercised.[131]

Printing the common law stems predominantly from two interlinked humanist desires. One for public legal education and an accessible legal text, associated with the humanism of the renaissance and the apparent open legibility of roman letterforms. The other for a Romanist codification, associated with prioritizing material texts as the stabilized source of law. The common law has generally come to be rendered in printed form, but it resists both the humanist openness to rational analysis and, along lines established by Coke, the authoritative codification characteristic of Roman law. Coke's insular vision of law reporting builds upon previous practices of legal reportage established in the year books and the emergent nominate reports in the latter half of the sixteenth century, of which Plowden is an innovative and influential example. The significant legacy of Coke's *Reports* serves as a relay and augmentation of the earlier watershed evident in the material register of Plowden's typography. As the first modern law report, printed in a face that is materially linked to both the humanism of Rastell and the Roman codification championed by Bacon, and caught between the potential authority of a standardized text and the traditional practices of manuscript culture and professional expertise, Plowden's *Commentaries* occupies a space in common law history where authority and typography explicitly overlap and, in their overlap, are implicated in the tensions inherent in 'romanizing' the law.

While Plowden's visual style expresses an authority grounded in a desire for humanism, the printing of reports expresses precisely the opposite, staging authority by referring to an absent source beyond any humanist text or code. On the one hand, the roman font in Plowden signifies a law that is not only written and disseminated, in the model preferred by Rastell and other early publicists, but one written in a codified form, authored by the sovereign, to be further elucidated and understood through scholarly study and the setting of other institutional texts to surround and support the primary code. The civilizing efforts of law become dependent on scholarship, on the textual work of the code itself and its supporting sources – mediated through a written form with a particular renaissance heritage, visually contoured for legibility and ease of study. This is not an imperious blackletter text – hard to read, steeped in a 'timeless' tradition and visual complexity – but an interpretively open roman one, able to be studied and examined through the endeavours of any reading subject. Such humanist roman letters have distinct implications in a legal context. They change the understanding of a text's status and its nature as a legal source, rendering law not invisible or determined elsewhere, or only accessible through a certain kind of cloistered proficiency, but as present in its very code. The law is made available for analysis by anyone who would care to make sense of it – by scholars and the wider population, not only the exclusive community of trained lawyers and judges. Yet on the other hand, the roman letterforms of Plowden only reveal a report of the law – not the law itself. The ideological trajectory implied by its humanist type is frustrated, the law fails to manifest itself, and the text remains at a distance from its authorizing source, only ever indicating the law as something decided elsewhere, by those with the proficiency to do so. Such a law remains invisible – and distinctly English.

We thus return to the initially frivolous associations of the 'english roman' of Plowden's printing. A terminological happenstance that actually does, upon fuller analysis, help signify much of the complexity and anxiety around the common law as an increasingly print-based tradition – regardless of the specific name that might be attached to the 'body' of the font in use. Encountered and developed in light of the humanist and Roman histories of the letterforms of Plowden's opening *iudicium*, and connecting to the wider debates of the propriety and effect of legal print, the opening words of the printed common law display in their visual form a structural relation between law's visibility and invisibility that is freighted with the complex tensions surrounding the qualities of the common law tradition. The text of the *iudicium* appears as a humanist roman text on an unseen english body: it is characterized by a Roman face or visible surface, supported or held together by an invisible, unprinted body of English principle, which can only be divined – in Coke's rendition, at least – through the expert study of trained jurists in line with immemorial tradition.

The printed reports of the common law only codify that law to the extent they are visible, and remain contingent upon that which is not printed: the invisible body that supports the visible face. Weaving a tricky path within the heritage of both unwritten and written traditions of law, under the seemingly unstoppable impetus of a proliferating communications technology, the first printed words of the English common law both codify and resist codification: they present the law in text in the same moment they resist the capacity of text to reveal the law. And, moreover, as found in their typographic meanings, they embed this contradiction in the aesthetics of their contingent visual form, signifying an (imperfect) Roman-style code for the unwritten common law of England.

Conclusion

More than mere decoration or practical necessity, the visible surface of the common law texts encountered within the legal institution, the design and appearance of their letterforms, manifest enduring questions worthy of legal attention and that go to fundamental debates as to the nature and study of the common law tradition. The style and design of common law typography, as exemplified in Plowden's opening imprint, are not without legal consequence, and have complex histories and associations. As we have seen, these trajectories meaningfully encounter core questions of common law authority, form, and method, captured here under the term 'romanizing'. These typographic dimensions of common law texts tend to sit in the background, or become suppressed through familiarity and convention, dismissed as 'mere style'. The analysis in this chapter – like the wider study this book undertakes – seeks to bring these aspects into the foreground. Often overlooked, their latent meanings linger, and can be extracted and elaborated through visual and contextual analysis. These meanings are not isolated from the substantive and authoritative qualities usually presumed to be the central, if not only, legally relevant dimensions of common law texts, and instead participate in the common law's material staging of authority. In the specific case of Plowden, the quality of this performance – expressed in humanist letterforms – reveals a claim that Latinate traditions are embedded in the material foundations of the modern common law, a tradition now beholden to the technology of typographically constituted law reports. This technology has had significant impact on the common law and its law reporting practices. Accordingly, in the next chapter we will examine how the technology of the press shaped the long-term practices of the common law through the nineteenth-century standardization of law reporting.

Notes

1. This chapter makes a consistent distinction between 'Roman' and 'roman', and between 'English' and 'english'. Where reference is to the national or geographic entity, the proper noun is used ('Roman', 'English'), while reference to general typographic categories uses improper nouns: 'roman' for the serifed style of typeface; 'english' for the body size (the body size of type is discussed below: see pp 61-62.
2. Dorsett and McVeigh, *Jurisdiction*, 34.
3. The literature is extensive. For an overview and practical guide, see Bringhurst, *Elements*. For an exemplary textbook, see Ellen Lupton, *Thinking With Type: A Critical Guide for Designers, Writers, Editors, and Students*, 2nd ed. (Princeton Architectural Press, 2010). For a wider range of critical perspectives and analyses, see Christopher Scott Wyatt and Dànielle Nicole DeVoss, eds., *Type Matters: The Rhetoricity of Letterforms* (Parlour Press, 2018). Appendix 1 also provides a brief primer on typographic concepts.
4. Bland, 'Appearance', 92. As Lyotard claims more generally, linguistic writing operates precisely through the suppression of text's visual form: see Lyotard, *Discourse, Figure*, 210. This is discussed in more detail in Chapter 1.
5. See, for example, Harvey, *The Law Emprynted*, 97. Tottel is better known for his poetic *Miscellany*: see, for example, Stenner, *Typographic Imaginary*, 128–43.
6. See Peter Goodrich, *Legal Emblems and the Art of Law:* Obiter Depicta *as the Vision of Governance* (Cambridge University Press, 2013).
7. See Mulcahy, *Legal Architecture*.
8. See Leslie J. Moran, 'Judicial Bodies as Sexual Bodies: A Tale of Two Portraits', *The Australian Feminist Law Journal* 29 (2008): 91–108. On law and dress more generally, see Watt, *Dress, Law and Naked Truth*.
9. See Philippopoulos-Mihalopoulos, *Spatial Justice*.
10. On the innovation and concomitant effects of language's written form, see Ong, *Orality and Literacy*. As he notes (at 87): 'Writing . . . moves speech from the oral-aural to a new sensory world, that of vision', thereby transforming both speech and thought. This is discussed further in Chapter 4. For a detailed study of evolving conventions in visual communication more widely (including text), see Charles Kostelnick and Michael Hassett, *Shaping Information: The Rhetoric of Visual Conventions* (Southern Illinois University Press, 2003).
11. On lawyers' professional immersion under the concept of '*nos erudition*', see Harvey, *The Law Emprynted*, 135–39.
12. Theodore F. T. Plucknett, *A Concise History of the Common Law* (Liberty Fund, 2010), 272–73. Judicial reasoning was 'off the record', with early records containing only the order of the court: see John Baker, 'Law Reporting in England 1550–1650', *International Journal of Legal Information* 45, no. 3 (2017): 212.
13. John P. Dawson, *The Oracles of the Law* (University Press of Michigan, 1968), 10.

14. Ian Williams, '"He Creditted More the Printed Booke": Common Lawyers' Receptivity to Print, c. 1550–1640', *Law and History Review* 28, no. 1 (2010): 42.
15. Ross, 'Commoning', 392.
16. See Harvey, *The Law Emprynted*, 42–44.
17. Harvey, *The Law Emprynted*, 44–47.
18. For detailed study of the early printing of the law in England, covering statute and common law, see Harvey, *The Law Emprynted*. Ross's overview of printing debates also covers both statute and common law: see Ross, 'Commoning'.
19. See Ian Williams, 'Early-Modern Judges and the Practice of Precedent', in *Judges and Judging in the History of the Common and Civil Law: From Antiquity to Modern Times*, ed. Joshua Getzler and Paul Brand (Cambridge University Press, 2012).
20. Ross, 'Commoning', 438–43.
21. Ross, 'Commoning', 379.
22. Ross, 'Commoning', 375.
23. Ross argues that resistance increased as printed texts became more commonplace in legal training and practice: see Ross, 'Commoning'. Indeed, extended anti-publicist sources are relatively rare, since they were not predisposed to publication: see Ross, 'Commoning', 385.
24. Hudson, quoted in Ross, 'Commoning', 358.
25. See Ross, 'Commoning', 361.
26. Ross, 'Commoning', 428, citing a 1610 proclamation by King James himself.
27. Ross, 'Commoning', 359.
28. Ross, 'Commoning', 428.
29. For examination of the bespoke qualities of legal language, divergent from everyday vernaculars, see Terezie Smejkalová, 'Legal Performance: Translating into Law and Subjectivity in Law', *Tilburg Law Review* 22 (2017): 62–76.
30. Goodrich, 'Emblem Book', 155.
31. In Gandorfer's terms, it is 'matterphorical' – law is not pure concept manifesting in material form, but is constituted as matter-discursive practice: see Gandorfer, *Matterphorics*.
32. Peter Goodrich, '*Imago Decidendi*: On the Common Law of Images', *Art and Law* 1, no 1 (2017): 28.
33. Zurcher, 'Spenser', 655–56.
34. Zurcher, 'Spenser', 657.
35. On law's 'geography of mental spaces', see Peter Goodrich, *Oedipus Lex: Psychoanalysis, History, Law* (University of California Press, 1995), 9–10.
36. We will return to this question in Chapter 5.
37. For a rich extended study of the revelation of law's formless form as a structural staging of the fiction of a divide between visible and invisible, see Legendre, *God in the Mirror*. This is engaged further in Chapter 5.
38. See Ross, 'Commoning', 329–42.
39. See, for example, Thomas Giddens, 'A Series of Unfortunate Events *or* The Common Law', *Law and Literature* 33, no 1 (2021): 23–48.
40. Ross, 'Commoning', 338.
41. See Ross, 'Commoning', 334–36.

42. See, for example, C. P. Rodgers, 'Humanism, History and the Common Law', *The Journal of Legal History* 6, no. 2 (1985): 131–32; Mark D. Walters, 'Legal Humanism and Law-as-Integrity', *The Cambridge Law Journal* 67, no 2 (2008): 357–60. See also Peter Goodrich, 'Intellection and Indiscipline', *Journal of Law and Society* 36 (2009): 460–80.
43. See Rodgers, 'Humanism'.
44. Ross, 'Commoning'.
45. On the repression of continental influences within the English tradition, and their critical return, see Peter Goodrich, 'Critical Legal Studies in England: Prospective Histories', *Oxford Journal of Legal Studies* 12, no. 2 (1992): 195–236.
46. Harvey, *The Law Emprynted*, 161.
47. See Harvey, *The Law Emprynted*, 160–61.
48. Baker, 'Law Reporting', 211.
49. Baker, 'Law Reporting', 212. On the immediate impact of Plowden, see Harvey, *The Law Emprynted*, 161–62. It is worth noting that an earlier text of importance might be *Bracton*, which from the thirteenth century provided lawyers with commentary on legal decisions drawn from the court record. However, *Bracton* – although significant – is beyond the focus of this study, since it does not 'report' on cases in the modern format that Plowden adopts, being piecemeal and polemical. See Plucknett, *A Concise History*, 259–60.
50. Baker, 'Law Reporting', 211.
51. The folio format is itself significant to note, for instance. The bare size and shape of the volume indicates the importance of the text, since folios were 'reserved for substantial works of serious intellectual, religious or political import', including 'lawbooks . . . classical literature and works of scholarship': Bland, 'Appearance', 117.
52. Note that 'judgment' at this time technically refers to the court's decision, not to the fuller concept of facts, law, reasoning, and justification that characterizes today's concept of 'judgment'; this underlying reasoning was 'off the record': see Baker, 'Law Reporting', 212. In this period, as the concept of precedent was still emerging, the 'record' of decisions was also clearly distinguished from reporting or commentary upon that record, with the record (that is, the court roll) being recognized as the most authoritative source: see Williams, 'Early-Modern Judges', 56–60. As Cormack also notes: because 'legal proceedings became a final and permanent record only when they were transcribed in Latin on parchment rolls, Latin was the principal linguistic sign of a document's status *as* formal record': Cormack, *A Power to Do Justice*, 70. Indeed, this is arguably why Plowden adopted his method of reproducing directly from the record – a practice now followed by modern full-text law reports that reproduce court transcripts, with clearly demarcated commentary and metadata. We discuss the typography of modern court transcripts in Chapter 4.
53. See Baker, 'Law Reporting', 211.
54. As Bland notes, 'italic was used . . . in order to convey the orality of the text': Bland, 'Appearance', 99–100. The current chapter does not engage with the

form and use of italics, but on the general development and spread of italic types from their Italian source, see Carter, *Early Typography*, 117–26.

55. Kostelnick and Hassett, *Shaping Information*, 6.
56. See n 1, above, on the use of 'Roman' vs 'roman'.
57. A subsequent report of this case, translated from Plowden's initial version, can be found at *Reniger v Fogossa* 75 ER 1.
58. The translation is reproduced from *Reniger v Fogossa* 75 ER 1, 33.
59. See n 49 above, and Baker, 'Law Reporting', 212.
60. See Carter, *Early Typography*, 3.
61. For comprehensive diagrams detailing the complex anatomy of a piece of type, see Figure 1 of Carter, *Early Typography*, 127. For fuller details and discussion of the complex techniques of printing and typographic production, and their early development, see Carter, *Early Typography*, 5–22; Febvre and Martin, *Coming of the Book*, 45–76.
62. Other elements may also contribute to this spacing, such as any 'leading' used between lines to widen them. See Febvre and Martin, *Coming of the Book*, 61. See also n 73, below, on size variation in early printing.
63. On traditional size terminology, see briefly Febvre and Martin, *Coming of the Book*, 60; Frank Isaac, *English Printers' Types of the Sixteenth Century* (Oxford University Press, 1936), vi. See also, on their origin, Morison, *Type Designs*, 12–14. For fuller analysis of the development of the modern conventional 'point' system, arguably emerging from the traditional printing sizes, see Kinross, *Modern Typography*, 22–33.
64. See n 1, above, on the use of 'English' vs 'english'.
65. On measuring type over 20 lines, see Isaac, *English Printers' Types*, xi.
66. See Isaac, *English Printers' Types*, 30–31. Note that Isaac's type classification uses 'Garamond' as a general style, not letters cut by Garamond himself. Isaac's taxonomy divides into 'gothic' and 'roman', with 'roman' subdivided into 'pre-Garamond' and 'Garamond' – indicative of the significance of Garamond's designs for the evolution of roman type: see Isaac, *English Printers' Types*, xii–xiii. This chapter uses 'post-Garamond' to accommodate this nuance in Isaac's particular terminology.
67. Carter, *Early Typography*, 84. Note that Garamond did not invent out of nothing, and it is generally thought he derived his work from the types cut for the (undercelebrated) Italian printer Aldus: Alexander Lawson, *Anatomy of a Typeface* (Hamish Hamilton, 1990), 132–33.
68. See Craig Eliason, 'A History of the "Humanist" Type Classification', *Printing History* 18 (2015): 3–26.
69. For an overview of Haultin's roman types and general significance, see Hendrick D. L. Vervliet, 'Printing Types of Pierre Haultin (ca.1510-87) Part I: Roman Types', *Querendo* 30, no. 2 (2000): 87–129. On his underratedness in type histories, see Carter, *Early Typography*, 86–87.
70. A matrix is the set of moulds for casting type. Letters are initially cut on 'punches' of hard metal, which are then used to create moulds by striking them into softer metal (e.g. copper). Hence the term 'punchcutters' for those who

craft letterforms. For the technicalities of early print, see Carter, *Early Typography*, chapter 1.

71. Carter, *Early Typography*, 86.
72. See Vervliet, 'Pierre Haultin', 114.
73. Printing is not an exact science. 92mm over 20 lines is approximately 4.6mm per line (roughly 13 point). Aberdeen's copy of Plowden was measured at 95mm over 20 lines, and 47mm over 10 lines, with individual lines varying between 4.5 and 5mm. It is conventional to measure type over 20 lines: see Isaac, *English Printers' Types*, xi. Yet Isaac also notes at n 1 – citing McKerrow, who prefers to measure over 10 lines – that 'english' size varies between 45 and 47mm for 10 lines (13–13.5 point). Most informatively, as James Mosley explains in his preface to Carter, *Early Typography*, 13: 'On the printed page, type appears in a variety of conditions, new or worn, over- or underinked. Type from identical matrices may look very different if it is cast in a mould for a larger or smaller body, or if a different setting . . . makes it appear more widely or closely set. The extent to which the dimensions of the impression have altered when the paper it is printed on has shrunk in drying, perhaps unevenly, after having been printed damp make it unwise to rely on exact measurements from the page'.
74. Vervliet, 'Pierre Haultin', 94. Vervliet observes these typical characteristics emerging from about 1550.
75. Vervliet, 'Pierre Haultin', 94.
76. The 'bowl' refers to the loop on letters such as P and R. See Appendix 1.
77. See Vervliet, 'Pierre Haultin', 114.
78. See Vervliet, 'Pierre Haultin', 113.
79. Isaac notes that most of Tottel's fonts can be matched to those also held by other London printers: Isaac, *English Printers' Types*, 31.
80. See John Dreyfus, ed., *Type Specimen Facsimiles [1–15]: Reproduction of Fifteen Type Specimen Sheets Issued Between the Sixteenth and Eighteenth Centuries* (Bowes, 1963), sheet 15.
81. Garamond's letters are sampled from a number of specimens contained in John Dreyfus, ed., *Type Specimen Facsimiles [16–18]: Reproductions of Christopher Plantin's 'Idex Sive Specimen Characterum' 1567 and Folio Specimens of c.1585, Together with the Le Bé-Moretus Specimen, c. 1599* (Bodley Head, 1972). The M comes from specimen 24 of Plantin's 1567 *Index Characterum.* The sampled T and P are from specimen 26 and 32, respectively, in Plantin's 1585 *Folio Specimen*, but represent the same font: Garamond's 'english' size roman (90mm over 20 lines) – see ibid 4. The R is from specimen 38 in the 1585 *Folio Specimen*: this specimen is of Garamond's smaller 'pica' size roman (80mm over 20 lines). It thus does not match the 'english roman' size of the M, T, and P, but shows the longer 'tail' on the R which is characteristic of Garamond's cuts.
82. There are some letters that do not fit this analysis, such as the occasional M lacking a top-right serif, or R that has a longer tail. There also appear to be at least two different versions of the capital C, one with a narrower aperture

than the other. Figure 2.2 gives good examples: the R in the final 'Regis' (cf 'Recognitio'), the M in 'Maroma' (cf 'Meryke' and the first 'Martini'), and the C in 'Carell' (cf 'Coseworthe' and 'Concessum'). These letters are more in line with Garamond's style – especially the asymmetrical M which, as Carter notes, was a feature that Garamond removed when he recut many of his fonts in 1550: see Carter, *Early Typography*, 85. Lawson also notes the addition of the right serif to the M in Garamond's later cuts: see Lawson, *Anatomy*, 133. It may be that different sets of type owned by Tottel became mixed, or that he purchased fonts of the same body from different sources. Carter does note that, while Haultin's faces were more common, some of Garamond's did find their way to London in the first half of the sixteenth century, prior to the 1550 recut: see Carter, *Early Typography*, 86. Regardless, for the purposes of the argument in this paper, the style of these other letters remains humanist: see Figure 2.6.

83. Bringhurst, *Elements*, 123. Appendix 1 has further introductory examples of typographic axis.
84. Bringhurst, *Elements*, 123.
85. See Bringhurst, *Elements*, 123. Bringhurst's example diagrams also show that as type evolves into the seventeenth-century baroque – and beyond – the axis becomes more generally variable or is omitted altogether (e.g. with modernist geometric letters). See Bringhurst, *Elements*, 12–15.
86. See Lawson, *Anatomy*, 35.
87. See B. L. Ullman, *The Origin and Development of Humanistic Script* (Edizioni di Storia e Letteratura, 1960), 11–12, quote at 12. See also Febvre and Martin, *Coming of the Book*, 79.
88. Bonnie Mak, *How the Page Matters* (University of Toronto Press, 2011), 23.
89. See Ullman, *Humanistic Script*, 11–19.
90. Ullman, *Humanistic Script*, 12.
91. Mak, *How the Page Matters*, 23, 29.
92. See Teresa De Robertis, 'Humanistic Script: Origins', in *The Oxford Handbook of Latin Paleography*, ed. Frank T. Coulson and Robert G. Babcock (Oxford University Press, 2020), 515.
93. De Robertis, 'Humanistic', 518.
94. De Robertis, 'Humanistic', 510.
95. See, generally, Ullman, *Humanistic Script*.
96. Ullman, *Humanistic Script*, 127. See also Bringhurst, *Elements*, 122–23.
97. De Robertis, 'Humanistic', 518.
98. Ullman, *Humanistic Script*, 134.
99. De Robertis, 'Humanistic', 515.
100. Ullman, *Humanistic Script*, 133.
101. Bringhurst, *Elements*, 122–23.
102. Bland, 'Appearance', 92.
103. Lupton, *Thinking with Type*, 15.
104. On standardization into the press, see Parkes, *Pause and Effect*, 50–61.
105. Febvre and Martin, *Coming of the Book*, 77.

106. Humanism has contended meanings, not simply those linked with human origin. In type, the 'humanist' label is similarly contentious, although does have a significant root in the renaissance humanism that influenced Jenson. See Eliason, 'A History'.
107. We return to questions of 'legibility' in Chapter 4.
108. Bland, 'Appearance', 104. See also Febvre and Martin, *Coming of the Book*, 78–83.
109. Bland, 'Appearance', 93.
110. Bland, 'Appearance', 104.
111. This change in style, Bland continues, was associated with 'a combination of Italianate fashion, economic prosperity and type replacement [that] finally changed the typography of literary publications . . . between 1588 and 1593': Bland, 'Appearance', 94.
112. Bland, 'Appearance', 93.
113. Febvre and Martin, *Coming of the Book*, 88.
114. For more on Garamond, including other Parisian figures such as the printers Estienne and Plantin who were instrumental in Garamond's fame and subsequent influence, see Lawson, *Anatomy*, 129–40.
115. On the trust the legal profession placed in Tottel, seemingly due to his affiliations with the legal community via Rastell's son William, see Harvey, *The Law Emprynted*, 98–101.
116. As Plowden's prologue puts it: his manuscript 'came to the handes of some printers who ment (as I was informed) to sett them forthe for gain. And because the cases were written by . . . ignorant persons, that perfectly did not understande the matter, the copies were very corrupt . . . Therefore to preuent and eschewe these defectes, I did deliberate whether it weare my parte to put this booke in print myself. . . . [Meanwhile,] all the Judges of both the benches & Barons of the Eschequer' sent him requests 'to put the woorke in print', which he dutifully did. (I have regularized the long 's' in this quotation, but otherwise maintained spelling.)
117. Helgerson, *Forms of Nationhood*, 75.
118. Helgerson, *Forms of Nationhood*, 75.
119. See Helgerson, *Forms of Nationhood*, 76–77. As he notes (at 77): 'When customs are registered at the king's behest, they become text law and the king becomes their author.'
120. Harvey, *The Law Emprynted*, 221.
121. See Harvey, *The Law Emprynted*, 220–34.
122. Helgerson, *Forms of Nationhood*, 85.
123. Coke, as cited in Helgerson, *Forms of Nationhood*, 84.
124. Rodgers, 'Humanism', 137.
125. Helgerson, *Forms of Nationhood*, 84.
126. On the general humanist connection between study and virtue in the common law, see Giddens, 'A Series of Unfortunate Events'.
127. See Helgerson, *Forms of Nationhood*, 97–100. As Coke puts it: 'the common law is itself nothing else but reason . . . [but] an artificial perfection of reason, gotten by long study, observation, and experience' (98, citing Coke).

128. Helgerson, *Forms of Nationhood*, 100.
129. See Helgerson, *Forms of Nationhood*, 83–84.
130. Rodgers, 'Humanism', 136.
131. On the control of sovereign power through law's textual form, see Augsberg, 'Reading Law'. On the variable understanding of the relation between law and sovereign authority, see, for example, Karl Shoemaker, '*The King's Two Bodies* as Lamentation', *Law, Culture and the Humanities* 13, no. 1 (2017): 24–35.

Chapter 3

Copying the law: the romance of empire

Introduction

In 1889, a steam-powered printing press, housed within the industrial infrastructure of the printing company Clowes and Sons, struck thousands of pages with carefully contoured pieces of metal adorned with ink. Each strike of the press left a particular trace upon a sheet of paper. These individual pages were then collated with others and distributed widely across the British Empire, operating as authentic evidence of the common law. The question of authentic encounters – with law, with nature, with meaning – is characteristic of the romantic. While contested and difficult to sharply define, romanticism can be understood to function as a range of reactions to the technological and rationalizing shifts of the Enlightenment, notably those related to the printing press. The mass duplication of texts troubles the authenticity of literary meaning that many romantic authors sought to challenge by prioritizing, amongst other things, authentic encounters with nature or a recall of humanist letters. The quest for authenticity, however, also results in the seemingly opposite impetus towards standardization practices that, by securing a unified source (*fons*), enable authentic encounters with meaning via a textual source (*fundere*) distributed at scale. In the standardization of law reporting in the nineteenth century, these divergent forms of romanticism come together in the expressive forms of common law typography.

By the nineteenth century, English law reporting had come a long way from the hesitant publication of Plowden, with reporters and printers now vying for a share of the common law readership under a rampant market-based system that increased both the cost and number of reports. Despite Francis Bacon's efforts to create a team of official reporters,[1] the English common law existed without official promulgation and in an uncodified form: it was a law *ex non scripto*,[2] accessible only through its patient (re)construction via the labours of textual reading, as established by Coke (see Chapter 2). Yet, in the competitive market of reports, this not only meant that there were too many law reports to read, but also that the professional practices of the English Bar had to be undertaken on the whims of unregulated commerce rather than the public good it was supposed to serve.

The wide distribution of the law as a mass of material sources, reproduced under the operation of modern systems of print production, raises significant questions for the development of the common law. While reports and their technologized reproduction were the main processes by which common law decisions became available at the time, this chapter focuses on a particular exemplary trace as a means of examining the dual legal and typographic questions these processes raise. This focal trace is a fragment pressed onto multiple pages in 1889 as part of the report of the decision in *Cooper v Stuart*, typically remediated as a quotation of the words 'practically unoccupied'.[3] The case of *Cooper v Stuart* appears at the tail end of the romantic period that sits in the temporal shadow of the Enlightenment, a period when law reporting (*inter alia*) was heavily affected by the ostensibly revolutionizing technologies of print production.[4] By the time *Cooper* was printed, however, the negative effects of print had apparently been tamed by the English Bar who standardized reporting and the printed dissemination of reports. At the same time, *Cooper* is a case about the industrial project of modernity and the spread of empire into an uncivilized beyond filled with natural resources ripe for exploitation. Nuancing understandings of the romantic as being exclusively a resistance to such centralizing projects, this chapter develops its understanding through the romantic typeface of *Cooper* that encompasses a broader range of responses to the technologized media environment following the Enlightenment, notably in relation to the desire for authenticity. *Cooper* is an apt choice to examine at this particular point in the history of common law typography, sitting as it does in relation to the forces of rational modernity as they emerge through the print industry, to which romanticism is often contrasted, as well as the standardization of common law sources undertaken in an effort to render them authentic. It is also a case primarily about the consolidation of the common law's imperial jurisdiction, seeking a single, authentic law at the frontier. Within a broader context of romantic literary production and typographic design that foregrounds the question of medial form, and thus how we might live with the technologies of the press, *Cooper*'s visual text encodes both the desire and the impossibility of a single, standardized source for the expanding common law.

The typographic legality visually and materially expressed as the pages of *Cooper v Stuart* are complex. This chapter seeks to map these complexities in four stages. First, the question of the common law's encounter with 'other laws' at the colonial frontier in *Cooper*'s legal substance is connected to the more general problem of finding authenticity in a context of excess that this chapter takes to be characteristic of the romantic period ('Too many laws'). This, in turn, foregrounds the medial quality of printed texts and how romantic questions about how to live meaningfully with modern communications technologies manifest in typographic practice and design ('Typographic romances'). In the third section ('Standardizing the source'), the question of 'too many laws' results in not only *Cooper*'s suppression of indigenous legalities, but also the overwriting of the market in law reports by a system of standardized and thus authentic reports, which are then duplicated on a mass scale. The practice of copying the law, however, is seen finally ('Distributing the law') to undercut the attempt to produce a single authentic source or origin for the common law, reinscribing the problem of 'too many laws' into a mass network of materially unique typographic artefacts.

The romance of empire is thus seen as a complex of elements related to contrast and authenticity: the elaboration of western civilization over the savage beyond, the encounter with nature at the frontier, the suppression and standardization of legal systems, and of the law reports that seek to authentically evidence them, and the processing of new industrial print technologies as the conditions of writing and the encounter with meaning. Recognized as a typographic artefact, *Cooper v Stuart* is a case industrially printed under the newly centralized law reporting system in England, substantively and contextually concerned with the elaboration of the British Empire into the uncivilized beyond. The romantic face of *Cooper*, itself a product of industrial print technologies, stages its authority as a claim to a standardized and thus authentically singular source (*fons*) distinct from others: one true law that overwrites all others and conditions lawful relations across the British Empire's widely distributed population. Ultimately, however, recognizing *Cooper v Stuart* as a typographic source (*fundere*) reveals it to be an exemplary expression of romanticism's complex question of how to live with modernity's rational project that, in the context of the common law, signifies the impossible fiction of a unitary source.

Too many laws

The 1889 case of *Cooper v Stuart* holds a particular position in the colonial heritage of the common law, situated as one of a series of cases that reformulated the concept of *terra nullius* to facilitate the violent occupation of the landmass now known in the west as Australia.[5] Ostensibly, the case concerns a parcel of land granted by the Governor of New South Wales, within which the colonial government reserved the right to reclaim the land and its resources for various public goods: timber for ships, land for roads, and 'any quantity of water and any quantity of land, not exceeding 10 acres . . . as may be required for public purposes', providing the water mills and watercourses on the land were not injured.[6] According to Lord Watson's judgment, the goal was to further the colonial project: 'The object of the Government in giving off public lands to settlers, is not so much to dispose of the land to pecuniary profit as to attract other colonists.'[7] Lord Watson ultimately argues that the aim of the colony is to perpetuate itself, to grow civilization in the outposts of empire – an aim facilitated by the granting of land to colonial settlers. To demand land be returned, even for specific 'public purposes', undermines the wider public purpose of colonial governance itself.[8] The legal question the judgment answers on the way to this conclusion is which law applies in the colony: specifically, whether the common law rule against perpetuities applies, which would mean the crown's reservation had expired.

The question as to 'which law' is load-bearing for the legal reputation of *Cooper v Stuart*, as it is for its typographic analysis. In both cases, the issue is one of there being too many laws. The laws present are indigenous and colonial, with the common law itself being duplicated in multiple copies by the technologies of print. For Lord Watson, as for Blackstone, the typographic duplication of the common law is not considered sufficiently relevant to discuss. There can be only one law, and the law that is taken to apply rests on the manner of settlement, which in turn rests on whether there was already a civilization and legal system occupying the land in question.[9] Lord Watson holds that a land occupied by cessation or conquest, 'in which there is an established system of law', retains that law unless expressly overwritten; meanwhile, a 'tract of territory practically unoccupied, without settled inhabitants or settled law, at the time it was peacefully annexed to the British dominions', automatically adopts the law of England[10] – including the rule against perpetuities that animated the specific dispute in the case. It is to this second category that Lord Watson infamously assigns the landmass now known as Australia, ultimately resulting in the dismissive encoding of the existential, cultural, and legal presence of all the first nations peoples already inhabiting the land at the time into the typographic artefact remediated in Figure 3.1.

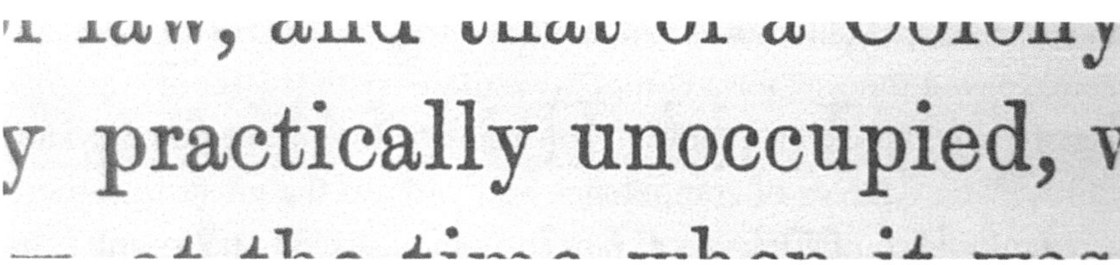

Figure 3.1: The fragment 'practically unoccupied', reproduced from the 1973 photolitho reprint edition of 1889 Appeal Cases, vol 14, housed in the Library at the University of Dundee. Image is detail of *Cooper v Stuart* [1889] 14 Appeal Cases 286, at 291.

This typographic artefact was no doubt taken by Lord Watson, as by the community of legal readers, as signifying a singular common law and thus of little relevance beyond its legible evidencing of that law. The common law gains its authority from its heritage, descending to us through the march of cases from its font (*fons*) in time immemorial – print's function is at best to ensure the law embodied by decision is accurately recorded and transmitted. Where the common law meets other legal traditions, it overwrites them, as in *Cooper* – or, as Shaunnagh Dorsett has argued, absorbs those traditions by retrospectively claiming them as always already part of the common law itself.[11] The plurality of multiple legal systems at the frontier, where the existence of multiple normative orders becomes starkly apparent, resolves to a single jurispathic system.[12] The problem of there being 'too many laws', it seems, is easily solved: there is one law, as embodied in Lord Watson's own decision, and as now evidenced by the report of that decision found in any copy of the fourteenth volume of the 1889 Appeal Cases one might care to consult. This is not an unfamiliar story, and is of course contrasted to postcolonial efforts to recentre indigenous knowledge and law.[13] But it is not a story restricted to the conceptual stratum of the common law: it is also a story of typographic appearance and the standardization of legal media.

In the first half of the nineteenth century, before the printing of *Cooper*, the reporting of the common law in print was a plural affair – there were too many law reports. The reporting system, such as it was, operated on the basis of a free market. The royal patent granted for the printing of common law texts had dissipated across the sixteenth century, as legal texts were produced outside of the patent's confines and the limits of its monopoly were proven to be impractical as the common law's professional literature expanded.[14] This practical erosion of the licence paved the way for a competitive industry of law reporting. Any barrister who fancied it could start up a series of reports, and many did, with varying degrees of competence and care, to the effect that there were multiple competing sets of reports of inconsistent quality and content. Reliable evidence of judicial decisions that could enable authentic encounters with the common law principles they were taken to embody was hard to find.

The common law's media environment was one in which there were both too many and not enough copies of the law. There were 'too many' in the sense that, as one contemporary account has it, the 'monstrous absurdity' of the plethora of competing publications were 'smothering the law in a mass of printed Reports',[15] making it impossible to access and know the law accurately. The landscape of the common law's printed sources had become a 'wilderness of single instances'.[16] On the other hand, there were 'not enough' in the sense that the common law was in 'no respect *officially* promulgated.'[17] On the practical level concerning lawyers and administrators, the problem was one of conflicting reports: if a case was reported in multiples and inconsistently, how were they, or indeed the public, to confidently rely on any particular report and thus know the law? As at the colonial frontier, the question is one of establishing which of the available laws – which report, which tradition – can be taken to be authentic. In legal print, as in the common law's imperial tendency towards a singular or unitary tradition, the project across the nineteenth century was to standardize the system of law reporting: to craft a single set of authoritative reports or sources (*fundere*), duplicated in the printing press, that could enable authentic encounters with the *fons* of common law itself.

The conceptual and material impetus towards a singular, unified, or standardized law corresponds to the wider centralization evident in the project of rational modernity, of which both colonialism and the development of print technologies of mass production can be understood as an expression. In the post-Enlightenment context characterized by an excess of both textual production and legal systems, the quest for standardization becomes a quest for an authentic version. It is this quest for authenticity that connects the efforts of industrial standardization with seemingly contrasting efforts to craft or find authentic meanings in romantic literature and art. A core example of this is seen in the romantic encounter with nature that in a literary sense invokes a lived uniqueness, while also generating a rational and standardized hierarchy of categories.

For Alan Bewell, it is in the colonial project that these aspects of romanticism flow together. The colonial project is both romantic and ecological,[18] as evident in the preoccupation with 'nature feelings' and the authentic encounter with nature in romantic writings: the romantic is 'inseparable from . . . an ecological awareness.'[19] The colonial project follows a similar line, in its encounter with natural phenomena previously unknown to Europeans and the expansion of natural history projects and resource extraction. Colonial expansion thus resulted in a 'proliferation of colonial natures' at the frontier that subsequently appeared 'both in print and material culture'[20] and began to 'disrupt European natural history classification.'[21] As with legal encounters at the frontier, colonial nature presented a problem of there being too many natures, putting into question the authenticity of the rational European ordering of the natural world.[22] In the texts of romanticism, Bewell argues, the encounter with nature as something mysterious and exotic drew its inspiration from a supposedly alien wilderness at the colonial frontier.[23] To resolve this plurality, natural history became '*the* colonial science *par excellence*',[24] seeking to integrate different natures into a standardized modern version of 'nature': a singular source of authorized (that is, European scientific) evidence for what nature was. Indigenous knowledge and culture were transformed into European natural history, just as much as plants and animals were translated into western scientific hierarchies.[25] Natural history became 'a world-making activity, which mediated colonial natures through their more portable forms – via inscriptions, print, specimens, and other forms of material culture' – enabling the British to know and act on 'the world from a distance'.[26]

Understood as part of a romantic project of natural history, the ecological discourse in *Cooper v Stuart* is concerned with the European exploitation of natural resources for the good of empire. Natural history, Bewell reminds us, was not just about a trade in exotic artefacts and specimens or the literary inculcation of nature feelings, but also 'provided knowledge necessary for colonial settlements and for the successful global exploitation of natural resources' by Europeans.[27] *Cooper* is not merely concerned with whether certain common law doctrines apply or not, nor with its dismissed question of whether first nations peoples 'occupied' the land. It is not just a question of there being too many laws, overwriting other extant laws with a common law right to land and resources, but also addresses the question of European resource extraction. Namely, whether the extended hand of the British state is able to reach out to the frontier and take what it needs, or whether these resources remain the purview of the good British subjects who have volunteered to help push back the outer reaches of European civilization. In either case, the land is understood as property in a western sense, and moreover as a pool of resources always already conceived as ripe for harvest by Europeans – the question is simply *which* Europeans. Taken as a romantic text, the story that *Cooper* navigates is the purportedly authentic encounter with both an untrammelled nature and a standardized expression of the common law. It is an entangled narrative of a beyond, replete with value for Europeans to take for the good of western civilization, to fuel the continued unfolding of the modern European project of centralization in the wake of the Enlightenment, performatively expressed in a medial form that both expresses a standardized law while, as this chapter argues, concomitantly undermining the very standardization of which it is a symptom.

Typographic romances

Too many laws, too many natures – and too many books. The problem of excess can be seen to permeate the romantic in general as much as in *Cooper v Stuart* specifically. In its substance and form, *Cooper* is preoccupied with the cultural processing of the new project of modernity: articulated through modern technologies of print as a resource-driven, imperial encounter with the beyond that produces 'too many' things. Indeed, *Cooper* was printed in a 'romantic' typeface, although the identification of a typeface as 'romantic' is not straightforward. Just as the romantic sits within an aesthetic and ideological framework that encounters the complexities of attempting to define the romantic in general, the claim that a font is romantic also retains a certain ambiguity or contested quality.

Hard to define in the abstract, the features of the romantic emerge from a particular historical set of cultural – predominantly literary – productions across the eighteenth and nineteenth centuries. Defining the romantic tends to resolve into questions of its relationship with the modern and the rational, and is also connected with contrast – the contrast between reason and sentiment, between civilization and its beyond, between industry and authenticity. For typographer and poet Robert Bringhurst, romantic fonts are characterized by round terminals, a vertical axis, and, significantly, a dramatic contrast in line weight.[28] These features can be seen in the printing of *Cooper* in Figure 3.2. Design thinking, of which modern type design is a key specialism, is often caught between ideals of 'rational planning' and being more 'artistically oriented'.[29] Ellen Lupton provides a high-level summary of type history that categorizes the 'humanist' (correlated with the renaissance and linked to the movements of the hand, discussed in Chapter 2), the 'transitional' (associated with an increased contrast in line width and sharper serifs[30]), and the 'modern,' linked to the Enlightenment period and characterized by sharp contrasts in thick and thin lines and abstract, display-oriented letterforms.[31] The broad movement is from letters that are organic and humanist towards those that are rationalist and geometric, enabled by typographic technologies.[32] Bringhurst follows a similar schema, but is more fine-grained, dividing up the Enlightenment into neoclassical and romantic, with sharp contrast in line width (as opposed to more gradual modulation of stroke) tending to be found in the romantic period.[33] 'Dramatic contrast,' Bringhurst tells us, 'is essential to much Romantic music and painting, [and] is essential to Romantic type design as well.'[34]

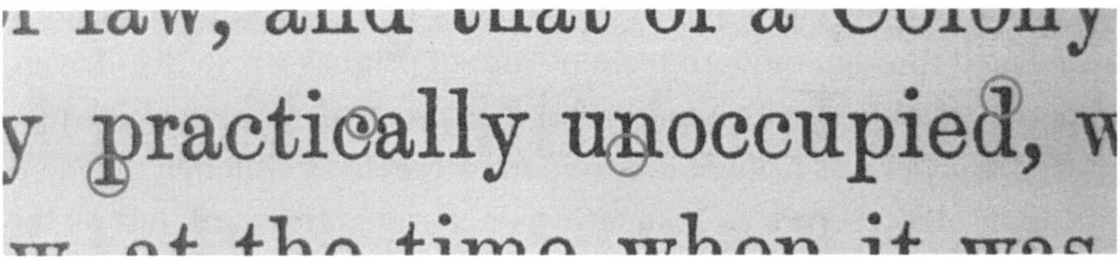

Figure 3.2: Applying Bringhurst's 'romantic' criteria to *Cooper v Stuart*. Mark-up produced by Thomas Giddens using the 1973 photolitho reprint edition of 1889 Appeal Cases, vol 14, housed in the Library at the University of Dundee.

The romantic letter is one to be viewed in its statue-like form against the uninscribed backdrop of the page, rather than entered and substantively navigated as the organic flows of preceding humanist letters encouraged, derived more immediately from their handwritten precursors.[35] Yet this claim is troubled by revival projects such as William Morris's Kelmscott Press in the 1890s, which in its deep resistance to the standardization and the mass production of print[36] arguably typifies 'romantic' responses to modern rationalized technologization.

> Romanticists protested against the idealization of pure logical reason and against the mechanical empiricism associated with ideas of social and natural progress which dominated the ambitions of [the 1800s].[37]

Morris himself 'idealized . . . communitarianism, authentic work ethics, and knightly romance' as a counter to industrialization.[38] As his manifesto for Kelmscott explains, he aimed for 'a letter pure in form' that avoided 'the essential fault of the ordinary modern type' that had become 'compressed laterally . . . owing to commercial exigencies'.[39] This type aspiration was coupled with Morris's own prose romances to produce typographic expressions in direct opposition to the industrial mass production of commercial print that, for Morris, signalled a decline in aesthetic standards in favour of 'cheap, fast printing engendered by the Industrial Revolution'.[40] The modern, rationalized and geometrically contoured letterforms of post-Enlightenment type design were what the priorities of Morris's romantic project sought to counter,[41] and the continued influence of his arts and crafts ethic remain evident as an enduring counterpoint to, or underpinning intuition in, the pure functionalism and rational geometry of 'modern' design thinking.[42]

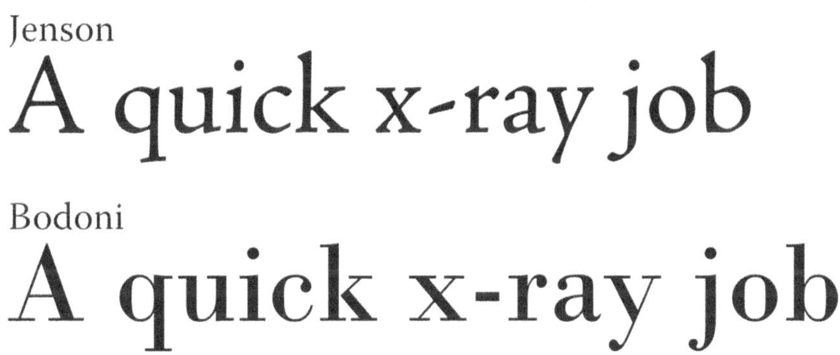

Figure 3.3: Contrasting typefaces: the smooth brackets of humanist Jenson versus the sharp contrast of modern, romantic Bodoni. Image credit: Thomas Giddens (reproduced with permission).

The tendency in modern typography in the nineteenth century was towards the contrast of thick vertical and thin horizontal lines identified by Bringhurst as 'romantic'. A comparison between a traditional humanist face (Adobe's revived version of Jenson's early roman fount) and a modern, romantic face (Bodoni) can be seen in Figure 3.3. The tendency for thick vertical and thin horizontal lines can produce something approaching vertical stripes on the page, resulting in a phenomenon that has been termed typographic 'dazzle'. Repeated patterns on the page are a marker of typographic unreadability, as they distract the eye from the discursive level of the text. With dazzle, as the white and black

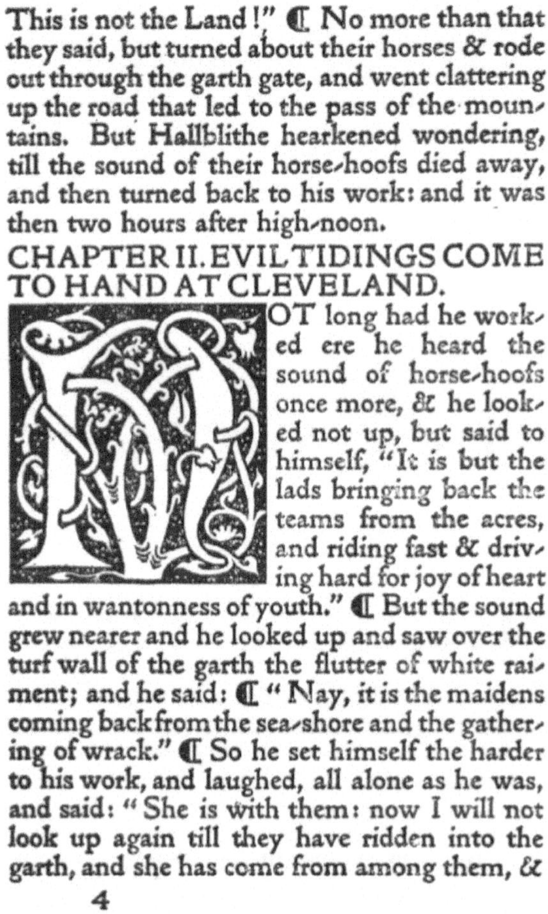

This is not the Land!" ❡ No more than that they said, but turned about their horses & rode out through the garth gate, and went clattering up the road that led to the pass of the mountains. But Hallblithe hearkened wondering, till the sound of their horse-hoofs died away, and then turned back to his work: and it was then two hours after high-noon.

CHAPTER II. EVIL TIDINGS COME TO HAND AT CLEVELAND.

NOT long had he worked ere he heard the sound of horse-hoofs once more, & he looked not up, but said to himself, "It is but the lads bringing back the teams from the acres, and riding fast & driving hard for joy of heart and in wantonness of youth." ❡ But the sound grew nearer and he looked up and saw over the turf wall of the garth the flutter of white raiment; and he said: ❡ "Nay, it is the maidens coming back from the sea-shore and the gathering of wrack." ❡ So he set himself the harder to his work, and laughed, all alone as he was, and said: "She is with them: now I will not look up again till they have ridden into the garth, and she has come from among them, &

4

Figure 3.4: An example page produced by the Kelmscott Press in 1891. Source: Wikimedia Commons (public domain). URL: https://en.wikipedia.org/wiki/File:SGP_ch_2_1891.png

spaces of the verticals approaches an equal balance it confuses the eye, producing 'a blurred muddle of black and white, figure and ground . . . the greater the number of vertical parallel lines that show up between and within the letters, the more dazzling and unreadable' typographers would judge the text to be.[43] The loose setting of this modern type, for Morris and his collaborator Emery Walker, further muddles the balance between figure and ground, letter and page, with pools and 'rivers of white' forming amidst the text.[44] The letter and page designs of the Kelmscott Press explicitly avoided such phenomena, borrowing from earlier humanist examples such as Jenson to craft lines of more modest and gradual variation[45] and setting the heavy text more closely to produce a densely textured page (see Figure 3.4).[46] The dramatic contrast that Bringhurst sees as definitional of romantic faces is precisely what the romantic resistance to modernity at the Kelmscott press sought to suppress, as a material symptom of modern industrial printing. Yet while Morris's Kelmscott pages may have been romantic in their resistance to modern technologies, the letterforms themselves overtly aimed at a humanist ideal.

In its statuesque form and the phenomenon of 'dazzle', the sharp contrast of romantic type design produces a letter that is increasingly oriented towards its own display, self-consciously aware of its own medial quality and thus foregrounding the concern with printing technologies in the wake of the Enlightenment. In Andrew Piper's study of the establishment of the bibliographic imagination that came to underpin western identities,[47] the romantic period is framed specifically in terms of the study of books and the foregrounding of medial form. Romanticism, Piper observes, encounters a division between creative imagination and the technics of form, between 'what happens in the mind', and the 'stuff of dissemination':[48] the contrast between the ideational and the material. According to Piper, it is in the romantic period that European culture transitions to an environment with 'too many books to read',[49] forcing recognition not only of the distinctly bookish form of literature and the material conditions of writing, but also the ways in which romantic writing processed the new writing technologies of print and book publishing.[50] On this level, as Gilles Deleuze recognizes, the confusion of figure and ground in Morris's 'modern letter' is not just an issue for the eye, but challenges the distinction between matter and idea: 'form distinguishes itself from matter or from the ground . . . [but if the] ground is no longer below, it acquires autonomous existence' and reveals the divisions at work in its delineation.[51] This concomitantly reveals the constructed nature of the division between the 'idea' that the form purports to transmit and the 'matter' of its articulation: the stuff in the mind becomes entangled with the stuff of the page. Where modernity might prioritize an internal rational order against an irrational outside, an imagined outside that fuels the desire for progress and expansion,[52] the visual-material technologies of the 'modern letter' reveal a continuum with no outside in which it is instead the affirmation of difference that generates the structures of meaning and form.[53] In this sense, just as Kelmscott's humanist revival can be seen to challenge rational industrialization, the 'rising ground'[54] of Bringhurst's 'romantic' letter can be understood to express questions about the stability of the modern rational order itself. Indeed, as Lupton notes, questioning how 'visual form get[s] inside the "content" of writing' is a distinctly deconstructive gesture.[55]

The theme of the romantic reaction to the Enlightenment project of rational modernity is commonly connected with a revolution against the rationalist and empiricist structures of Enlightenment knowledge: 'romanticism', we are told, 'is characterized by a revolt against modernity'.[56] So much is evident in projects like Kelmscott, but while romanticism does rebel against Enlightenment rationalism in many senses, the transition to post-Enlightenment culture is not so clear cut. 'Romanticism was revolutionary', Brown tells us, but 'in that older and more encompassing sense in which a revolution gathers up and recollects, as it sweeps all with it towards the future'.[57] Not only were overt elements of romantic writing – such as nature-feelings, descriptions of wildernesses, and subjective emotionality – present in and through the Enlightenment, but the Enlightenment was itself a story of an unknowable background against which human endeavour strived for knowledge – a project that was continued and refined in romantic writings,[58] including the literary establishment of new book-oriented subjectivities[59] and the colonial expansion of European civilization[60] as facilitated by *Cooper*. The historical period of the Enlightenment produced a contingent set of conceptual and medial tools through which the romantic period was able to express concerns of how to live in response to this radical historical and technological shift.[61] The romanticism of *Cooper*'s letters is not simply due to their adherence to Bringhurst's model, but that this model – in its foregrounding of rationalized medial forms – reveals romantic typography to be a site of expression of the technological inheritance with which the diverse projects of nineteenth-century literary and legal media were attempting to grapple, in both the colonial project and the standardization of sources.

Standardizing the source

The problem of having too many laws results in the suppression of not just other legal traditions, but of proliferating law reports. Examining the media form of *Cooper* encounters not only the romantic qualities of its letter design, entangled with imperial and literary responses to the project of modernity, but also the romance of its production as an authentic source within a modern industrial infrastructure. Once it has been established 'which law', as Lord Watson does in *Cooper*, this law must be authentically evidenced for lawyers and administrators. The question of common law typography thus extends beyond the shape of letters to the entangled material dimensions of law's typographic expression[62] – as both a printed and a discursive artefact, legal type is the material evidence of an immaterial world of norms.[63] In the case of *Cooper v Stuart*, its printerly production is part of a much larger project of legal standardization that sought to overwrite the emergent plethora of unregulated law reports with a single, authentic expression of common law decisions. The fruit of this project, established in the nineteenth century to standardize common law sources in England, remains in place today: the Incorporated Council of Law Reporting (ICLR).

The lawyer and barrister W. T. S. Daniel provided much of the impetus behind the creation of the ICLR. A dominant theme of his contemporaneous account relates to the tensions surrounding the creation of what was perceived as a monopoly on law report publication that would undermine the vested interests in the extant system of market-led competition.[64] Juridically, the concern was with the authority of common law sources, but the question was also one of industry and trade. Across

Daniel's account – which is itself a play of sources, as a set of reprinted letters, articles, recorded minutes of meetings, and committee reports, packaged in a sparse narration – there is presented a robust defence of the ICLR's standardization project as a legitimate exercise of the office of Barrister, grounded in the service of the public good. In a reproduction of a missive he first circulated to the Bar in 1863, Daniel distinguishes the 'evils of a monopoly' (either commercial or governmental) from 'the principle that the proper preparation and publication of . . . the law *ex non scripto* is a public duty.'[65] A duty, moreover, necessarily precluded by commercial interests.[66] As he subsequently wrote of commercial reporters in an open letter to the Solicitor-General calling for reform: 'The public interest is not their concern nor the object of their care.'[67] As conduct that produces resources for professional practice, reporting the law is a species of the Barrister's professional privilege of addressing the court from their knowledge of the law – a privilege held in check in the courtroom but liable to abuse[68] when mediated through printed reports. It is the Bar's obligation to regulate and control the exercise of this privilege,[69] which necessarily extends to the materialization of law reports, for 'the public benefit.'[70]

The structure of the common law as '*ex non scripto*'[71] – as unwritten – means it is always in need of authentic evidence.[72] The common law's reason, lest judicial decisions remain 'mere air',[73] needs to be registered in materiality, in a singular and reliable form. And this registered form needs to be distributed, to be accessible by legal subjects. The project of the ICLR was not just to reign in rampant private interest, but to manifest and distribute the means by which practitioners and administrators could have authentic encounters with the common law. This distribution was via the technology of print and the standardized reproduction that printing techniques enabled.[74] It was – and remains – a distinctly typographic project.

The 'authentic form'[75] of a law report functions by overwriting the variable manifestations of free trade with a standardized, unitary order of legal appearance. Like Louis XIV's *romain du roi*, the letters of the law should not suffer forgery (*fundere*) but flow unadulterated from a genuine source (*fons*). To achieve this, the ICLR based their model on the premise that, for evidence to be authentic, there must only be one unique, authorized version, replacing the multiple competing versions of the market. 'Writing what was unwritten,' however, acts as 'a way of simultaneously affirming and effacing . . . origins'.[76] The act of cancelling previous versions, as Cornelia Vismann has shown, functions to hide law's origin and to restrict access to the formative power that shapes it in order to authorize its updated, visible expressions.[77] For Vismann, legal authority requires overwriting a space where many potential laws might manifest with a singular medial version. For the practical purposes of administration, this singular version must also be widely distributed: copied and shared so it can be received, accessed, understood, and applied within communal life. The ICLR's reports function to cancel and overwrite the preceding uncertainty, securing an updated and authoritative distribution of judicial texts through the mass reproduction of a single report.

Crafted under the ICLR's system of authentic reports, the mass reproduction of the decision in *Cooper v Stuart* was implemented by Clowes and Sons, a printing company that, by the late nineteenth century, was a behemoth of modern technologized production – diametrically opposed to projects such as Kelmscott. Initially asked only to comment on the viability of the scheme, as a printer known to a member of the Bar, Clowes emerged as the only printer willing to tender for the ICLR's contract. The existing law publishers all refused to support reforms seen to undermine their vested interests in the free market in law reports. Despite the ICLR's aims to operate the system solely for the public benefit – with only funds to cover basic costs going to Clowes – the volumes pressed by Clowes in the late nineteenth century are more than mere objects of legal or textual interpretation. They are also the material symptoms of the on-going evolution of a large-scale industrial culture in the shadow of the Enlightenment, the outcome of attempts to rationalize the printing process towards the goals of efficiency and the replication of standardized forms that, in their standardization, enable authentic encounters with the meanings they purport to distribute. As such, produced in the common law context, the ICLR's reports are also an expression of an attempt to secure their own authority by staging their singularity, in contrast to the preceding multiplicity of legal sources. They are the seal of their own authenticity: just as molten metal is set in the font (*fundere*) of the press, the formless authority of the divergent market of reports becomes set in the crisp typographic form of the law reports printed by Clowes.

In the nineteenth century, printing involved multiple steps, from setting the type, to inking, to pressing, to various finishing processes such as cutting and binding.[78] Robin Kinross describes the nineteenth century as a period of 'leapfrog' developments in the mechanization of the various processes of printmaking, rather than a wholesale automation.[79] While there were some successful experiments with steam-powered presses in the early part of the century, notably in the faster-paced world of newspaper printing,[80] it was William Clowes who fully exploited the steam engine as a means of mass producing printed books.[81] Samuel Smiles's 1884 overview of Clowes's contribution to nineteenth-century industrial development provides an account of his motives and method:

> What Mr Clowes principally aimed at . . . was accuracy, speed, and quantity. He did not seek to produce editions de luxe in limited numbers, but large impressions of works in popular demand – travels, biographies, histories, blue-books, and official reports, in any quantity . . . he [thus] early turned his attention to book printing by machine presses, driven by steam power.[82]

Increased speed and mechanization meant text was measured in quantity rather than meaning.[83] Smiles describes Clowes's output through a statistical description of resource consumption: 'From his gigantic establishment were turned out not fewer than 725,000 printed sheets, or equal to 30,000 volumes a week. Nearly 45,000 pounds of paper were printed weekly.'[84] Now called CPI William Clowes, it is part of the global CPI group, a conglomerate that produces – so boasted by CPI's website – 450 million books per year[85] – including the current volume.

Clowes is a printer bound up in both Europe's narratives of industrial progress and resource extraction, and romanticism's bibliographic problem of having 'too many books'. Clowes represents a typographic project opposed to that of Kelmscott – yet both are examples of the media processing of the communications technologies developing since the Enlightenment. Where Morris revives carefully crafted humanist pages printed by hand, Clowes crafts a heady industrial edifice of rationalized efficiency, reliant upon the larger networks of resource extraction that fuelled England's industrial empire more broadly, to generate standardized copies. The employment of a large-scale commercial organization to print standardized, and thus authoritative, expressions of the law demonstrates the typographic confluence of industrial and legal concerns in the Enlightenment's romantic wake. And just as the impetus towards authenticity finds expression in Clowes's standardizing industrial practices, as it does in a different form in Kelmscott's performative resistance to such an impetus, it is also found in the ICLR's overwriting of the market in law reports and the colonial suppression of other traditions of law to leave only the 'authentic' normative order of the British Empire. All of which is entangled in the typography of *Cooper*. Typography that, moreover, also resists the fiction of a unitary law in its manifestation as a network of unique print artefacts.

Distributing the law

Although aiming to secure an authoritative common law source, the printed duplication of the law (*fundere*) troubles the singularity of its origin (*fons*). The ICLR's system aimed to stop there being 'too many' law reports, and to fill the void of 'not enough' with its single, authoritative set. Yet the common law's resultant typographic evidence, while claiming to represent just the right amount, remains caught in the romantic media conundrum of there being 'too many' reports. The problem is indicated clearly in the question of 'where' a literary or legal work is: to paraphrase F. W. Bateson, if the *Mona Lisa* is in the Louvre, where is *Cooper v Stuart*?[86] Although instituted to provide authentic evidence of the common law, the mechanical reproduction of common law reports under the ICLR is a process by which specific instances of legality are distributed through material relays across the common law world, a practice that confounds any attempt to locate a unitary law in a single, authoritative source. While the standardized appearance of *Cooper* stages the illusion of a single, unchanging, and thereby authoritative law, printed law reports actually involve a distributed series of multiple unique manifestations that, once recognized, undercuts the sense of law's uniqueness as a singular (conceptual) object. Any such sense rests on the construction of an idealized unity that necessarily suppresses the material fact of the common law's distributed form, a form to which the medial quality of *Cooper*'s romantic face draws attention.

Repetition refers to a series of unique instances. 'Repetition', Gilles Deleuze tells us, 'concerns non-exchangeable and non-substitutable singularities' that 'do not belong to the domain of resemblance or equivalence'.[87] It is not just that 'no two typewriters have the same strike',[88] as Deleuze describes, but that there is no identity between two strikes of the *same* typewriter. Each strike – of typewriter or printing press – is a unique event producing a non-exchangeable impression. This claim can be substantiated by careful examination of multiple copies of the 'same' text. Figure 3.5 remediates three separate copies of *Cooper*'s infamous fragment, 'practically unoccupied', as printed in 1889 and now consigned to three separate common law archives. Looking closely, it is possible to see material differences in the appearance of the letters: the different thicknesses of the tail of the first a; the varying appearance of the tail of the first u; the different shape of the top of the second c of 'occupied'; the various areas of patchiness in the ink saturation; the variable fibres of the three different sheets of paper; *inter alia*.

Material differences can be seen even more clearly in the example of the second a from 'practically', reproduced in Figure 3.6. The most notable differences (as marked up on the figure) are found on the outer

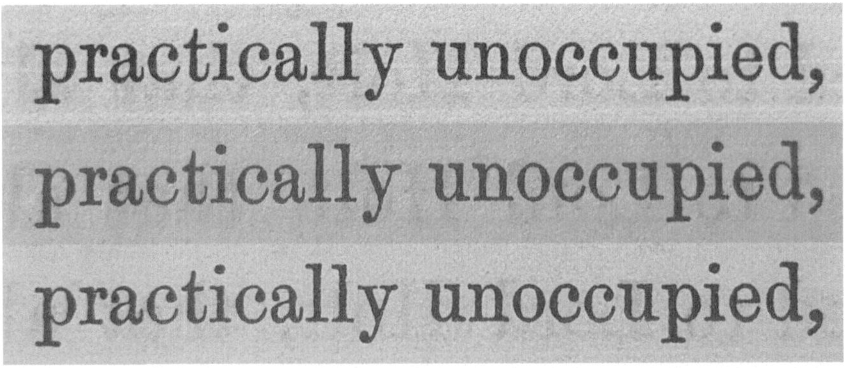

Figure 3.5: Variations of *Cooper*'s infamous fragment from its 1889 printing. Respectively, from top to bottom, these copies are held at: the Library of the Honourable Society of Gray's Inn (stock no. 32292; reproduced with permission); the Library of the Institute of Advanced Legal Studies (Accession No. 105160; reproduced with permission); and the Library at Lincoln's Inn (no accession number; only one copy held; reproduced with the permission of the Honourable Society of Lincoln's Inn). Each image is a detail of page 291 of 1889 14 Appeal Cases 286.

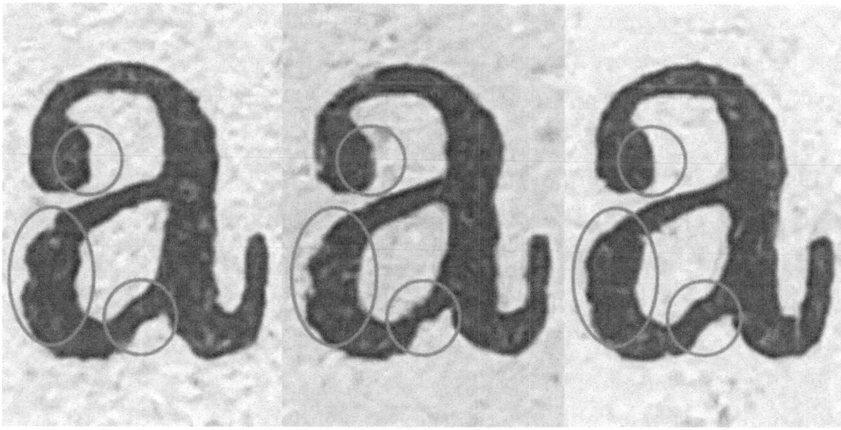

Figure 3.6: Spot the difference. Detailed comparison of the second a of 'practically'. Mark-up produced by Thomas Giddens using, respectively from left to right, copies held at: the Library of the Honourable Society of Gray's Inn (stock no. 32292; reproduced with permission); the Library of the Institute of Advanced Legal Studies (Accession No. 105160; reproduced with permission); and the Library at Lincoln's Inn (no accession number; only one copy held; reproduced with the permission of the Honourable Society of Lincoln's Inn). Each image is a detail of page 291 of 1889 14 Appeal Cases 286.

left-hand side of the bowl, at the lower edge near where the bowl joins the stem, and on the contours of the terminal – but careful readers can undoubtedly detect further differences. Even from this limited set of examples, it is clear that no two copies of *Cooper v Stuart* – or of any printed law report – are materially or visually identical, but instead vary from copy to copy. Each repetition, as Deleuze demonstrates, is its own unique instance.

If no two strikes of the press are the same, the common law becomes distributed across a wide set of incommensurable materials that troubles the idea of a singular origin or source. 'As the unwritten drama is written, the unpublished note published', or, we can add, the unwritten law reported, 'writing is reconceived as a practice of media translation.'[89] Law is translated into materially unique products of the press, with no two copies of a case report, no two accounts of the law, being the same. In the minor variations between copies, in the small material differences of the print, is expressed the lack of a single source: the common law's *fundere* expresses the fictional nature of its mythical *fons*. The unitary source of the common law flows into a sea of pluralizing copies, becoming replaced or staged only by its material instantiations. Typography 'puts law into question, it denounces its nominal or general character',[90] as it manifests legality as a multiplicity of single instances through repetitive production.

This multiplicity can be understood as a network. Piper's examination of the work of Goethe is instructive in relation to the tensions between book-as-singular and book-as-materially-distributed, framed under the concept of the network. Goethe's publication practices are spatially and temporally dispersed, representing a 'network' of typographic objects in a way that radically reorients understandings of literature. For Goethe, Piper argues, 'writing did not solely encompass the patient imagination of complex narrative tapestries but involved attention to the available technologies of dissemination and preservation.'[91] In this way, Goethe 'redefined the literary work as something material, processual, and spatially dispersed.'[92] Such reworkings focused priority on material processes:

> They located literary work, and thus the 'work' itself, not in some ideal and crucially immaterial space, but instead in the material event of publication – the circulation, distribution, and reproduction that shaped its reception. They reoriented the reader's gaze to the mobile artifacts of literary life.[93]

In this way, books came to be understood as 'technological compounds', objects that 'transcended a single author's control.'[94]

With the common law, its single instances in print are, paradoxically, of a universal form: repetition is 'always revealing a singularity opposed to the particulars subsumed under laws, a universal opposed to the generalities which give rise to laws.'[95] While each strike of the press is materially unique, resulting in a media network of typographic artefacts, each is an instance of a supposedly unitary and universal law. The movement is opposed to the common law's usual structure: it is a single universal finding expression in each distinct strike, rather than the multiplicity of instances being bundled together and abstracted into a general and unitary set of principles.

Yet, if we follow Deleuze, there is no 'original' term as such of which the printed law is a copy: 'There is no first term which is repeated', says Deleuze; there is 'nothing repeated which may be isolated or abstracted from the repetition in which it was formed.'[96] The first instance of a repeated series – what we might posit as the 'origin' of law – is itself a repetition. It is not the case that there is a 'first' version of a printed case, or even an 'original' unwritten law that is 'copied' in print, because the first instance must be defined in relation to the other copies if those duplicates are understood to be copies *of* anything. Repetition is found in the difference between instances: a thing is only a repetition to the extent it is different from that which it repeats (otherwise it becomes the thing, rather than repeating it).[97] This difference is not between 'the repeated and the repetition, but between these types of repetition' such that 'the first time is no less repetition than the second or the third.'[98] The result is that we do not encounter a 'repetition of successive elements or external parts, but totalities which coexist on different levels or degrees.'[99] Each term in the series is a totality in itself, each copy or impression is the law in itself, disguised or clothed in its representational form. As a totality, each material copy is thus a duplicated origin. The common law's transmission (*fundere*) becomes its source (*fons*), but 'prolonged like so many reproductions' in the distributed network of material impressions.[100]

Each strike of the press manifests a singular instance of law's universal form. The material dissemination of the common law is thus opposed to the structure of the common law itself. The common law proceeds by similarity and resemblance, by the production of 'generalities' from the particulars of specific cases. In legal print, however, we have a universal law continually manifesting as singular instances, each similar only to itself, each its own source. Accordingly, 'in each new expression . . . the seamless web of law is constantly being redrawn, enacted, changed and expanded'; 'new meaning' is inscribed into the law with each impression.[101] Each strike of the press continues the elaboration of a shifting network of expressions, embedding in legal print an unresolved tension between the singular 'idea' of law and the typographic reality of its duplication.

Despite being a series of unique elements, the multiples of a law report hold together as unitary legal form, a contraction or synthesis of individual instances that stages an imagined singularity. Books are materially distributed, but there remains 'the *imaginative* possibility that something stayed the same and that this sameness was . . . juridically and aesthetically legitimate.'[102] This copy of *Cooper* is taken to be the same as that copy, as that copy, as another, and through this suppression of their actual differences they perform the existence of 'the case' in itself as an ideational object to be invoked as an authoritative 'source' or node of argumentation.[103] The material distinctions are forgotten in the quest for the legal principles the copy is taken to hold or index, that it stages as present. As Nietzsche puts it: 'Every concept arises from the equation of unequal things', in particular 'by forgetting the distinguishing aspects' of those things.[104] This feature of mass-produced reports is symptomatic of a more general feature of repetition:

> The sensed quality is indistinguishable from the contraction . . . but the object perceived implies a contraction of cases such that one quality may be read in the other, and a structure in which the form of the object allies itself with the quality at least as an intentional part.[105]

Explicitly transposing this to common law print, to the performance of the common law within the theatre of the archive, when one encounters a printed case report the quality 'sensed' in that object becomes that of 'law' – more precisely, a specific bit of law, such as the fragment 'practically unoccupied' – with this same quality concomitantly implied as being found in all other copies of that same report and the fact of their unique materiality being suppressed. Each material copy of a law report, each strike of the press, stages the implication both that the same law is readable in another copy, and that this commonality is contingent on its duplicated form as a printed document that forgets its material uniqueness. Just as written language suppresses its visuality in favour of the conceptual register of a linguistic system, as discussed in Chapter 1, the law report suppresses its variable form in favour of the system of unitary and thus authoritative legal principles that it instantiates as a distributed material register. Moreover, it is by means of repetition, by the material distribution of copies, that the idea of a law that transcends matter is generated.

While we might (re)construct law's immaterial unity from its printed copies, the repetition of the law in its distribution takes place on both material and conceptual levels: the ideational law is also repeated in each strike of the press. 'We repeat twice simultaneously,' Deleuze tells us; 'first we repeat the parts, then we repeat the whole on which the parts depend.'[106] And these 'two forms of repetition'[107] have distinct features, dividing themselves between the material and the ideational. Repetition is defined by the difference between instances. How this difference is structured determines the two kinds of repetition: put in terms of law reports, the first kind of repetition is defined by the difference between the material copies of the same case, while the second is defined by the difference that marks out 'the law' itself as a distinct ideational form.[108] There is both a mechanical repetition of the printed form of law, and a conceptual repetition of the idea of law staged by the material artefact: 'One is a "bare" repetition, the other a covered repetition, which forms itself in covering itself, in masking and disguising itself.'[109]

The 'bare' repetition of print is a dead materiality, identifiable simply by its accuracy of physical repetition as a distribution or multiplication of forms that are sufficiently similar for their differences to be suppressed so they can be linked together or animated into a single concept; the other is a repetition of a distinct ideational form, requiring materialization so it can be encountered.[110] The unitary law, meanwhile, requires the 'disguise' of form to be sensed or imagined – the material duplication of law reports, in its duplicated form as print, re-presents the unitary law in a covered form. As Legendre elaborates, the foundation of institutional images is a double movement in which the invisible law is shown only by veiling the ideational law in perceptible images that necessarily cover its formless form with a perceptible one.[111] The text, as Goodrich puts it, is the 'costume' the law needs to wear to enter the theatre of social governance.[112] The question, if the law is only appearing in costume, is how one is to tell that the mask is hiding (revealing) the actual law: a romantic question of authentic encounter. While the 'bare' repetition is easy to spot in its material relation to other copies, the ideational form is masked in its image. Accordingly, the *idea* of law, as Deleuze puts it, 'has authenticity as its criterion.'[113] The manifested law, if it is to be authoritative, requires some evidence that it is a genuine instance and not a forgery.

Overtly responding to the romantic problem of authorizing multiplied copies of judicial decisions, the ICLR put itself into existence in order to authenticate the printed form of the common law. In a context characterized by a radical diversity of media sources, the unitary law could not be knowingly sensed by those concerned with its administration and application. The ICLR represents the institution of a practice whereby single renditions of each case were confirmed as accurate by the judges who made them, thereby 'authorizing' those accounts as genuine – what could be more accurate, or more romantic? These authentic accounts were then translated into mass-produced typographic form for distribution to a common law readership to aid their interpretative, argumentative, and administrative activities. The authentic original became one copy amongst many: the source became forged in its transmission, with the goal of producing authorized evidence repeatedly undercut by the medial productions of the press. In the paginal strikes, what was actually distributed was a series of unique forms that as bare repetitions exist as a collection of different objects, and as markers of a repeated ideation express the unanswered question of their authentic quality as law.

Conclusion

Contrary to the common law's desire to be the only show in town, there remain in place too many laws and too many sources. Following the advent of the printing press, and the modern flourishing of printing technologies that expanded the production of texts and their widespread distribution, romanticism emerged as a complex and conflicted set of tools for making sense of this new media environment. Where romantic poets and arts and crafts projects like Kelmscott sought a retreat from the mass duplication they saw in modern technologies, back to the authenticity of the singular, industrial pioneers like Clowes embraced the possibility of standardization via the steam-powered press, and the British state saw the unfettered expansion of a centralized empire. The ICLR, meanwhile, sought both: an authentic singular law manifested authentically on an industrial scale. They wielded the new typographic technologies under a modernist impetus, seeking to construct rationally reliable evidence of the common law as embodied in judicial decisions, from which lawyers and administrators alike could derive genuine understanding of the principles that ordered modern society and government. But the typographic artefacts their efforts produced, of which *Cooper v Stuart* is a key example, did not solve the problem of romantic media, did not remove the plethora of divergent legal texts and leave a singular source in their place. The romance of a single law, and of a centralized system of mass-produced reports of that law, is a tragic story of highly proficient lawyers manifesting accounts of an unwritten legal tradition as a network of material instances that, in their technological specificity, constantly resist their own authenticity as rationalized and standardized indexes of univocal legality.

Copying the law pushes the problem into the background, suppressing the diversity of law's material entanglements into the small details of common law print. The typographic form of *Cooper v Stuart* stages the existence of a singular law on an ideational level, overwriting the plurality of laws at the frontier, but in its romantic form as a modern letter that foregrounds its own medial quality, and that is materially unique in each instantiation, it undercuts the success of its own jurisdictional performance. The question of the authority of the common law's texts, which the ICLR's project hoped to solve, is exacerbated by its romantic typography. Instead of standardizing the common law within the project of empire, each copy manifests an unanswered question about its own authenticity as a common law source, of the law itself as singular rather than radically plural, and thus of the imperial project itself.

The theatre of jurisdiction is decentralized; it is distributed and encountered across the network of material artefacts that constitutes the common law's medial network. In the material distribution of *Cooper v Stuart*, then, is the undoing of its own substantive argument. Far from there being only one law, as Lord Watson claims, there are many. The law is pluralized in its typographic distribution as a sea of single instances that must be suppressed, like the indigenous laws supressed by *Cooper*'s claim that Australia was 'practically unoccupied', in order to permit the idea of a unitary law to persist. It is only by forgetting their radical pluralism that these divergent texts are able to stage and maintain the fiction of the common law as a singular authority in the theatre of the archive. And this is a forgetting, as we will see in the next chapter, that is not only enabled by the techniques of typographic design, but enhanced in the specific modern example of Times New Roman.

Notes

1. See Baker, 'Law Reporting'.
2. See W. T. S. Daniel, *The History and Origin of the Law Reports* (William Clowes and Sons, 1884).
3. *Cooper v Stuart* [1889] 14 App Cas 286, at 291.
4. For the classic articulation of the (perhaps overstated) revolutionary effects of the press, see Elizabeth Eisenstein, *The Printing Press as an Agent of Change* (Cambridge University Press, 1980). More pertinent for lawyers is the impact of the press on legal practice, for which see Harvey, *The Law Emprynted*.
5. The jurisprudence of *terra nullius* ostensibly runs from Blackstone (land that is 'desert and unoccupied') through *Cooper v Stuart* ('practically unoccupied') and *Coe v Commonwealth* (unoccupied 'by European standards'), to the problematic distinction of conquest and its consequences in *Mabo*. On this trajectory, see Gerry Simpson, '*Mabo*, International Law, *Terra Nullius* and the Stories of Settlement', *Melbourne University Law Review* 19 (1993): 195.
6. *Cooper*, at 288, per Lord Watson.
7. *Cooper*, at 293, per Lord Watson.
8. *Cooper*, at 293, per Lord Watson.
9. See Simpson, '*Mabo*', 199.
10. *Cooper*, at 291, per Lord Watson.
11. Dorsett, 'Since Time Immemorial'. This point is also nicely expressed by Cormack: 'the common law came to see alternative legal frameworks as possessed of an authority that could be said to be valid just to the extent that the common law itself acknowledged and controlled those alternatives': Cormack, *A Power to Do Justice*, 27.
12. See Robert M. Cover, 'Foreword: Nomos and Narrative', *Harvard Law Review* 97 (1983): 4–68; 4.
13. See Irene Watson, 'Re-Centring First Nations Knowledge and Places in a Terra Nullius Space', *AlterNative: An International Journal of Indigenous Peoples* 10, no. 5 (2014): 508–20.
14. Harvey, *The Law Emprynted*, 250–51.
15. Hemming, in a letter to the Bar Committee, reproduced in Daniel, *History and Origin*, 107.
16. Quoted in Daniel, *History and Origin*, 183.
17. Pulling, reproduced in Daniel, *History and Origin*, 5.
18. See Alan Bewell, 'Romanticism and Colonial Natural History', *Studies in Romanticism* 43, no. 1 (2004): 5; Alan Bewell, *Natures in Translation: Romanticism and Colonial Natural History* (Johns Hopkins University Press, 2017).
19. Bewell, 'Romanticism', 5.
20. Bewell, 'Romanticism', 6.
21. Bewell, 'Romanticism', 7.

22. Bewell, 'Romanticism,' 8.
23. See Bewell, 'Romanticism,' 13–15.
24. Bewell, 'Romanticism,' 11.
25. See Bewell, 'Romanticism,' 20.
26. Bewell, 'Romanticism,' 17.
27. Bewell, 'Romanticism,' 28.
28. Bringhurst, *Elements*, 13.
29. Ida Engholm and Karen Lisa Salamon, 'Design Thinking Between Rationalism and Romanticism,' *Artifact* 4, no. 1 (2017): E1.1.
30. A 'transitional' style of typeface is discussed in Chapter 4.
31. Lupton, *Thinking with Type*, 46.
32. See, for example, Morison, *Type Designs*, 30–44.
33. See Bringhurst, *Elements*, 13.
34. Bringhurst, *Elements*, 130.
35. See Bringhurst, *Elements*, 130. See also the fuller discussion on humanist letters in Chapter 2.
36. See Kinross, *Modern Typography*, 45–53.
37. Engholm and Salamon, 'Design Thinking,' E1.2.
38. Engholm and Salamon, 'Design Thinking,' E1.2.
39. Morris, quoted in Lawson, *Anatomy*, 47–48.
40. Lawson, *Anatomy*, 49.
41. Aaron Donachuk, 'After the Letter: Typographical Distraction and the Surface of Morris's Kelmscott Romances,' *Victorian Studies* 59, no. 2 (2017): 268.
42. See Engholm and Salamon, 'Design Thinking.'
43. Donachuk, 'After the Letter,' 271.
44. Kinross, *Modern Typography*, 46–47.
45. Donachuk, 'After the Letter,' 272–73; Kinross, *Modern Typography*, 46.
46. Kinross, *Modern Typography*, 47.
47. See Andrew Piper, *Dreaming in Books: The Making of the Bibliographic Imagination in the Romantic Age* (University of Chicago Press, 2009).
48. Piper, *Dreaming*, 12.
49. Piper, *Dreaming*, 12.
50. Piper, *Dreaming*, 12–13.
51. Gilles Deleuze, *Difference and Repetition* (Continuum, 1994), 37.
52. See Andreas Philippopoulos-Mihalopoulos, 'The World Without Outside,' *Angelaki* 18, no. 4 (2013): 165–77.
53. See Deleuze, *Difference and Repetition*, 77.
54. Deleuze, *Difference and Repetition*, 37.
55. Lupton, 'Post-Mortem,' 46.
56. Warren Breckman, 'Marx and Romanticism,' *Critical Review* 34, no. 1 (2022): 37.
57. Marshall Brown, 'Romanticism and Enlightenment,' in *The Cambridge Companion to British Romanticism*, 2nd ed., ed. Stuart Curran (Cambridge University Press, 2010), 55.
58. See Brown, 'Romanticism and Enlightenment.'
59. Piper, *Dreaming*, 12–13.
60. Bewell, *Natures in Translation*.

61. See Clifford Siskin and William Warner, 'If This Is Enlightenment Then What Is Romanticism?', *European Romantic Review* 22, no. 3 (2011): 281–91.
62. The breadth of what 'typography' animates as a discursive category, as a wider economy of practices, technologies, discourses, and design traditions, is ably demonstrated by Kinross's history of modern typography: see Kinross, *Modern Typography.*
63. Goodrich, *Advanced Introduction*, 24–41.
64. See Daniel, *History and Origin.*
65. Daniel, *History and Origin*, 24.
66. 'Law Reporting is, in our system of jurisprudence, an essential part of the proper promulgation of the law *ex non scripto*, and therefore a function of the State . . . [and not] an object of commerce and the subject of individual enterprise': Daniel, *History and Origin*, 54.
67. Daniel, *History and Origin*, 36.
68. The desire that animates commercial reporting, Daniel concludes, is not the care of the law incumbent on the jurisprudential office of the Barrister, but 'the Pleasure of seeing one's name in Print' – a desire that harms 'the body of the living public' the common law is supposed to serve: Daniel, *History and Origin*, 49. To apply commercial practices 'to a system of Law Reporting *intended for citation as authority* . . . [is] an abuse' and must give way to reforms in the public interest: Daniel, *History and Origin*, 53.
69. Daniel claims law reporters should be 'appointed exclusively for the office', an office he likens to 'the Judicial Office itself': Daniel, *History and Origin*, 55. Commercial interests manifestly undermine the public quality of law reporting as an official function.
70. Daniel, *History and Origin*, 56.
71. Daniel, *History and Origin*, 24.
72. As Dorsett and McVeigh put it: 'There is no text of the law, but rather a set of textual practices, whereby writing functions as a kind of evidence of law beyond the written': Dorsett and McVeigh, *Jurisdiction*, 61.
73. *The Times*, 2 December 1863, reproduced in Daniel, *History and Origin*, 78.
74. See Ong, *Orality and Literacy.*
75. Pulling's report on 'Law Reporting Reform' (1849), as reproduced in Daniel, *History and Origin*, 21.
76. Piper, *Dreaming*, 147–48.
77. See Vismann, 'Cancels'. This is discussed in more detail in Chapter 5.
78. On the general process of mechanization across the nineteenth century, see Kinross, *Modern Typography*, 34–44.
79. Kinross, *Modern Typography*, 35.
80. As Kinross notes, 'the first powered cylinder press was in use at *The Times* in 1814': Kinross, *Modern Typography*, 35. The history of *The Times* is discussed in more detail in Chapter 4, but for a detailed rendition see Stanley Morison, *Printing The Times Since 1785* (Printing House Square, 1953).
81. Samuel Smiles, *Men of Invention and Industry* (John Murray, 1884), 210–12.
82. Smiles, *Men of Invention*, 212.
83. Kinross, *Modern Typography*, 36.

84. Smiles, *Men of Invention*, 218.
85. See https://www.cpi-print.co.uk/ (accessed 1 May 2024).
86. F. W. Bateson: 'If the *Mona Lisa* is in the Louvre, where is *Hamlet*?' Quoted in Piper, *Dreaming*, 9.
87. Deleuze, *Difference and Repetition*, 1.
88. Deleuze, *Difference and Repetition*, 29.
89. Piper, *Dreaming*, 145.
90. Deleuze, *Difference and Repetition*, 3.
91. Piper, *Dreaming*, 24.
92. Piper, *Dreaming*, 25.
93. Piper, *Dreaming*, 45. This is in contrast to the aspiration in some areas of bibliography to construct an imagined 'ideal copy' from an issue's diverse expressions: see, for example, Thomas Tanselle, 'The Concept of "Ideal Copy"', *Studies in Bibliography* 33 (53): 18.
94. Piper, *Dreaming*, 50.
95. Deleuze, *Difference and Repetition*, 6.
96. Deleuze, *Difference and Repetition*, 19.
97. As Deleuze puts it: 'The interior of repetition is always affected by an order of difference: it is only to the extent that something is linked to a repetition of an order other than its own that the repetition appears external and bare, and the thing itself subject to the categories of generality': Deleuze, *Difference and Repetition*, 29. If something is the same as something else, it becomes that thing, not a repetition of it.
98. Deleuze, *Difference and Repetition*, 367.
99. Deleuze, *Difference and Repetition*, 367.
100. Deleuze, *Difference and Repetition*, 252.
101. Goodrich, *Advanced Introduction*, 64–65.
102. Piper, *Dreaming*, 56.
103. On law's material sources as actually denoting conventional reasoning, disregarding their materiality, see Bell, 'Sources of Law'.
104. Friedrich Nietzsche, 'On Truth and Lies in a Nonmoral Sense', in *The Rhetorical Tradition: Readings from Classical Times to the Present*, ed. P. Bizzell and B. Herzberg (Bedford Books, 1990), 891.
105. Deleuze, *Difference and Repetition*, 93.
106. Deleuze, *Difference and Repetition*, 362.
107. Deleuze, *Difference and Repetition*, 26.
108. 'But in one case, the difference is taken to be only external to the concept; it is a difference between objects represented by the same concept, falling into the indifference of space and time. In the other case, the difference is internal to the Idea; it unfolds as pure movement, creative of a dynamic space and time which correspond to the Idea': Deleuze, *Difference and Repetition*, 26–27.
109. Deleuze, *Difference and Repetition*, 27.
110. 'One is bare repetition which can be masked only afterwards and in addition; the other is clothed repetition of which the masks, the displacements and the disguises are the first, last and only elements': Deleuze, *Difference and Repetition*, 359.

111. See Legendre, *God in the Mirror,* 101. Legendre is returned to in further detail in Chapter 5.
112. Goodrich, 'Imago Decidendi,' 28.
113. Deleuze, *Difference and Repetition*, 27.

Chapter 4

Delivering the law: all roads lead to Times New Roman

Introduction

The common law should appear in properly formatted Times New Roman, a fact made explicit by both the English Court of Appeal and the UK Supreme Court. That court transcripts in England and Wales are invariably set in Times New Roman is rarely commented upon, but Lloyd LJ's overt engagement with typographic form in the case of *Baigent v Random House*[1] advertises the institution's concern for typographic propriety, a concern made even clearer by the Supreme Court's conscious typographic experiments. Within the theatre of the archive, the words of judicial decision must arrive from the past – from the inaccessible moment of judgment or from time immemorial – in the correct face. Times New Roman, moreover, is not a neutral face, but one that not only reflects the humanist heritage of the legal institution, with its complex tensions of romanization,[2] but that also effectively stages the immaterial strata of legal principle and inculcates a (presumed) community of individual, abstract subjects under the imperialism of an invisible reason. It is a face that emerges from and prioritizes the western imperial project. Delivering the law in another form thus not only breaches a common typographic convention, but undermines the civilizing project of the modern legal order.

In order to articulate what is at stake in this institutional preference for Times New Roman, this chapter undertakes analysis of the face's design and heritage, in particular its connections with modern civilizing order. It does this across four sections. The first section ('Typographic transcripts') sets out the institutional preference for Times New Roman through engagement with typographic variations in *Baigent* and the transcripts of the UK Supreme Court that draw attention to the active maintenance of Times New Roman as the default style for court transcripts in England and Wales more generally. Deriving from its generative context of industrial newsprint, Times New Roman is introduced in the second section ('A civilizing container') by highlighting its connections to the imperial spread of nationhood via the artefacts of print-capitalism that enable the imagination of modern communities. The emergence of imagined communities is contingent on an older and more general feature of textual technologies that stage rational discourse and inculcate the structure of the modern (male) subject's rational interiority, a process that resonates with central features of the common law ('Staging the subject'). These broader contexts in place, the chapter finally demonstrates how they manifest and are enhanced in the typographic details of Times New Roman itself, the use of which embeds an ideal of modern, rational, patriarchal dominance of western civilization into the jurisdictional expression of the common law as it appears in the court transcripts of England and Wales ('The imperial face of the common law'). In the spread of western civilization and the delivery of the common law judgments that support it, as in the spread of western text in general, it appears that all roads lead to Times New Roman.[3]

Typographic transcripts

There is a secret message encoded in the typography of *Baigent v Random House*,[4] an English case involving a copyright claim against Dan Brown's *The Da Vinci Code*.[5] The cryptophilic novel inspired the trial judge Smith J to transmit a secret 'smithy code' of his own by strategically formatting bold and italic letters throughout his transcript (see Figure 4.1).[6] These typographic variations were given short shrift by the Court of Appeal: Lloyd LJ mentions the 'smithy code' solely to denounce its substantive relevance – a determination that also denies any legal significance to the visual formatting that encodes the message. As

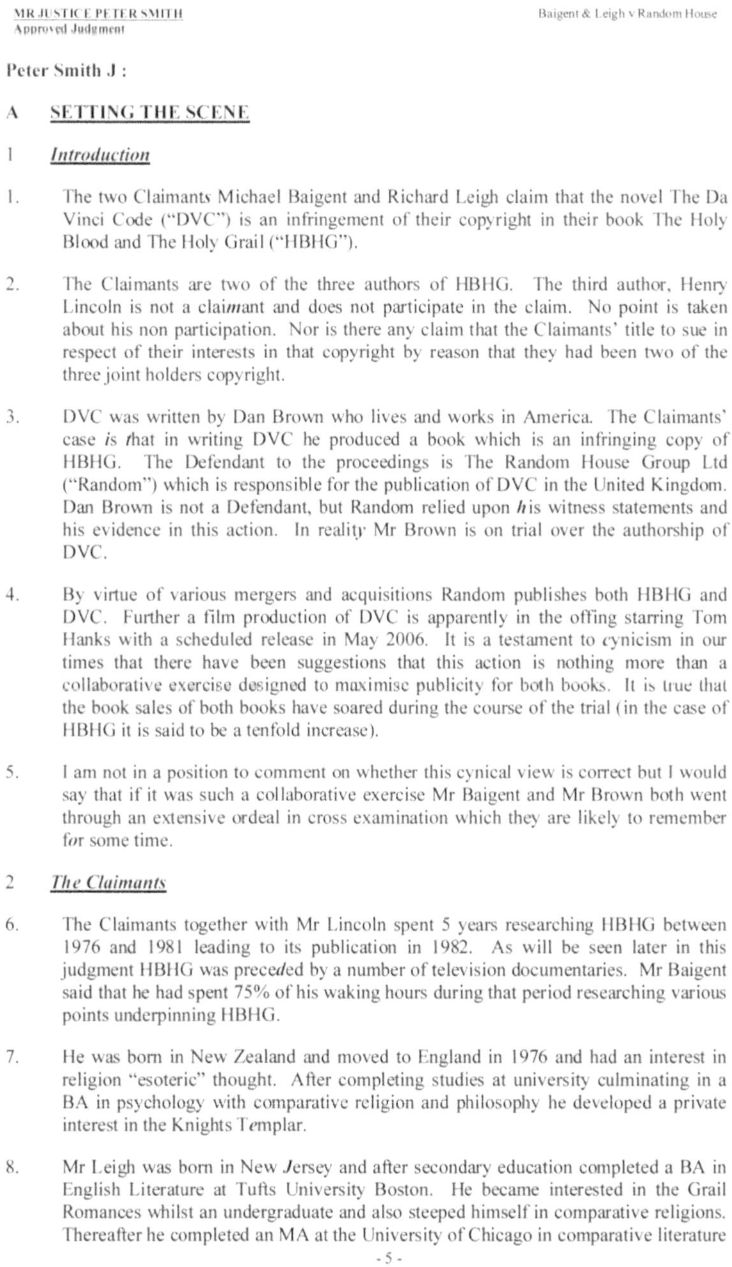

MR JUSTICE PETER SMITH
Approved Judgment

Baigent & Leigh v Random House

Peter Smith J :

A SETTING THE SCENE

1 *Introduction*

1. The two Claimants Michael Baigent and Richard Leigh claim that the novel The Da Vinci Code ("DVC") is an infringement of their copyright in their book The Holy Blood and The Holy Grail ("HBHG").

2. The Claimants are two of the three authors of HBHG. The third author, Henry Lincoln is not a claimant and does not participate in the claim. No point is taken about his non participation. Nor is there any claim that the Claimants' title to sue in respect of their interests in that copyright by reason that they had been two of the three joint holders copyright.

3. DVC was written by Dan Brown who lives and works in America. The Claimants' case is that in writing DVC he produced a book which is an infringing copy of HBHG. The Defendant to the proceedings is The Random House Group Ltd ("Random") which is responsible for the publication of DVC in the United Kingdom. Dan Brown is not a Defendant, but Random relied upon his witness statements and his evidence in this action. In reality Mr Brown is on trial over the authorship of DVC.

4. By virtue of various mergers and acquisitions Random publishes both HBHG and DVC. Further a film production of DVC is apparently in the offing starring Tom Hanks with a scheduled release in May 2006. It is a testament to cynicism in our times that there have been suggestions that this action is nothing more than a collaborative exercise designed to maximise publicity for both books. It is true that the book sales of both books have soared during the course of the trial (in the case of HBHG it is said to be a tenfold increase).

5. I am not in a position to comment on whether this cynical view is correct but I would say that if it was such a collaborative exercise Mr Baigent and Mr Brown both went through an extensive ordeal in cross examination which they are likely to remember for some time.

2 *The Claimants*

6. The Claimants together with Mr Lincoln spent 5 years researching HBHG between 1976 and 1981 leading to its publication in 1982. As will be seen later in this judgment HBHG was preceded by a number of television documentaries. Mr Baigent said that he had spent 75% of his waking hours during that period researching various points underpinning HBHG.

7. He was born in New Zealand and moved to England in 1976 and had an interest in religion "esoteric" thought. After completing studies at university culminating in a BA in psychology with comparative religion and philosophy he developed a private interest in the Knights Templar.

8. Mr Leigh was born in New Jersey and after secondary education completed a BA in English Literature at Tufts University Boston. He became interested in the Grail Romances whilst an undergraduate and also steeped himself in comparative religions. Thereafter he completed an MA at the University of Chicago in comparative literature

- 5 -

Figure 4.1: Manifesting the 'smithy code'. Page extracted from *Baigent v Random House* [2006] EWHC 719 (Ch). Note the s in in para 1 ('Claimants'), the m in para 2 ('claimant'), and the i, t, h, and y in para 3, *inter alia*.

highlighted in Chapter 1, legal matter tends to give way to the imaginary world of reason: the appearance of law's words is of negligible significance in relation to their doctrinal and analytical meanings. According to Lloyd LJ, while font and page layout may articulate meanings, for the common law they are meanings 'on which nothing turns'.[7] In this determination, Lloyd LJ lodges a judicial determination regarding common law typography in the archive of decision. However, although Lloyd LJ's statement criticizes Smith J's visual presentation as irrelevant, that presentation does not impact the basic legibility of the text. While Smith J's judgment 'is not easy to read or understand', the appellate court is clear this is not because of its typographic appearance, but because Smith J rushed his text: he produced it in 'less than three weeks', complete with complex and irrelevant code, and should have spent more time on its 'preparation, checking and revision'.[8] If we are to take Lloyd LJ's seemingly offhand statement seriously, as a critical reading would demand,[9] there must be something beyond legibility at stake for the Court of Appeal in Smith J's typography. Noting that bold and italics are commonly used in transcripts, for example for headings, emphasis, or case names, Lloyd LJ's reaction to their manifestly improper use indicates a concern not with bold or italics per se, nor with legibility, but with the proper appearance and form of a common law transcript.

Code notwithstanding, the instant and appellate transcripts of *Baigent* are set in 12-point Times New Roman (see Figure 4.2 for a sample), which is common practice for judicial transcripts in England and Wales whose body text follows the same default appearance.[10] In one sense, then, Lloyd LJ's preference merely repeats the default convention, displaying a kind of rhetorical apathy, as legal typographer Matthew Butterick argues is inherent in any use of Times New Roman given its broadly 'default' status in western culture.[11] However, as we saw in Chapter 2, conventions signal an authorization of that particular style as fundamental to the practice or context in which it is conventional.[12] A demand for the default setting of court transcripts thus shows the opposite of apathy: it shows the deep importance of typographic form in general, and the proper application of Times New Roman in particular, for the common law's institutional expression in the matter of the archive.

Times New Roman

A quick x-ray job to map
the King's civilized law font

Figure 4.2: Times New Roman sample, complete with topical pangram. Image credit: Thomas Giddens (reproduced with permission).

The concern in *Baigent* is not an isolated incident. The same stylistic preference is revealed in the commitment of the UK Supreme Court to Times New Roman. In 2021, the UK Supreme Court experimented with Calibri, Microsoft's successor default to Times New Roman, before reverting its transcripts to Times New Roman in 2023.[13] This change, its online reception in legal circles, and its relatively hasty reversal, express further concern over not only the appropriate appearance of the primary manifestations of common law decisions, but that this appearance should be in the forms of Times New Roman.

Anecdotally, Times New Roman is associated with authority and knowledge,[14] and online reactions to the Supreme Court held its traditional qualities were undermined by the modern friendliness of Calibri's rounded, geometric style (see Figure 4.3 for a sample).[15] Use of Calibri is often in the interests of readability, yet the question of readability is not necessarily contingent on serifs per se.[16] Indeed, legibility was a primary concern in the design of Times New Roman, which followed leading medical research on print legibility and was finalized in consultation with readability experts.[17] Its subsequent popularity arguably owes much to its readability across multiple contexts. Removing serifs, then, 'signals a change in tone of voice' rather than readability, a choice that 'will have emotional impact' on a text's readership.[18] The change away from serifs, then, is not necessarily to do

Calibri

A quick x-ray job to map
the King's civilized law font

Figure 4.3: Calibri sample, complete with topical pangram. Image credit: Thomas Giddens (reproduced with permission).

with legibility – but, like *Baigent*'s defence of the convention for court transcripts, with a preference for a particular style of letter.

Like the Supreme Court's transcripts, the appellate critique of Smith J's use of bold and italic betrays a concern not with a reader's ability to decipher the letters, but with the visual propriety of the common law's typographic form. The critique is not only found in Lloyd LJ's statement, but also in the appeal's own typographic performance. In its re-setting of the m in the word 'claimant', for instance (see Figure 4.4 and Figure 4.5), the Court of Appeal's transcript demonstrates for the legal community how it should be done, visually overruling Smith J's instant formatting and the contingency it revealed in his judicial craft.[19] What is really at stake in Smith J's typography is not how much legal substance might 'turn' on the letterforms – but the proper appearance of a court transcript as an expression of the more general institution of the western common law. By undertaking to say nothing turns on it, within a wider context where Times New Roman is evidently both the default and the active choice, this judicial slip[20] reveals a concern for typographic style that underpins not only the Court of Appeal's specific ruling (the code is not legally legible because it is outside normal forms of expression), but the edifice of western common law itself. If we trace the unspoken line of appeal from Smith J to the Court of Appeal to the Supreme Court, to the Supreme Court reversing its own decision, the institution's position is clear: the common law should appear in properly formatted 12-point Times New Roman.

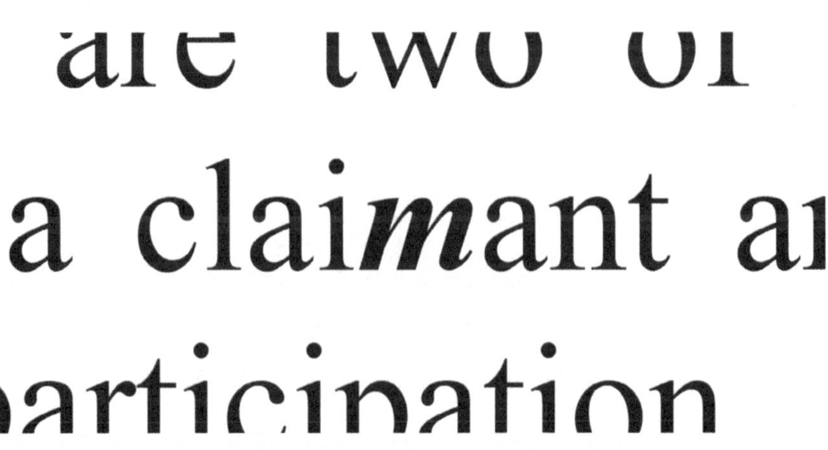

Figure 4.4: Excerpt from *Baigent v Random House* [2006] EWHC 719 (Ch) at para 2.

Figure 4.5: Excerpt from *Baigent v Random House* [2007] EWCA Civ 247 at para 26.

Transcripts are the initial form in which judicial decisions are typographically encoded, of which law reports such as those of the ICLR are then edited and typeset remediations. Far from the romantic face of *Cooper*, the contemporary reports of the ICLR are now set in Sabon[21] – a traditionally humanist letterform (see Figure 4.6 for a sample, and this endnote[22] for a brief analysis), acting as an on-going institutional relay for the romanizing tensions of Plowden discussed in Chapter 2. The entrenched typographic conventions of judicial transcripts, however – the material record closest to at least one version of the common law's lost source, in the crucible of judgment – authorize and carry with them a different set of meanings. Before they become set in Sabon, or otherwise appear in the vanishing faces of digital typography (see Chapter 5), judicial texts are set in Times New Roman and become laden with the qualities and the history of meanings that have accreted to Times New Roman as a visual form. These are qualities and meanings that go beyond anecdotal connections with 'formality' or 'tradition'. Instead, as we will see, they encompass the letterforms' staging of imagined community and modern subjecthood, as well as the font's visual expression of its capitalist heritage and the

Figure 4.6: Sabon sample, complete with topical pangram. Image credit: Thomas Giddens (reproduced with permission).

imperial dominance of western civilization. The explicit preference for Times New Roman in the court transcripts of England and Wales authorizes the central role of this imperial face in the heart of the common law institution's jurisdictional performance. What is thus at stake in the matter of court transcripts is not an arbitrary stylistic preference or an aesthetic desire for neat formatting, but a normative demand that the common law's typographic performance contribute to its general project of promoting an imperial and patriarchal community of modern rational subjects.

A civilizing container

Times New Roman was first created for *The Times* newspaper between 1929 and 1932 under the direction of Stanley Morison.[23] While the creation of Times New Roman is typically attributed to Morison's design vision,[24] the letters themselves were drawn by Victor Lardent (under Morison's instruction; see Figure 4.7), and adapted through the complex re-drafting processes at the Monotype Corporation to fit their technical requirements (see Figure 4.8).[25] Nevertheless, Times New Roman did follow Morison's broad aesthetic and ideological direction, and expresses his civilizing aspirations for modern typography. Morison was 'modernist to the core' and deeply driven by his 'desire for principles';[26] accordingly, typography should not hinder the reader's access to the text, but should be 'a transparent and civilizing container'.[27] A prolific type designer and historian, Morison's general project includes, notably, his 'doctrine of self-effacement and obedience',[28] which in Times New Roman manifests as the visual form falling into the background of the reading experience while remaining robustly utilitarian across the variable contexts of *The Times*'s printed surface. Times New Roman has arguably fulfilled Morison's goals many times over. From the rigorous crucible of industrial newspress, it has spread widely – thanks not only to its robust design, but also its inclusion from the early 1990s as the default font in Microsoft Word. From their inception in London, the forms of Times New Roman have colonized texts across the globe,[29] becoming a default font of the technologized west and fading into its cultural background.

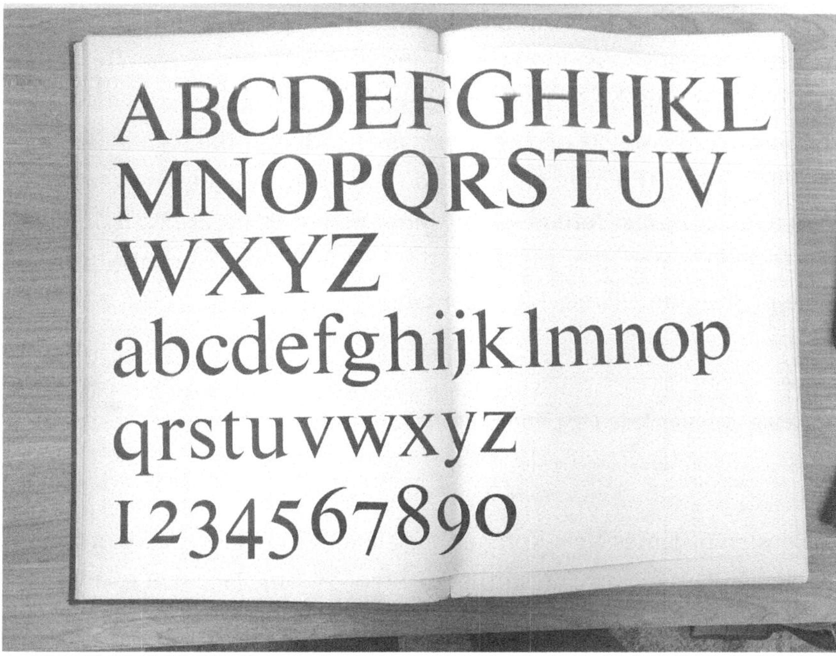

Figure 4.7: Victor Lardent's drawings for Times New Roman, reproduced under fair use from *Morison, Printing the Times Since 1785.*

Times New Roman emerges out of the capitalist and technological developments of the romantic period explored in the previous chapter, connected with the development of the modern sense of rational community and empire. Morison's history of designing Times New Roman (like his wider histories of newsprint[30]) is preoccupied with industrial processes[31] and presents an overarching narrative of technological innovation.[32] He traces John Walter I, II, and III as successive generations of industrial problem-solvers, enabling daily newspapers to be printed at high speed and mass volume. From the paper's beginnings in

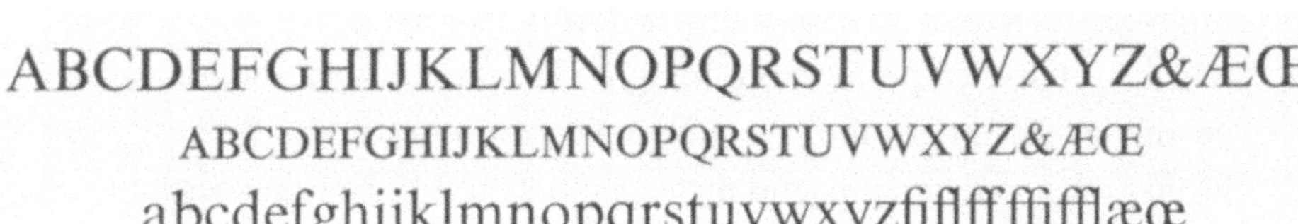

Figure 4.8: Monotype Specimen 327 (Times New Roman). Image © The Board of Trustees of the Science Museum, London. Reproduced with permission.

1785 under Walter I, 'commercial utility' took precedence over 'typographical accuracy'.[33] Walter II subsequently shepherded *The Times* into the steam age, and by 1828 the paper could print 4,000 sheets an hour.[34] The industrial context of *The Times* is encoded in the forms of Times New Roman, with letterspace – and thus profit – being of paramount importance: thinner letters meant more news per square yard of paper. As Morison states, this maximization of profit was of central importance in designing Times New Roman:

> The primary editorial requirement is space . . . no design could be considered satisfactory that failed to bring in at least as many characters in an equivalent space as that taken by the design it was intended to supersede.[35]

The design of Times New Roman thus balances 'legibility', 'economy', and 'mechanical efficiency',[36] resulting in a typographic face that expresses a 'capitalistic intention'.[37]

As a civilizing newspaper face with capitalist intentions, Times New Roman falls squarely in the context of Benedict Anderson's study of modern imperial imaginaries. Anderson follows the spread of 'print-capitalism', a phenomenon that describes the colonial spread of typographic materials that allowed an imperial population to imagine themselves as part of a single community.[38] Communities are not concrete objects, but are imagined – and determined in particular 'by the *style* in which they are imagined'.[39] The quality of community is not arbitrary, it is not some free-floating imaginary dream-world – but is shaped by the common material forms that inspire its putatively shared hallucination. While print in general can enable the imaginary membership of a shared communal order, it was capital-driven newspress that was central to this process. With the spread of the newspaper and its increasingly daily production and ephemerality, of which *The Times* is the most long-running example, there emerged an 'extraordinary mass ceremony' in which widely distributed populations imagined the contents of the newspaper 'in the lair of the skull'.[40] The imagined community was thereby 'conjured up by lexicography and print-capitalism'.[41] With the newspaper as its leading form, the imperial nation unfolded as a particular quality of community. Events in newspapers are not witnessed first-hand, but are remediated in text and imagined 'from the print',[42] shaped by the conflation of seemingly arbitrary happenings drawn, in early newsprint, from across the commonwealth. The glue that held together their contents 'was the very structure of the colonial administration and market system' upon which newspapers reported, and that accordingly produced an imagined community conditioned by imperial capitalism.[43]

The printed forms of common law texts are also located within this broad context of the production and maintenance of an imagined community, albeit along different lines from Anderson's model of print-capitalism. For James Boyd White, as a practice of constitutive rhetoric, legal reading is always concerned with the imaginary constitution and maintenance of community. While law tends to be 'abstracted and conceptualized',[44] with its body of rules then acting on the world as a machine of governance,[45] recognizing law as a rhetorical practice foregrounds the contingency of legality, its materials as 'a set of resources for thought and argument',[46] and its practice as always constitutive of its own language of argumentation.[47] Law's rhetorical practice is always specific to particular contexts and materials;[48] it is not made by a sovereign and given to lawyers to use, but is always made by lawyers in the act of lawyering.[49] Power is thereby mediated through the specifically textual form of law and its concomitant interpretive practices.[50] The rhetorical practices of law thus not only resolve disputes, but also claim the language in which disputes should be resolved, and in doing so express the mode in which community should be imagined.[51]

> It is the true nature of law to constitute a 'we' and to establish a conversation by which that 'we' can determine . . . what kind of community we should be, with what values, motives, and aims. It is a process by which we make ourselves by making our language.[52]

Crafting the materials of legal language – the expressive register of jurisdiction – is a rhetorical practice that, ultimately, contributes to the constitution of lawful community.[53] Legal matter enables the imagination of a community in line with the values and norms to which that law aspires.

Like printed content in general, and the shared hallucination of the modern nation in particular, access to law's immaterial structures of principle and doctrine, and the community they engender, is enabled by analysis of the visual surface of its pages. From the typographic images set on the page or screen, the unseen, invisible, or otherwise ideational structure of thought, concept, and virtual form unfold in the imagination. Anderson makes clear that it is specifically print that 'invents nationalism' by generating feelings of shared encounters, rather than the use of any particular vernacular.[54] Yet print, for Anderson, is treated monolithically as the mechanically reproduceable form of written text in the printing press. Anderson's study, like modern lawyers and readers in general, overlooks the meaningful associations and heritage of printed forms as visual artefacts.

Widespread typographic convention offers 'an unconscious yet ubiquitous means of persuasion and identification.'[55] Yet arguably, as Jake Cowan notes, when generating imagined communities the specifics of a font are not as relevant as their shared or default quality: 'The ideological force of the typeface lies in the banal pervasiveness of sign after sign at the edge of consciousness,'[56] rather than its vexillological status as a flag or emblem of nation.[57] But while the specifics of a given form may not be relevant in terms of generating a shared imaginary per se, the particular style of a common form is relevant to the quality of that imaginary. As we have seen, a default is not meaningless just because it is a default, but rather signals the profound importance of an entrenched convention. As Cowan admits: 'the imagined community is flagged when a . . . choice in font has stopped being a choice at all' and has instead become 'the unquestioned, self-evident standard.'[58] The specificity of a shared form that helps provide a common basis for an imagined community contributes to the manner in which that community is imagined.

In the jurisdictional imagination, the forms of print function not only on the level of the reading subject, but on the level of community: the contours and meanings of the literal images that constitute typographic legality shape the quality of discourse and community those images inspire. Just as the specific content of newspapers shape the manner in which a community is imagined, so the specific design of a court transcript contributes to the manner of lawful community it constitutes – even and especially if that design is a default convention. The abstract 'content' of a common law text is imagined under the conditions of the page,[59] supervised and managed by the forms of legal expression.[60] Both Lloyd LJ's reaction in *Baigent* to Times New Roman's improper use and the UK Supreme Court's reversion to Times New Roman in general reveal that the default convention is not merely nominal, but should actually be adhered to. By setting court transcripts in Times New Roman, the civilizing ethos of Morison's project and the imperial mechanics of print-capitalism are embedded in the modern law's constitution and management of its community, sanctioning the face's blended heritage as part of the common law's jurisdictional performance. If law is a rhetorical process by which we make ourselves by making our language, to make that language 12-point Times New Roman is to constitute a modern, rational community of capitalist empire.

Staging the subject

The visual order of the page stages the imaginary order of thought. The production of the imagined community of the colonial west mapped by Anderson draws upon an older and more general feature of the technology of writing: the production of the modern subject as a being of rational interiority. Prior to written language, memory and thought – including legal thought[61] – were conditioned by conventional patterns of speech.[62] Under such conditions, performing analysis without an external storage device threatened the loss of what was sedimented in oral formulae.[63] Written text, however, 'freed' the mind for 'abstract thought.'[64] Analytical reasoning, as Walter J Ong's extended study of oral and literate cultures demonstrates, derives specifically 'from text-bound thought,'[65] distinctly a product of 'the technology of writing,'[66] such that the page comes to embody the conceptual order of what is taken to be its abstract content.

The form of the written text is the 'materialization of abstraction,' mirroring in its aesthetic appearance the order of what it is imagined to transmit.[67] Calculated layouts project 'mentally organized and quantified patterns of "knowledge" onto the empty space of the page,'[68] with pages providing the 'visual architecture' for their presumed content[69] that is taken to have an 'autonomous existence,' distinct from typographic matter.[70] Preserved by the emulation of written manuscripts in early typecutting, this conventional patterning reflects or stages the conceptual order of modern thought. As they developed, print technologies enhanced the generated sense of ordered thought made visible on the page. Print afforded a control of space that increased the impression of 'tidiness and inevitability' without visible use of guides or borders.[71] While visual writing results in graphically contingent usages distinct from oral practice,[72] print consolidated and emphasized these 'grapholects' by attributing them with 'a special normative power for keeping language in order'.[73] The shift to abstraction is a product of earlier shifts in reading and textual practice, and the many effects of print function to consolidate and evolve the cognitive revolution that writing had already started.[74] In the imagined community of the west, it is the order of thought that is staged by the repeated materials of print-capitalism, producing a shared unitary space of reason that establishes the illusory existence of community and its membership.

In Chapter 3, the industrial repetition of printed forms generated the idea of a unitary version of an (immaterial) legal text in tension with the material distribution of its copied instances. The simulated immaterial version of a text is a product not just of the repetitions of the press facilitated by print-capitalism, however, but also of writing techniques in general that the press enhanced. Various manuscript innovations with no oral precedent – such as subject indexing, ordered page layouts, headings, summaries,[75] as well as regularized punctuation systems[76] – operated to render the text as a visual artefact distinct from oral speech, and thereby helped it to function as a stage for an imagined conceptual structure rather than as a score for an oral performance.[77] Numbering paragraphs in printed judgments, for example, follows the same trajectory, as if 'the' judgment exists somewhere as a conceptually ordered object, with this conceptual object indexed by the visual page that is taken to permit communal access to it. Through such techniques, the matter of legal transmission stages the existence of an imaginary order of law that comes to exist beyond the page, with its source in the thought of the author, the communal expertise of the profession, or the objective world of reason itself.

The technology of visualized text demands that individuals adapt to its formal requirements. Ivan Illich's study of writing technologies forms part of a more general critique of industrial society,[78] mapping how inequality and injustice are produced by a shift in the relationship between individuals and their tools: where tools are 'convivial', they remain useful extensions of human will and capacity; where they are 'manipulative', they require individuals to adapt to their systemic demands.[79] As Samerski summarizes, modern technological society has generally passed this tipping point: 'today's institutions, machines and technogenic structures form a technological system that colonizes our imagination, reshapes self-perception, patterns human activity and damages social relations.'[80] The technology of the page – from manuscripts to the digital – is a 'powerful interface' between the reader and its formal arrangement,[81] and, like other sufficiently complex tools of modern society, demand a specialist training and conditioning of the subject who makes use of them.[82] Textual technologies, including the typographic figures that are central to their functioning, thus demand particular habits of their users, a process that, on a broad scale, produces modern subjects with particular qualities and capacities.

While particular typefaces can have specific histories of meaning they (unconsciously) retransmit,[83] the technologies of material text can be linked to the formation of the modern subject in general. The page is a specialist technology: reading becomes a 'technical activity of deciphering' in which individuals relate their mind to a document's imagined content.[84] 'The modern reader', Illich observes, 'conceives of the page as a plate that inks the mind, and of the mind as a screen onto which the page is projected.'[85] Words on pages are understood as 'a repertory of the author's thought',[86] staging conceptual discourse outside its material articulation. Modern reading, which aims at knowledge and understanding, generates a kind of secular faith in the presence of reason and thought made apparent by the signs on the page.[87] In this way, writing and print have become 'deeply interiorized, made a part of our own psychic resources.'[88] Freud's discovery of the unconscious corresponds with the development of inner life in post-typographic culture,[89] such that writing functions as an x-ray that visibly stages the invisible interior of the self.[90] Typography is thus a 'symbol for thought'[91] and the subject is restructured to have an immaterial yet secular inner life,[92] conditioned by the abstractions of rational thought that are staged by technologies of visible text.

The production of the rational modern subject interacts with questions of difference and inclusion that run through the imperial project. The goal of civilizing is one linked with the improvement of 'savage' or under-developed cultures, to update them to the level of development characteristic of modernity. Significantly, though, the standards of modernity have traditionally been those of white male Europeans. The emancipation projects of modernity may seek equality, but it is not inherently or necessarily the case that this aspired society of equals includes those of different genders, races, or other characteristics. Modernity is often understood to hold an 'inner logic' of equality that 'drives us towards the completion of modern ideals'[93] – we are always progressing towards an increasingly inclusive and equal community. Yet there is clear historical evidence that through the processes of modernism there was a shift towards both 'explicitly racist accounts of human difference' and an 'intensification of gendered differences',[94] with colonial others being categorized as incapable of modern standards and women excluded from the ever more sharply defined public sphere.[95] The ideal of the abstract, rational subject seems on the one hand to support an equal inclusion, free from bias based upon embodied differences. Yet the abstract individual 'is never as disembodied, degendered, or deracialised as he claims', but due to its abstraction makes it harder to challenge existing inequalities.[96] Insofar as its technologies are connected with the ideal of the modern rational individual characterized primarily by their abstract, disembodied interior life, the page is both racialized and gendered. While such a technology may appear to promote a free inclusion in the intellectual realms of knowledge, law, and principle, at least in early modernity this realm of 'equality' and the concept of the abstract individual that supported it were inhabited by white males. In line with this, the subject inculcated by the techniques of the page thus unfolds along European and masculine lines.

The ideals of rational subjecthood become embedded in the common law via the use of Times New Roman. The particular style in which common law texts appear, understood as part of wider traditions of visual expression and governance via the technologies of the page,[97] is of primary significance in the institution's jurisdictional performance. If we recall Ridler,[98] the success of a jurisdictional performance does not rest on the actual supplication of individuals, but instead on the text's form of address. In the design of Times New Roman, modern industrial heritage overlaps with the textual production of the modern subject, resonating powerfully with modern law's ideals of an abstract civilizing reason that governs the rationally individual subject.[99] Accordingly, if we pay attention to their typography, the presumed subject to which the court transcripts of England and Wales is addressed has a particular form, as expressed in the contingent design of Times New Roman. This expression invokes not only the rational interiority of modern subjecthood staged by printed forms, and linked with a racialized gendering of that rational space, but also the wider imperial community of which the (white male) subject is imagined to be a part within the civilizing project of the west.

In the details of its design, as we will see in the next section, Times New Roman foregrounds and intensifies these broader trajectories of the western civilizing project. Within the context of print-capitalism, the specific design of Times New Roman enhances this feature of writing, invoking both a general heritage of civilizing reason and the specific mechanics of its own backgrounding on the page during reading. These features of Times New Roman not only express Morison's own modernist preferences and desire for a rational, principled order, but condone and enhance the wider technological and cultural production of modern subjecthood as the secular internal life of the reasoning subject familiar to conceptions of western legal subjecthood. By staging its own disappearance – into the background of the page as much as the background of modern western culture – Times New Roman signals a desire to inculcate modern rational subjecthood and – in its distinctly print-capitalist heritage and use – thereby facilitate the imperial spread of western civilization.

The imperial face of the common law

As a tool for focusing the mind on the imaginary, writing technologies provide the productive conditions for generating conceptual knowledge, the structures of the modern rational subject that come with it, and the imagined community this (shared) interiority of the subject enables. The typographic matter of the legal institution stages the existence not only of rational discourse in general, but of the conceptual structures and principles of law in particular. As introduced in Chapter 1, in a legal context, attention is shifted away from paginal matter into law's immaterial structure of reason – and textual technologies facilitate this. As Olaf Tans notes, we continually use sophisticated 'props', such as 'using a novel to experience a fictional world'.[100] For lawyers, typographic text enables access or imagination of law as a normative order: props 'such as codes, statutes and jurisprudence . . . function as objects that trigger the imagination of an ultimate normative foundation' for law.[101] With the dressing of court transcripts in Times New Roman, the staging of the common law's authoritative presence explicitly includes the staging of its imagined source (*fons*) in the civilizing structures of reason: Times New Roman's invocation of its heritage, coupled with its deliberate self-effacement, is not only part of this larger project, but seeks to actively enhance it. When found on the pages of court transcripts, within the institution of western law that adheres to the premise of rational subjecthood, Times New Roman is a meaningful expression not only of the wider structures of rational modernity and empire, but of their place within the common law's rhetorical claim to authority in its typographic practice of jurisdiction.

Legal understanding rests heavily on the ordering benefits of reason, and the demand that the common law appear first in Times New Roman ensures that reading subjects and the constituted community continue to be expressed as a rational imperial order. Attending to the specifics of its form, Times New Roman can be seen to intensify the features by which a page stages the existence of an abstract order of thought upon which imperial community is built. The broad design heritage of Times New Roman is a blend of 'modern' and 'old face', crafted to minimize the ideological disruption to the readers of *The Times* and thereby background the textual form to ensure that readers' imagination of the paper's news content remained unimpeded. The particular design of Times New Roman seeks to maximize the ease with which reading subjects imagine the existence of a conceptual structure of discourse, staged by but taken to be independent from the matter of the page. This backgrounding functions not only in relation to the face's high-level principles and the typographic heritage it draws on, but also in the details of its functioning as a readerly object. By actively backgrounding itself, the visual form of Times New Roman enhances the page's staging of its invisible structures. In this way, the design of Times New Roman not only recalls a heritage of design, but actively facilitates the production of the modern subject and the imagination of imperial community.

In tension with his modernism, the historical influences on Morison's vision for Times New Roman predate the 'modern' in typographic design history, recalling earlier humanist and pre-rationalized models of letterform. Even if typographers wish to avoid historical styles, they must still grapple with traditional alphabetic shapes and the five-plus centuries of heritage they come with – 'the ancient forms', as Bringhurst puts it, 'are living in the new'.[102] Morison is explicit in recalling earlier models, and also makes the observation that the sharp, flat style of serif he claims is characteristic of 'modern' types[103] can be found in sixteenth-century manuscripts, two and a half centuries before they were supposedly invented by typographers like Bodoni.[104] For Morison, the modern forms of roman typography derive from an earlier model – specifically the development of the *romain du roi*, discussed earlier.[105] This face was the product of submitting 'the traditional roman form . . . to the discipline of the rule and compass'.[106] This strict rationalism was then tempered by the punch-cutting craft of Philippe Grandjean who 'preferred the guidance of his own trained eye'.[107] The resulting font was thus a blend of rational geometric form and traditional craft expertise, sharply cut and mechanically regular. The design of Times New Roman aspires to a similar ethos.

In relation to its broader heritage, Times New Roman is derived from its own 'concept of what constitutes a letterform'.[108] In line with Morison's modernist desire for principled order, it draws together a varied history of typographic design and places it in the print-capitalist context of modern technological production and empire. Morison's rationalist vision draws together historical influences, blending them into an aesthetic of civilizing modernism. Coupled with *The Times*'s desire for profits was a concern for the heritage of the paper and its typographic dress. There was a desire not to alienate its readers who were used to an essentially unchanged letter style since the turn of the nineteenth century.[109] The result, then, needed to invoke older faces, updated to modern standards, under the controlling limits of the paper's capitalist existence as a commercial enterprise.

Where Morison's account provides specific engagement with the letterforms, he focuses on the adaptations made from older models rather than the details of their design heritage. The brief, Morison recalls, was to avoid novelty and be 'absolutely free from faddishness',[110] continuing the tradition of *The Times* as isolated from populist trends (not just in typography) and generally 'resistant to frivolous change'.[111] According to Morison, Times New Roman achieved this by mixing 'old style' Plantin[112] with not-quite-modern Perpetua[113] within the capitalist requirements of *The Times*, resulting in a distinct historical and industrial blend. By blending the 'old style' with the modern, Times New Roman exploits a widespread cultural familiarity with humanist letterforms that have been dominant, as we saw in Chapter 2, since at least the sixteenth century to ensure the face generally passes below the notice of western readers, and *Times* readers in particular. At the same time, in updating to modern standards, Morison's vision produced a rationalized and industrially robust system of modern figures.

Where Morison's account is a vague invocation of typographic history, Robert Bringhurst's leading guide offers some more specific clues as to the inherited meanings living in the forms of Times New Roman. The face, he summarizes, is a 'historical pastiche', consisting of 'a humanist axis' (see Figure 4.9), 'Mannerist proportions', 'Baroque weight', and a 'sharp, Neoclassical finish'.[114] Mannerism, Bringhurst explains, was popular following the renaissance and is characterized by 'subtle exaggeration' in length, shape, and angularity,[115] and in Times New Roman describes the apparent increase in height due to squashing the letters to maximize profits. Later Baroque style commonly featured an enlarged x-height,[116] which Times New Roman employs to gain much of its legibility at the small sizes used in a profit-bound newspaper. The Baroque also involves modulation and restless variation, typically in axis,[117] but in Times New Roman's case the weight of the line itself varies between thick and thin, comparatively more than heavier renaissance letters (see Figure 4.10) but without the sharp contrast of the modern or

Figure 4.9: Times New Roman's humanist axis. Image credit: Thomas Giddens (reproduced with permission).

Figure 4.10: Times New Roman has a more varied line width compared to an 'old-face' like Plantin. Image credit: Thomas Giddens (reproduced with permission).

romantic. The brackets of Times New Roman's serifs exemplify this, blending a modern with an older style to produce curves that invoke something of the heavy tradition of the renaissance without succumbing to the novelty of a sharp contrast (see Figure 4.11). Times New Roman is thus 'transitional', retaining the antique within the modern.[118] The 'sharp, Neoclassical finish' describes the small brackets on the serifs,[119] and also captures the 'static and restrained' quality of Times New Roman's 'rationalist' letters that, despite their humanist axis, are shaped not by conventional writing anatomy – but by Morison's ordering principles[120] combined with his panoptic view of print history.

As Morison emphasized above, the context of newspaper production left its material imprint on Times New Roman's design: maximizing

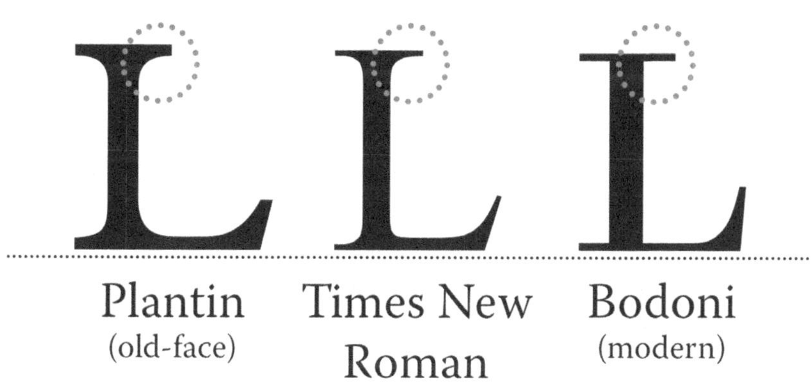

Figure 4.11: Times New Roman's 'transitional' serifs, situated between the 'old' and the 'modern'. Image credit: Thomas Giddens (reproduced with permission).

profit by minimizing letter width was a central concern. This resulted in a thinner set of letters than traditional book faces, and a newspaper that could sell more (imagined) news per square yard of paper – a quintessential expression of print-capitalism. This compression, however, also produces a sense of proficiency for the reader. By compressing letters into words, and generating a relative increase in the space between those words, Times New Roman enables 'the eye to more quickly take in whole words as shapes, see them as outlines and whole units rather than assemblages.'[121] This technique recalls and enhances specific shifts in the earlier arrangement of written letterforms that contributed to the staging of abstraction: the early innovation of putting spaces between words meant readers 'could grasp single words with their eye as if they were ideograms.'[122] The thing-like quality of words is emphasized in Times New Roman and the reader's access to both the conceptual layer of meaning and the imperial imaginary is made more efficient, reducing the distraction of the contingent material forms of Morison's civilizing design.

This technique also infuses Times New Roman with a colonial gaze. In backgrounding the perception of text's visual dimensions, Lyotard argues that modern reading challenges 'the visibility of the legible.'[123] Times New Roman enhances this process, actively working to aid the reader's suppression of material form in favour of content by visually and materially subsuming individual letters under the priority of words. Alphabetic writing in general suggests that words are not embodied speech events, but things present (via the page) as independent forms.[124] Typographic print exacerbates this change: type units physically preexist the words they manifest, thereby suggesting that 'words are things far more than writing ever did.'[125] Print thereby reifies the word, but Times New Roman's particular staging of the conceptual existence of words as rational objects works to efface the individuality and difference of letters themselves. A high-level gaze is embedded into the reading experience, rendering individual letters anonymous and subordinate to the rational order of modern civilized discourse. Coupled with the imperial spread of empire through the networks of print-capitalism in which Times New Roman was forged, and the panoptic perspective evident in Morison's cherry-picking from the history of type design, this managing of typographic perception embeds a colonial gaze into its visual expression, offering 'the reader a sense of mastery' over the text[126] and the imaginary world it stages.

Under the organizing principles of Morison's project, pages of matter are suppressed and dominated by readers on a quest for rational content, asserting a document's masculine competence along with its performative claim to modern rationality. As we saw above, the production of an abstract realm of reason has historically gendered connotations, connected with the priority of white male subject positions as populating the community of modern equals (for example, 'all men are created equal' does not automatically apply to non-white men, women, the poor, and so on).[127] As in modernist literature, where being modern is 'best exemplified by the male',[128] in its brief to Morison *The Times* asserted that any new typeface should be explicitly 'masculine'.[129] This desire is arguably undercut by the highly skilled draftswomen of Monotype's Type Drawing Office through which Morison's ideals were filtered.[130] As Kinross observes, 'while Morison could make proposals and then urge corrections, the final forms of a typeface', even one like Times New Roman that he was heavily involved in designing, 'were in the hands' of the predominantly female staff at the Monotype works.[131] Yet the forms retain their domineering aesthetic and their prioritization of a characteristically male reason. For Hawkins, 'Times New Roman was created to be efficient and powerful'.[132] Words set in Times New Roman signify a masculine 'prowess' – a feature further accumulated by its print-capitalist success as much as its subsequent ubiquity in other contexts, but also established aesthetically in the 'domineering elements' of its 'tall, compressed, thin form'[133] that facilitates readers' control of the textual content. The patriarchal dominance expressed in the figures of Times New Roman is not the autonomous will of Morison, but emerges from a context of both the profit-driven industry of newspaper printing and the denigration of women's agency in typographic production and design, as well as the wider exclusion of women and colonial others from the public spheres of rational thought. In its domineering prowess and global spread, Times New Roman becomes the print form of patriarchal imperialism, encoding an 'assumed superiority of [modern] Western thought and accomplishment', itself a symptom of historically privileged male subject positions, 'with clear material connections to hegemonic, colonialist sensibilities'.[134]

To use Times New Roman in court transcripts is to stage jurisdiction, and concomitantly constitute the subject and the communal order, in a particular manner. In the example of *Baigent*, jurisdictional staging takes place not only in its overlooked textual conventions, as it does in other transcripts, but also more overtly in the m of 'claimant', set in 12-point Times New Roman, that overrides and forcefully replaces the incorrectly italicized m used by Smith J in the same word (see Figure 4.4 and Figure 4.5). Jurisdiction takes place, too, in the wholesale shift from Calibri back to Times New Roman in the transcripts of the UK Supreme Court. In these typographic slips, the judicial institution reveals not only its concern with the contingent images in which the common law appears, but that the contingency of those seemingly default images must be actively managed and maintained. Adverted by these slips, but present across the archive of judicial transcripts in England and Wales, is the more general fact that formal judicial texts are not naturalized containers of legal meaning upon which nothing turns, but are contingent forms that – in their contingency as Times New Roman – reveal the structure of modern western civilization: as a capitalist, rationalist, patriarchal, and imperialist order. The quality of the common law institution is revealed not simply as a standardized platform upon which to stage the institution's intellectual content, or even as having a mere preference for visual neatness, but as the entangled forms of judicial typography that perform a particular civilizing function. The use of Times New Roman expresses the continued unfolding of empire and patriarchy, of strength and suppression, and of the prowess and paternalism of western civilization. In the court transcripts of England and Wales, this violent domination is repeated – in detail and at length – in the visual contours and style of the common law's typographic appearance.

Conclusion

Times New Roman is a tool for civilization. Its visual form contributes to the modern project of rational civilization, going beyond the updating of its forms to modern, rational standards of design. In all its details, the materialization of Times New Roman's letters visually encodes the heritage and ideas behind its design in a set of readerly mechanics that promotes the imperial imagination. Times New Roman enhances the staging of a conceptual text in both the intricacies of its letters and its broader ideological heritage, maximizing its own invisibility. Use of the font expresses an ideological preference for the virtues of the humanist tradition, the ordering force of modern rationalization, and the projection of a civilized order of empire. A page set in Times New Roman not only stages (*qua* text) the existence of an independent strata of rational content that inculcates the modern subject, nor just (*qua* print) the enhanced existence of letters as objective components for communication that have become detached from spoken language, but – *qua* Times New Roman – the ideological contingencies of the western desire for abstract reason and civilized order under which its forms were forged. While the common law can and does appear in other faces, in the court transcripts of England and Wales it does so in Times New Roman. Manifesting law in Times New Roman does more than communicate abstract principle: it expresses a range of western values – rational subjecthood, patriarchy, imperialism, principled order, the authority of precedent and tradition – within the institutional materials of the common law itself.

By fading into the background to become the default choice in the west, Times New Roman has become a common textual form that binds individuals into an imagined community hallucinated under the conditions of the page. As the default for court transcripts, it conditions the imagination of lawyers and judges as they exercise the constitutive rhetoric that grounds lawful community. To set a text in Times New Roman demonstrates that text's membership of the modern industrial order while hiding the contingency of this membership. It is a statement – conscious or otherwise – that a text is part of a tradition of textual governance and the homogenization of a supposedly fragmented globe under the auspices of empire. It is also a rhetorical feint that in its form of address naturalizes that order by shifting the visual forms of the text into the background of the readerly encounter, prioritizing instead the presumed subject's imagined belonging to the civilized order and the abstract structures of modern rational law, reaffirming the supposedly immaterial quality of modern legal power.

Notes

1. [2007] EWCA Civ 247.
2. See Chapter 2.
3. The title of this chapter is adapted from Jake Cowan's claim that, given the ubiquity of Times New Roman as a formatting convention, when setting an official text like a constitution, 'it seems only natural – which is precisely the point [of a convention] – that all roads would lead to Times New Roman.' See Jake Cowan, 'Typographic Nationalism and the Banal Uniformity of Imagined Communities', in *Type Matters: The Rhetoricity of Letterforms*, ed. Christopher Scott Wyatt and Dànielle Nicole DeVoss (Parlour Press, 2018), 248–49, quotation at 249.
4. [2006] EWHC 719 (Ch).
5. Dan Brown, *The Da Vinci Code* (Doubleday, 2003).
6. For a non-peer reviewed overview of the code, see https://en.wikipedia.org/wiki/Smithy_code. And, for extensive analysis, see Peter Goodrich, 'Legal Enigmas – Antonio de Nebrija, *The Da Vinci Code* and the Emendation of Law', *Oxford Journal of Legal Studies* 30, no. 1 (2010): 71–99.
7. *Baigent v Random House* [2007] EWCA Civ 247 at [3].
8. *Baigent v Random House* [2007] EWCA Civ 247 at [3].
9. See Desmond Manderson, 'Bodies in the Water: On Reading Images More Sensibly', *Law and Literature* 27, no. 2 (2015): 279–93.
10. There is no comprehensive repository of the courts' own transcripts of judgments, although many are available alongside their respective case reports in databases like WestLaw. More recent decisions have been archived online closer to the institutional source: see the PDF transcripts of judgments since 2019 provided by judiciary.uk (see https://www.judiciary.uk/judgments/), and for the House of Lords (forerunner to the UK Supreme Court), the Parliament website archive includes PDF transcripts for judgments since December 2004 (see https://publications.parliament.uk/pa/ld/ldjudgmt.htm#2004).
11. See Matthew Butterick, 'A Brief History of Times New Roman', in *Typography for Lawyers*, 2nd ed. (2018), https://typographyforlawyers.com/a-brief-history-of-times-new-roman.html.
12. Recall Kostelnick and Hassett's observation in Chapter 2 that 'convention carries the rhetorical weight of the discourse community that sanctions it': Kostelnick and Hassett, *Shaping Information*, 6.
13. The change to Calibri happened between 22 September and 6 October 2021. See *R (on the application of TN (Vietnam)) (Appellant) v Secretary of State for the Home Department and another (Respondents)* [2021] UKSC 41, manifesting in the usual Times New Roman on 22 September, followed by *Reference by the Attorney General and the Advocate General for Scotland – United Nations Convention on the Rights of the Child (Incorporation) (Scotland) Bill; Reference by the Attorney General and the Advocate General for Scotland – European Charter of Local Self-Government (Incorporation) (Scotland) Bill* [2021] UKSC

42, which appeared in Calibri on 6 October. Quietly, in 2023, the Supreme Court switched back to Times New Roman between 10 August (see *R (on the application of Worcester County Council) (Appellant) v Secretary of State for Health and Social Care (Respondent)* [2023] UKSC 31 in Calibri) and 20 September (see *Republic of Mozambique (acting through its Attorney General) (Appellant) v Privinvest Shipbuilding SAL (Holding) and others (Respondents)* [2023] UKSC 32 in Times New Roman). So quietly, in fact, that even *Legal Cheek* – who broke the original news of the change to Calibri – has not noticed: see, for a late 2024 reference to the Supreme Court still using Calibri, Rhys Duncan, 'Battle of the Fonts: What's the Best Typeface for Lawyers?', *Legal Cheek*, 23 December 2024, https://www.legalcheek.com/2024/12/battle-of-the-fonts-whats-the-best-typeface-for-lawyers/.

14. See Sarah Hyndman, 'The Ultimate Font Face-off: Serif vs sans Serif in the Psychological Battle of Font Personalities', *Type Tasting*, 16 February 2023, https://www.typetasting.com/blog-1/2023/2/16/the-ultimate-font-face-off-serif-vs-sans-serif-in-the-psychological-battle-of-font-personalities.
15. The Legal Cheek report, while brief, has a reasonable summary of different online comments at the time: Aishah Hussain, '"Legal Font Wars": Supreme Court's Switch to Calibri Sparks Debate among Lawyers', *Legal Cheek*, 22 December 2021, https://www.legalcheek.com/2021/12/legal-font-wars-supreme-courts-switch-to-calibri-sparks-debate-among-lawyers/.
16. While Calibri is often noted as an 'accessible' font, Granet, for example, lambasts the UK Supreme Court's shift away from Times New Roman as a problematic undermining of the accessibility of the Supreme Court's texts: see Elijah Granet, 'Despair at the Supreme Court', *Notes on the Style of the Law*, 27 December 2021, https://www.legalstyle.co.uk/2021/12/despair-at-supreme-court.html. His fervour is not without basis, since serifs are traditionally used to improve the flow of the eye in book typography. Indeed, there was early resistance to modern sans-serif designs for prioritising 'form' over the comfort of familiar readability: see Kinross, *Modern Typography*, 151–53. Recent psychological studies are equivocal on their effect on legibility in general: see for example Aries Arditi and Jianna Cho, 'Serifs and Font Legibility', *Vision Research* 45 (2005): 2926–33. Regarding accessibility, the style guide of American Psychological Association busts numerous myths about accessible typography – including the (non)use of serifs: see 'Accessible Typography', https://apastyle.apa.org/style-grammar-guidelines/paper-format/accessibility/typography (accessed 11 February 2025).
17. Morison discusses the use of the Medical Research Council's 1927 report into print legibility in his account of Times New Roman's design process: see Morison, *Printing The Times*, 165. See also Meredith Mann, 'Where Did Times New Roman Come From?', *The New York Public Library*, 9 December 2014, https://live-legacy-admin.nypl.org/blog/2014/12/09/times-new-roman.
18. Hyndman, 'Font Face-Off'. For an empirical study on the different personalities that readers perceive in typefaces, see Eva R. Brumberger, 'The Rhetoric of Typography: The Persona of Typeface and Text', *Technical Communication* 50, no. 2 (2003): 206–23.

19. On this point, see Goodrich, 'Legal Enigmas'. The use of italics itself is traditionally associated with orality, reinforcing the challenge to law's objective reason raised by adverting the matter of the text (see Chapter 2, n 54).
20. On the radical significance of slips, see Peter Goodrich, 'Oedipus Lex: Slips in Interpretation and Law', *Legal Studies* 13, no. 03 (1993): 381–95.
21. Paul Magrath, Head of Product Development and Online Content at the ICLR, email correspondence with author, 23 April 2025.
22. Sabon is a humanist font, recalling older models of letterform. This is evident in its regular axis, following the imagined right-handed writer as the human origin of the letterforms. Its terminals (e.g. at the end of the top line of the a and f) are modelled on pen strokes, rather than being crafted balls or teardrops. It does not have the heavy weight of classic renaissance faces such as in Plowden, but it retains that older model in its updated form. It was designed by Jan Tschichold in the 1960s, based on the model of Garamond and named after one of Garamond's pupils: see Bringhurst, *Elements*, 231. It is very appropriate for setting book text, as Bringhurst notes, with its 'calm and steady flow': Bringhurst, *Elements*, 104. Tshichold himself was a prolific type designer, whose modernist project sought to derive letterforms from the interior elements of typographic technologies, but always oriented towards the social purpose of a text: see Kinross, *Modern Typography*, 106; Jan Tschichold, 'The Principles of the New Typography', in *Texts on Type: Critical Writings on Typography* (Allworth, 2001). Leveraging the readability of humanist conventions within the book typography of law reports is an apt continuation of this ideal, locating it squarely within the tensions of romanizing discussed in Chapter 2.
23. Morison was famously requested to undertake the task after publicly observing what he saw as *The Times*'s typographic failings. For detailed narration of this conventional history, see Lawson, *Anatomy*, 270–76. On Morison's subsequent long-term involvement with *The Times*, see Kinross, *Modern Typography*, 79.
24. See, for a pithy account of the 'neat' version of the font's history, Alice Savoie, 'The Women Behind Times New Roman: The Contribution of Type Drawing Offices to Twentieth Century Type-Making', *Journal of Design History* 33, no. 3 (2020): 209. The myth of the single (typically white male) designer who manifests their visual will is widely criticized in design studies. As Savoie notes, citing Scotford's concept of 'neat history', the historiographical need for a single, clear narrative of creation tends to go against the collaborative nature of most design work: Savoie, 'Women', 210.
25. Savoie, 'Women'. Close comparison of Figure 4.7 and Figure 4.8 reveals numerous substantive differences in letter design, notably the serifs on the C, G, S, and s, and the terminal on the j. The capitals are generally wider in Lardent's drawings than the compressed final form. For some closer analysis of the differences, including a detailed comparative figure, see Mike Parker, 'W Starling Burgess, Type Designer?', *Printing History* 16, nos. 1–2 (1994): 63–68.
26. Ames Hawkins, 'Why I Hate Times New Roman, and Other Confessions of a Creative-Critical Scholar', in *Type Matters: The Rhetoricity of Letterforms* (Parlour Press, 2018), 164. For a more general critique of modernism in

typography, see Mr Keedy, 'Zombie Modernism', in *Texts on Type: Critical Writings on Typography*, ed. Steven Heller and Philip B. Meggs (Allworth, 2001).

27. Kinross, *Modern Typography*, 80.
28. Kinross, *Modern Typography*, 80.
29. Hawkins, 'Why I Hate', 165.
30. See Stanley Morison, *The English Newspaper: An Account of the Physical Development of Journals Printed in London 1622–1932* (Cambridge University Press, 1932); Morison, *Printing The Times*.
31. As he describes it:

> The designing of a new body type for use in a newspaper is not an easy matter. The preparation of such a design for mechanical composition involves a multitude of calculations forming the basis of the patterns that are used for the manufacture of the punches from which matrices, in turn employed on the casting machines, are driven. It is the punch, therefore, that governs the impression finally made on the sheet that comes before the reader. Above 14,750 punches, including those corrected (a large number), were cut by the Monotype Corporation. (Morison, *Printing The Times*, 68.)

32. For more recent discussion on the role of technology in the history of news-press, articulating the agency of the technology itself over that of individual pioneers, see Dallas Liddle, 'The News Machine: Textual Form and Information Function in the London Times, 1785–1885', *Book History* 19, no. 1 (2016): 132–68.
33. Morison, *Printing The Times*, 4.
34. Morison, *Printing The Times*, 28–36.
35. Morison, *Printing The Times*, 168.
36. Morison, *Printing The Times*, 64.
37. Hawkins, 'Why I Hate', 164.
38. Benedict Anderson, *Imagined Communities: Reflections on the Origin and Spread of Nationalism*, revised edn (Verso, 2016), 36.
39. Anderson, *Imagined Communities*, 6. Emphasis added.
40. Anderson, *Imagined Communities*, 35.
41. Anderson, *Imagined Communities*, 109.
42. Anderson, *Imagined Communities*, 32.
43. Anderson, *Imagined Communities*, 62. Morison's study of London newspaper history similarly observes how content mixed together foreign and domestic items: see Morison, *English Newspaper*.
44. White, 'Law as Rhetoric', 685.
45. White, 'Law as Rhetoric', 684–87. See also, on the imaginary of law as a machine, James Boyd White, 'Imagining the Law', in *The Rhetoric of Law*, ed. Austin Sarat and Thomas R. Kearns (University of Michigan Press, 1996).
46. White, 'Law as Rhetoric', 689.
47. White, 'Law as Rhetoric', 688–92.
48. White, 'Law as Rhetoric', 695.
49. White, 'Law as Rhetoric', 696.

50. See Augsberg, 'Reading Law'.
51. White, 'Law as Rhetoric'.
52. White, 'Law as Rhetoric', 698.
53. See Dorsett and McVeigh, *Jurisdiction*, 54–59.
54. Anderson, *Imagined Communities*, 134.
55. Cowan, 'Typographic Nationalism', 232.
56. Cowan, 'Typographic Nationalism', 245.
57. Compare, for example, the typographic 'branding' of South Africa: see Kurt Campbell, 'The Sociogenic Imperative of Typography: A "Face" for the New South Africa', *European Journal of English Studies* 17, no. 1 (2013): 72–91.
58. Cowan, 'Typographic Nationalism', 248.
59. On the 'extispicy' (the divinatory reading of entrails) of the visual, see Goodrich, *Judicial Uses*, 164–95. See more generally Benjamin Goh, 'Dream of the Legal Monograph', *Law, Culture and the Humanities* 21, no. 3 (2025): 421–437.
60. On the supervision of the reading subject by the textual forms of law, see discussion of Mussawir in Chapter 1.
61. Ong, *Orality and Literacy*, 35. On the function of memory as a precursor to writing in jurisdictional technologies, see Dorsett and McVeigh, *Jurisdiction*, 67.
62. Millman Parry's analysis of *The Odyssey* as using a formulaic pattern to aide oral recall is the typical example in this regard: see Ong, *Orality and Literacy*, 20–26. But it can also be seen in the usage of proverbs, sayings, and laws: see Ong, *Orality and Literacy*, 33–36.
63. Ong, *Orality and Literacy*, 39.
64. Ong, *Orality and Literacy*, 24.
65. Ong, *Orality and Literacy*, 54–55.
66. Ong, *Orality and Literacy*, 169.
67. Illich, *Vineyard*, 116.
68. Illich, *Vineyard*, 98.
69. Illich, *Vineyard*, 99.
70. Illich, *Vineyard*, 119.
71. Ong, *Orality and Literacy*, 120. The unmarked rational 'grid' that organizes page design is a core concept in typographic practice: see, for example, Lupton, *Thinking with Type*, 151.
72. Ong, *Orality and Literacy*, 104–6.
73. Ong, *Orality and Literacy*, 106. The printed dictionary is a leading example, establishing a relatively static 'official' version of a language.
74. See Ong, *Orality and Literacy*, 115–16. See also Illich, *Vineyard*, 116–18.
75. See Illich, *Vineyard*, 94–95.
76. See Parkes, *Pause and Effect*.
77. Indexes and lists, for example, do not have an oral counterpart, and function to divorce written appearance from spoken discourse: Ong, *Orality and Literacy*, 121–26. On the emergence of standardized punctuation as a uniquely graphic system, see Parkes, *Pause and Effect*, 20–29.
78. For an overview and discussion of his work, see Silja Samerski, 'Tools for Degrowth? Ivan Illich's Critique of Technology Revisited', *Journal of Cleaner Production* 197 (2018): 1637–49.

79. See Samerski, 'Tools for Degrowth?', 1638–39.
80. Samerski, 'Tools for Degrowth?', 1639.
81. Mak, *How the Page Matters*, 3.
82. On technologies in general, see Samerski, 'Tools for Degrowth?', 1640.
83. For example, Plowden's 'humanist' type (Chapter 2), *Cooper*'s 'romantic' type (Chapter 3).
84. Illich, *Vineyard*, 82.
85. Illich, *Vineyard*, 54.
86. Illich, *Vineyard*, 95.
87. Compare to pre-modern monastic reading which, for Illich, sought divine enlightenment: see Illich, *Vineyard*, 11–21.
88. Ong, *Orality and Literacy*, 152.
89. Ong, *Orality and Literacy*, 151.
90. cf Goodrich, who notes (from Benjamin) that the x-ray was invented around the same time Freud discovered the unconscious: see Goodrich, *Judicial Uses*, 167.
91. Illich, *Vineyard*, 119.
92. See Ong, *Orality and Literacy*, 129.
93. Anne Phillips, 'Gender and Modernity', *Political Theory* 46, no. 6 (2018): 846.
94. Phillips, 'Gender and Modernity', 847.
95. Phillips, 'Gender and Modernity', 845–48.
96. Phillips, 'Gender and Modernity', 853.
97. In parallel to this, Goodrich's reading of *Baigent* argues that the technical language of the common law is also derived from wider traditions of textual and linguistic practice, which the inclusion of Smith J's divergent code makes apparent: see Goodrich, 'Legal Enigmas'.
98. See Ridler, 'Exercise of Jurisdiction'. And see general discussion of this point in Chapter 1.
99. While reprehensive about Times New Roman, Butterick says that 'good' typography reinforces the message of a text: Matthew Butterick, 'What Is Good Typography?', in *Typography for Lawyers*, 2nd ed. (2018), https://typographyforlawyers.com/what-is-good-typography.html. Bringhurst, too, affirms that typography's function is to generate enlightening resonances with a text's content or themes: Bringhurst, *Elements*, 98–99. On this level, the typography of judicial transcripts is arguably a success.
100. Olaf Tans, 'The Imaginary Foundation of Legal Systems: A Mimetic Perspective', *Law and Literature* 26, no. 2 (2014): 133.
101. Tans, 'The Imaginary Foundation of Legal Systems', 134.
102. Bringhurst, *Elements*, 98. See Chapter 2 for more on the development of early letterforms.
103. See, for example, the 'romantic' face discussed in Chapter 3.
104. Morison, *Type Designs*, 32–33.
105. The *romain du roi* is the first example, for Morison, of a 'modern' serif (flat, thin, unbracketed). Grandjean's work was highly influential, and Morison traces its impact through Dutch typographers to the English typecutters Caslon and Baskerville, and on to the more famous 'modern' type styles of

Bodoni (often credited with its innovation) and Didot: see Morison, *Type Designs*, 36–43.
106. Morison, *Type Designs*, 34.
107. Morison, *Type Designs*, 34.
108. Bringhurst, *Elements*, 98.
109. Morison, *Printing The Times*, 64.
110. Morison, *Printing The Times*, 165.
111. Morison, *Printing The Times*, 65.
112. A design of the Monotype Corporation, created as 're-cuttings of historical originals from the sixteenth century': Morison, *Printing The Times*, 167.
113. A contemporary design from the infamous Eric Gill: Morison, *Printing The Times*, 167.
114. Bringhurst, *Elements*, 97. As we saw in Chapter 2, the humanist axis refers to the imagined line of a right-handed writer's hand and forearm resulting in thinner lines running diagonally up from left to right. See also Appendix 1.
115. Bringhurst, *Elements*, 126.
116. Bringhurst, *Elements*, 127.
117. Bringhurst, *Elements*, 127.
118. It is worth comparing Times New Roman's transitional serifs to the eclectic blend of this book's face, Warnock Pro, discussed in the Preface. By invoking a counter-modernist style of serif, Warnock Pro resists the modernism so clearly embraced by Times New Roman.
119. He uses the term 'adnate serifs': Bringhurst, *Elements*, 13.
120. See Bringhurst, *Elements*, 128.
121. Hawkins, 'Why I Hate', 165.
122. Illich, *Vineyard*, 88.
123. Lyotard, *Discourse, Figure*, 211. See also discussion in Chapter 1.
124. Ong, *Orality and Literacy*, 90.
125. Ong, *Orality and Literacy*, 116. And in doing so continues a process begun centuries before Gutenberg: Ong, *Orality and Literacy*, 117.
126. Hawkins, 'Why I Hate', 165.
127. See Phillips, 'Gender and Modernity', 848. As Phillips argues, such equality ideals need to be reworked and recreated through innovation outside of the modernist frame to develop new and properly inclusive social imaginaries: Phillips, 'Gender and Modernity', 850–56.
128. Phillips, 'Gender and Modernity', 845.
129. Morison, *Printing The Times*, 165.
130. Savoie, 'Women'. The draftswomen were central to Monotype's exacting standards and – given Monotype's dominant role – the development of typography across the twentieth century. They took original design drawings and scaled and adapted them into usable specimens for typographic production within Monotype's systems, work that involved substantive changes to size and shape of letterforms and an exacting eye for anticipating their effects at multiple scales. See, notably, Savoie, 'Women', 210–12.
131. Kinross, *Modern Typography*, 71. Morison acted as a design consultant for Monotype for numerous typefaces.

132. Hawkins, 'Why I Hate', 164.
133. Hawkins, 'Why I Hate', 165.
134. Hawkins, 'Why I Hate', 165. The gendering of reason is well established. On the widely acknowledged masculine qualities of reason, see, for example, Jean P. Rumsey, 'Re-Visions of Agency in Kant's Moral Theory', in *Feminist Interpretations of Immanuel Kant*, ed. Robin May Schott (Pennsylvania State University Press, 1997).

Chapter 5

Displaying the law: apparitions on the screen

Introduction

In its visual and technological contingency, which relies on the reduction of mathematically modelled curves to the discontinuous grid of an electronic display, the digital common law performs a claim as to how the law should appear. What if the common law was imaginary, it proposes, and appeared in material form at the demand of legal readers? What if the unseen 'body' of the common law was immaterial, yet still conditioned its visible 'face'? What if the common law archive held, on its substrate, data that indexed the law's immaterial form without substantiating it, and used this index data to model that form mathematically as a set of imagined and perfectly continuous curves that could, in turn, be reduced to a material approximation of the common law's jurisdictional form, ready for perception by its (presumed) audience of reading subjects? What if each moment of the common law's digital display (re-) performed this process, repeating as it does the foundational myth of western power as a staging of the division between the image and the invisible beyond? And what if that performance was constantly repeated, rendering the law's typographic image as a vanishing sign that relentlessly gestures towards law's absent and immaterial form? In short, what if the common law's transmission consisted of the constantly repeated reduction to matter of its invisible source?

This set of 'what if' speculations indicate the contingent parameters that condition the display of judicial texts on the screen.[1] In its reduction of the law's *fons* to its materialized *fundere*, this claim not only resonates with the typographic concepts of (invisible) 'body' and (visible) 'face',[2] but also the predominantly hermeneutic structure of common law meaning and authority. The law wants to appear, but cannot do so unmediated. Visible typographic form is contingent upon the unprinted 'body' of material type, but in digital typography the nature of the body – and concomitantly the face – is different. In the mechanical press, the body is stabilized as cast metal upon which the typeface is held. This cast body, when its face is pressed to the page, leaves the residue of set type as a static image, to be distributed and encountered by reading subjects who imagine the page's 'content' on the basis of that encounter. While each strike of the press may be materially and aesthetically unique (see Chapter 3), each element in the network of artefacts that constitute a set of 'copies' is as materially stable as the body itself. In digital typography, however, the material basis changes from the cast metal of type to the computational substrate of a digital system – solid cast metal and the paper of the page are both replaced by the constant cycling of a system of electronic processing and display. In this constant cycling, the texts of law are rendered as vanishing signs, expressing a repetitive desire not only for the typographic face of law to appear, but also that this face disappear – and permit the invisible source itself to enter the social world unfettered by material form.

To articulate this reading of the theatre of the common law's digital archive, and thereby round out this book's study, this chapter proceeds through four sections. The first ('The law's new body') introduces the material shift in the 'body' of the text that digitization brings about. In the second ('The moment of display'), the discussion considers the moment a digitally displayed typeface appears, as an expression of the more general myth of western law as the staging of the limits of visibility in the work of Pierre Legendre. The moment of appearance is then articulated in more detail through the process of rasterization ('Rasterization and authority'), which describes the translation of ideal forms into discontinuous images in digital display, a process this chapter reads as an expression of the claim to authority via Cornelia Vismann's understanding of the cancel. From here, the chapter concludes ('The vanishing face') by foregrounding the constant appearance and disappearance involved in digital display, thus rendering it a repeatedly vanishing sign that signifies the desire not simply to appear – but to move aside and allow forth the invisible source of law itself.

As the final study in this book, the jurisdictional performance of the digital common law indicates a shift. Across the archive of the common law, whether digital or print, the typographic theatre of jurisdiction unfolds relentlessly, but in the digital it takes on an increasingly rapid intimacy. Where the distribution of the law in print generates a wide-scale network of theatrical objects, with digital display it is in the very moment of perception that jurisdiction is staged. The authority of the law is claimed not in the crafted production of a document for distribution and subsequent witness by a (presumed) audience, but in the drawing of the lines of the text on the screen in the moment of witness itself. At the same time, the appearance of the common law's typography becomes unstable, able to be moved and resized and altered by user preferences. But, as this book has hoped to demonstrate, with any instance of the common law's typographic legality the crafted textual source (*fundere*) seeks to materially render the *fons*, the mythical source of authority beyond the visible. Thus, while the legal subject can intervene in the digital's jurisdictional staging, the structure of display retains its performative claim, and the common law's authority is intensified on the intimate scale of individual perception. Wherever the common law is displayed on screen, the jurisdictional staging of authority takes place as the repeated insistence of the impossible materialization of law's immaterial source.

The law's new body

Digitization changes the material basis of meaning. A screen's display is enabled by electronic and hardware systems and the computational processes those systems support. A display is not a window to a virtual reality, but is a directly encountered configuration of matter. A computer screen is no more a portal to another realm than is a book, television, or stage. The tendency, even in academic writing on 'new' media, to treat screens as essentially a window into an immaterial virtuality overlooks the material matrix of technological features that govern electronic writing.[3] Digital technologies are a particular material configuration that, like other media, can stage ideational meanings for its (presumed) audience. As Bonnie Mak's history of the technology of the page elaborates, a digitally displayed page is simply another 'materiality from which meaning is made'.[4] Print and digital artefacts, however, 'are underpinned by different systems and therefore shape the making of meaning in different ways'.[5] Seemingly disconnected from the material practices of typefounding and the mechanics of letterpress, it is computer code and display hardware that condition the display of digital law reports – from the shape and style of the letterforms, to their spacing, arrangement, and paginal context.[6] Rather than the strike of the press, judicial texts manifest on screen as 'the result of algorithmic code' and the sophisticated material systems that facilitate the processing of that code and the display of its output.[7]

As we have seen in the preceding chapters, typographic form is conventionally pushed into the background to prioritize readerly focus on the ideational 'content' of a text (see, in particular, Chapter 1). What is backgrounded even further, though, is that which leaves no visible trace on the page or screen: the material basis of the display, the 'body' that conditions the visible 'face' of the text. Suppressing or forgetting through repeated use the contingency of a form – its process of creation, production, or its material conditions – results in a reified or naturalized form that tends to be taken as given. As Mak says of page technology in general, whether print or digital: because we are 'habituated to its operation' we 'overlook how the page sets the parameters for our engagement with ideas'.[8] For Johanna Drucker, this means the page functions by 'effacing its mode of address to the viewer'.[9] As we saw in Chapter 1, attending to jurisdictional performance brings this mode of address (to the presumed subject) to the foreground.

Recognizing law's material mode of address situates it as one kind of artefact within a wider cultural record, and acknowledges the contingent visual knowledge practices that are central to technologies of jurisdiction and concomitantly the reading of legal texts. In digital display, this means foregrounding the assumed parameters of which a particular visualization is a product. Visual images, Drucker observes, 'have the capacity to produce and embody information' in their very form, and thereby 'perform . . . epistemological work'.[10] Visual form, space, and arrangement 'are themselves *arguments* about knowledge or belief',[11] caught up in the radical complexity of interpretation and epistemic construction:

> The information embodied in formatting features contains codes for reading, instructions on how to interpret each word or line depending on its placement. We rarely pause and consider these codes – or the multiple ways in which our reading of any text or image is governed by the site in which it appears.[12]

Working out of a critical humanist heritage, in which knowledge and meaning are the product of contingent norms and ideologies, Drucker's project seeks to unpack these codes and permit access to the contingent parameters of a display's construction.

For users of modern digital displays, the inner workings of the typographic environment they encounter is hidden from the critical reflexivity characteristic of humanist study. While concerned with wider practices of information and data display (for example, in constructing statistical claims), Drucker's work excavates a divide between 'pure' or 'objective' display of information (*mathesis*) and the recognition of the contingency and incompleteness of visual knowledge (*graphesis*).[13] There is a tendency towards objective display (*mathesis*) in digital displays, symptomatic of an unthinking adoption by digital humanists of display conventions designed for the physical and social sciences, resulting in the uninterrogated assumption that 'data' have a factual quality, overlooking the necessary production of data through contingent models of knowing.[14] This is true of typographic display in particular, as we will see in more detail over the next two sections: digital typography embodies the assumption not only that a particular letterform exists as an objectively stored shape in a font file (for example, the shape of this Warnock Pro A), but that the letter itself exists as a conceptual object (for example, the idea of the letter 'A' in general). The general concept of the letter is mapped onto the specific lettershape which is subsequently rendered visible via the rational and mathematical processes of display. For Drucker, rather than a factual ('this is') claim that leaves assumptions hidden, the visual expression of data (for example, in a chart or diagram, as much as a typographic image) is better understood as a 'what if' statement: this is how things look *if* we work from an acknowledged set of assumptions.[15]

The use of display methods derived from the sciences embeds the values of rational modernity into what is visible on the screen. For law, the relationship between technology and the human subject in the rational project of modernity is of particular significance. Kieran Tranter argues that the western complex of law, technology, and humans is embodied in the cultural prevalence of the *Frankenstein* myth, which – like science fiction in general – articulates anxieties about technological development, and should thus take a central place in discourses on law, technology, and humans.[16] Shelley's text captures early the tendency of the west to bundle together technology, humanity, and law, in a way that configures technology as 'monstrous', humanity as 'vulnerable' to the troubling impacts of this technology, and law as the (absent) heroic saviour that protects through regulation.[17] In dominant readings, it is Victor Frankenstein – not his morally ambivalent creation – that is understood to be monstrous, with Victor's monstrosity deriving in large part from his 'acontextual rationalism'.[18] We can go further: Victor is not a cypher for all of humanity, but of the particular set of values or ideological framework that animates him. It is his rationalist science, removed from any understanding of its contingency or of human vulnerability, that drives his monstrosity. Configured in this way, the warning of *Frankenstein* can be understood to be aimed at reification: the adherence to an idea of rational knowledge that suppresses its derivation from contingent assumptions and matter. The modern monster, expressed through the character of Victor Frankenstein, is the forgetting of origins, the loss of genealogy, which gives rise to the dangerous objectivity of reified forms of knowledge, floating free from their methodological and material tethers.[19]

In digital display practices, mainstream conventions bury their constructed nature through their repeated familiarity and leave the positivist desire for objectivity unchecked: 'Stealth positivism', Drucker observes, 'is rampant in digital work.'[20] Repeating display conventions from the sciences without interrogation or adaptation disables the critical work of humanist interpretation that seeks to construct meaning through a knowing engagement with the foundations and assumptions of the meaning produced. Following a convention, as we have seen before, authorizes that convention within the discourse practice in question. Because the presumption of a coherent, preexisting order of knowledge (as opposed to the nonlinear and affective quality of knowing as a constructed and political form) is underpinned by the Enlightenment rationalism of scientific understanding,[21] following scientific conventions of data display built on *mathesis* embeds the reifications of rational modernity into the dominant practices of digital visualization.

The rational methods of typographic display embed the modern monsters of reification and the suppression of origins into the display of digital law reports. But, as Tranter notes, to engage without the humanities – without science fiction myths like *Frankenstein* – disables the capacity for discourse to engage meaningfully with legal technology,[22] just as suppressing the contingent parameters of digital display undermines the meaningful adaption of digital technologies to non-scientific contexts. Indeed, in the history of the common law, as Jean Gaakeer elaborates, the humanities functioned to contextualize the dominant ideal of objective knowledge in the institutional project of justice that demanded certainty over the vagaries of interpretation, and developed tools to engage skilfully with the interpretive features of law.[23] Humanist study, Gaakeer argues, provides practical wisdom in the complex task of judgment, opening juridical knowledge to sources of justice and fairness unavailable within the confines of a rationally disciplined system of law.[24] The complexity of computer systems, the material basis of these emerging systems of display, tends to be hidden from view, a performance shaped by larger and older ideological preference for certainty and stabilized forms of modern knowing.[25] In both the critical analysis of legal substance and of its typographic display, the humanist unpacking of sedimented assumptions – the knowing adoption of a contingent foundation – can provide access to these hidden forces.

The display of digital law reports is not neutral or objective, and while variable between instances, relies on common techniques to which analysis should attend. We have already seen a number of examples of legal typography in print that have exposed the meaningful baggage that comes with law's medial form – from the conflicted romanization of Plowden,[26] via the romantic display of *Cooper v Stuart*,[27] to the civilizing imperiousness of modern court transcripts set in Times New Roman.[28] In digital law reports, however, the typeface is changeable: users can select their face when downloading from WestLaw, or can save as an editable document and visually manipulate the appearance of the common law's record. See, for example, Figure 5.1, in which the leading case of *Woolmington v DPP*[29] has been displayed in varying typefaces. In

House of Lords

Viscount Sankey L.C. , Lord Hewart L.C. , Lord Atkin , Lord Tomlin , and Lord Wright.

1935 April 5; May 23.

Criminal Law—Murder—Onus of Proof—Accident—Unlawful Intention—Direction to the Jury—Reasonable Doubt of Guilt— Criminal Appeal Act, 1907 (7 Edw. 7, c. 23), s. 4 .

In a trial for murder the Crown must prove death as the result of a voluntary act of the prisoner and malice of the prisoner. When evidence of death and malice has been given, the prisoner is entitled to show by evidence or by examination of the circumstances adduced by the Crown that the act on his part which caused death was either unintentional or provoked. If the jury are either satisfied with his explanation or, upon a review of all the evidence, are left in reasonable doubt whether, even if his explanation be not accepted, the act was unintentional or provoked, the prisoner is entitled to be acquitted.

House of Lords

Viscount Sankey L.C. , Lord Hewart L.C. , Lord Atkin , Lord Tomlin , and Lord Wright.

1935 April 5; May 23.

Criminal Law—Murder—Onus of Proof—Accident—Unlawful Intention—Direction to the Jury—Reasonable Doubt of Guilt— Criminal Appeal Act, 1907 (7 Edw. 7, c. 23), s. 4 .

In a trial for murder the Crown must prove death as the result of a voluntary act of the prisoner and malice of the prisoner. When evidence of death and malice has been given, the prisoner is entitled to show by evidence or by examination of the circumstances adduced by the Crown that the act on his part which caused death was either unintentional or provoked. If the jury are either satisfied with his explanation or, upon a review of all the evidence, are left in reasonable doubt whether, even if his explanation be not accepted, the act was unintentional or provoked, the prisoner is entitled to be acquitted.

House of Lords

Viscount Sankey L.C. , Lord Hewart L.C. , Lord Atkin , Lord Tomlin , and Lord Wright.

1935 April 5; May 23.

Criminal Law—Murder—Onus of Proof—Accident—Unlawful Intention—Direction to the Jury—Reasonable Doubt of Guilt— Criminal Appeal Act, 1907 (7 Edw. 7, c. 23), s. 4 .

In a trial for murder the Crown must prove death as the result of a voluntary act of the prisoner and malice of the prisoner. When evidence of death and malice has been given, the prisoner is entitled to show by evidence or by examination of the circumstances adduced by the Crown that the act on his part which caused death was either unintentional or provoked. If the jury are either satisfied with his explanation or, upon a review of all the evidence, are left in reasonable doubt whether, even if his explanation be not accepted, the act was unintentional or provoked, the prisoner is entitled to be acquitted.

Figure 5.1: Typographic variations on the headnote for *Woolmington v DPP* [1935] AC 462.[32]
Image credit: Thomas Giddens (reproduced with permission).

such instances, the display of the law is contingent upon the shifting options of WestLaw and Lexis, or the typographic manipulations of any end-user lawyer or reader armed with a word processor. Beyond these preferential settings, in the digital archive the 'baggage' of the common law's specific face is more generally mutable: the common law not only appears in the sanctioned font of the court transcript, or via user-preferred formats, but also in the PDF options within WestLaw and Lexis, the revived humanism of the PDF versions of the ICLR's series of reports,[30] or the ICLR's preferred hierarchy of browser fonts.[31] Even with supposedly stable PDFs, while the particular face may be set, the display of any particular case remains contingent on the actual font data available within a given system and the material techniques of digital display themselves. Accordingly, whether PDF, DOC, or RTF, and regardless of which face a user might select where this is possible, the material display of the common law's typographic form relies upon the same contingent technological substrate.

Although one might wish to examine the specific typographic style of particular digital law reports (and hopefully the preceding chapters have provided sufficient demonstration of how one might go about deciphering the design heritage of a particular font), given their broad recognition as law regardless of their formatting, what is more significant is the material basis by which these reports appear. To unpack the broader jurisdictional theatre of the common law's digital display, the remainder of this chapter focuses analysis on the material basis of display. To account in detail, as Drucker so passionately argues, for the methods or parameters towards which any instance of legal display is an argument: the 'what if' of the common law's medial possibility.

The moment of display

The sprawling instantiations of digital legal media repeatedly argue for the common law's immateriality and its jurisdictional veridiction. Whenever a user-lawyer calls up a case report on Lexis or WestLaw, opens a saved PDF on their laptop, or checks a headnote in their browser, in each moment of display the argument is repeated. The digitally displayed letters and words of the common law are enabled by the coding within that display's hardware and software infrastructures, and become visible as recognizable text only in the moment they appear on the screen. Just as a mechanically printed page is conditioned by the technologies of the press, the law's digital display is conditioned not simply by the 'content' of a document file (for example, the words of a document stored in a PDF or a DOC file, or the imagined schema of legal principle they stage), but by the data file in which the shapes of letters are indexed and from which a digital environment (or other display technology, such as a printer) is able to manifest their typographic forms for perception by an anticipated subject-user. It is in this moment of appearance that jurisdiction takes place, that the common law 'speaks' in images and stages its authority. Taken as a whole, the common law's digital display is a spatially and temporally distributed performance of the foundational moment of legal appearance.

The appearance of institutional images is the foundation of legal presence as (self-)authorized power. This moment of appearance, for Legendre, is the theatrical manifestation of a beyond that grounds the normative order of legal presence. Myth is 'the code of the normative system,'[33] and in Legendre's model this myth unfolds as a complex staging of the void, of the immaterial or invisible that remains outside possible articulation. The foundational myth of law shows the subject both a void without law and the divine source of authority that comes from beyond, while at the same time protecting them from that void and barring them entry to the (divine) space of power by immersing them in the simulated order of legality.[34] Being a subject, as Goodrich observes, means being an 'image amongst images.'[35] The subject witnesses itself mirrored in the institutional simulation,[36] experiencing a 'gap' between their being as a living individual and their representation as a subject in the imaginary order of legality staged by institutional materials.[37] The gap is reflexively framed by the discourse it authorizes, thereby rendering it perceptible for the subject.[38] The subject thus becomes bound 'to the system of images' that shows them their place within the institutional order, the divine (invisible) authority from which it derives, and the (imageless) void this order shields them from.[39] Law's visible text is thus positioned as 'the zero point of all reference,' taking the practical or material place of the divine and the invisible, thus staging for its (presumed) subjects the 'myth' that 'shores up the whole edifice of culture'.[40] Common law images, as Goodrich's study of their genealogy demonstrates, descend ultimately from the divine source of authority, and include the typography of judgments.[41] With digital law reports, the structure of this materialized foundation of law's normative order is conditioned by the techniques of digital typographic display. These techniques and their features are common to digital typographic systems, but their resonance with the theatrical veridiction of western institutional power is heightened where they are used to render visible the texts held in the common law's digital databases.

Visual form emerges under an impetus that animates the mark-making trajectory of its materialization, conditioned by its medium of appearance. Any line is radically shaped by 'a formative force, prior to any other determination or quality',[42] resulting in the formation of something new, not the mere repetition or mimesis of some precedent shape or idea. What matters is not what is purportedly 'represented' by the form, but rather 'the movement that detaches [the form] from the formless [*informe*]',[43] and interrupts sense as the ideational seems to break through into visual space.[44] In this way, the inscription of a line is an expression, best understood as 'the opening of form',[45] with this inscription conditioned by its medium. An inscription – even a digital inscription – is the expressive mattering of a formative force.

Even apparently mimetic representation, Jean-Luc Nancy says, is not a representation of a precedent object or idea, but a technique that exposes the process of 'coming into view or into the world, the birth to form': the line reveals not some prior truth, but appearance itself.[46] A form's '*essence* consists entirely of the manner, mode, and allure of its gesture, the force of its movement, the weight and lightness of its mark [*trait*]'.[47] The materialized embodiment of a text has its own specific communicative properties,[48] embedded in their instantiated design.[49] Thus, as Bonnie Mak explains, digital pages 'are not digital surrogates' for print, 'but are instead isolated moments' of display in themselves.[50] Each individual page performs its own mattering.[51]

Insofar as it appears as a digital text, then, the common law's process of appearance relies upon the techniques of typographic display. These techniques unfold using letterform or 'glyph' data unseen by the user. Stored in font data files, these indexed glyphs are an invisible structure behind the scenes of the digital stage. Font data files come in a range of formats, of which OpenType is the most standardized: it stores multiple permutations of the same font, enabling implementation of the most compatible format within a given system.[52] Historically, individual letters – their forms stored as founts cast on a metal body – were arranged in a physical grid for manual typesetting. This painstaking arrangement process involved letterforms stored in gridded trays from which a compositor could retrieve letters by hand to arrange them for printing (see Figure 5.2). In the OpenType format, data are organized into a sequence of tables,[53] with the 'character map' table and the table of glyph data being the most significant in terms of visual display. The character map (or 'cmap' table) links specific letter outlines to the indexes of abstract alphabetic letters within an operating system,[54] thereby emulating the material history of type composition by arranging imagined letterforms in a conceptual grid ready for use on the page.

The glyph data, on the other hand, is what controls the shape of typographic characters. If the character map is the metaphorical compositor's tray, the glyph data are the pieces of type in that tray.

Figure 5.2: Metal moveable type. Image credit: Willi Heidelbach, reproduced from Wikimedia Commons under Creative Commons Attribution 2.5 Generic license (https://creativecommons.org/licenses/by/2.5/deed.en).

Figure 5.3 is an example extracted from a CFF and TrueType encoding of the glyph A (a capital A rendered in Adobe's Source Sans). Despite the apparent discrepancies in coding format, each operates on the same core principle. Whether viewing in Word, Pages, a web browser, or as a PDF,[55] letterforms are captured as coded coordinate data that are processed to enable the characters of a written language to be displayed at any scale. It is via this technology of display – font files and operating

CFF

```
<CharString name="A">
  580 213 72 342 73 hstem
  3 574 vstem
  240 700 rmoveto
  -237 -700 rlineto
  91 hlineto
  67 213 rlineto
  255 hlineto
  66 -213 rlineto
  95 hlineto
  -237 700 rlineto
  -157 -415 rmoveto
  33 107 24 79 24 75 22 81 rlinecurve
  4 hlineto
  22 -81 23 -76 25 -78 34 -107 rcurveline
endchar
```

TrueType

```
<TTGlyph name="A" xMin="3" yMin="0"
  xMax="577" yMax="700">
  <contour>
    <pt x="240" y="700" on="1"/>
    <pt x="340" y="700" on="1"/>
    <pt x="577" y="0" on="1"/>
    <pt x="482" y="0" on="1"/>
    <pt x="416" y="213" on="1"/>
    <pt x="161" y="213" on="1"/>
    <pt x="94" y="0" on="1"/>
    <pt x="3" y="0" on="1"/>
  </contour>
  <contour>
    <pt x="394" y="285" on="1"/>
    <pt x="360" y="392" on="1"/>
    <pt x="320" y="518" on="0"/>
    <pt x="290" y="627" on="1"/>
    <pt x="286" y="627" on="1"/>
    <pt x="258" y="527" on="0"/>
    <pt x="233" y="449" on="1"/>
    <pt x="228" y="430" on="0"/>
    <pt x="216" y="392" on="1"/>
    <pt x="183" y="285" on="1"/>
  </contour>
  <instructions><assembly>
  </assembly></instructions>
</TTGlyph>
```

Figure 5.3: Encoding the letter A in Source Sans in CFF and TrueType formats. Taken from https://simoncozens.github.io/fonts-and-layout/opentype.html (accessed 1 May 2025).[56]

systems, cmap tables and glyph data – that the typographic images of the common law are manifested in digital environments, and the presence of legal authority is performed for a presumed subject of address.

The process of law's appearance in the jurisdictional performance of its typographic lines constitutes a 'theatre of attachment'.[57] The visual appearance of the legal institution is the medium by which legal authority enters the subject[58] that is presumed to be the audience of that appearance. Law's images are structured in a way that aims to generate subjective attachment to the institution of law, and thereby facilitate successful governance. In Goodrich's rendition, the 'individual must become attached, must be held internally and so become faithful' to the law, a project which is effected by images: 'the law binds through emblems'.[59] The emblem is that which 'throws signs inside', enabling the (staged) immaterial or beyond to enter material space (as the discursive staging of the immaterial),[60] while also facilitating the entry of signs within the subject. As a staging of authority, typographic legality is 'a montage of words proffered in the public space'.[61] And as a staging of the moment of appearance out of the void, this montage is directed at the interior of the subject, at that by which the subject is animated.[62] The address and interpretation of law creates a public sphere for the 'transmission of myth',[63] and the staging of the subject's place within the 'massive simulation' of the legal institution that protects them from the abyss without form.[64]

Despite typography's persistent materiality, it is in the simulation, generated by the repeated instantiations of the legal text, that the subject imagines itself going forth as an expression or part of institutional law, as caught within an imaginary structure or edifice of reason and principle. This internalized fabulation then controls the conduct of the body. Institutional matter generates an imagined realm of legal order in which the audience-subject sees themselves as a part, and acts accordingly. The subject's imagined belonging produces appropriate conduct under the staged authority of law: the theatre of the institution leads the subject 'to act, to speak in the name of' law's divine source, its absolute and authorizing reference,[65] signified by '*the absolute symbolic Other* staged by the institutional theatre'.[66] In encountering and making meaning from the material image of the common law's letterforms, constituted by the complex elaboration of lines on the screen, the individual takes on the role of the presumed subject and participates in the establishment of legal meaning and authority: the lines on the screen enter the subject, where their impetus is 'reborn'[67] and the performative expression of law becomes relayed by judges, lawyers, and other reading individuals alike.

The digital technologies of display enhance and make overt the repeated quality of legal images that sets up a harmonization within the subject and expresses a desire for law to both appear and disappear. As a specific technology of the page that stages the existence of rational structure and interior life,[68] it is in the mind of the anticipated subject that the law's fantasy of reason is generated by the material techniques of the legal display. The individual is turned: first, into a modern subject, complete with inner life; and, second, into an embodied expression of the law itself.[69] The authority of law, staged by law's typographic matter in the moment of display, resonates within the individual and subjectivates them, producing not simply docile or faithful subjects, but nodes that re-articulate authority in their entangled performances of right and obligation.

Rasterization and authority

In design contexts, the term 'rasterization' describes the reduction of a continuous, mathematically modelled form to the discontinuous contingency of a digital display. In the context of the common law's display, it also denotes the reduction to materiality of law's imaginary structure and source. Legal knowledge cannot be transmitted directly: the law must be updated, remediated in graphic form as a technique of jurisdiction. This is most commonly done as typography, which in its display is rasterized in both a design and a jurisdictional sense. Persuasion, and thus effective governance as law rather than as a 'tyranny of rules',[70] requires, in the typographically evocative words of Julia Chryssostalis, 'setting the word of law in poetry'.[71] To enter the social stage of governance, to convince the subject of its authority, law must dress itself up in words, and by the theatre of its setting, as a leading part in a larger performative apparatus, enter the mind of its audience to bind from within.[72] Yet all graphic systems of remediation, through processes of rasterization, result in a 'loss of information that . . . is considerable'.[73] As the law becomes 'set in poetry' – materialized in literary form[74] – the law is rasterized and reduced to the limitations of the material and the concomitant vagaries of interpretive practice. While it might be possible to conceive of a formal system in the abstract, upon entry into inscriptive matter, 'where an image is produced as a material trace' via the rasterization process, any formal perfection is necessarily lost.[75] Just as the general abstractions of law cannot survive their specific application, becoming concrete outcomes for parties seeking resolution in place of general rules, in the case of legal sources themselves the supposedly universal form of law is replaced by the unique material trace of transmission.

Law must appear as material form before it can be received as intellectual content. As Gaakeer observes, 'there is no immediate, unmediated access to truth and reality' – what is required is study and engagement with the technologies of language that mediate and enable the construction of truth and reality in their encounter with the subject.[76] Accordingly, as the work of Cornelia Vismann recognizes, jurisprudence is ultimately a question of media. It is, she says, a transfer science, and asks the same underlying question as Drucker: 'of which processes of transfer is the law in its concrete shape an effect?'[77] If we are to understand the staging of legal authority in law reports, the typographic theatre of jurisdiction, the question is not simply one of argumentative rhetoric, as if law entirely consists of the ideational 'content' of a text that argues for its own power – but fundamentally one of its display.

Any digital display, as Drucker frames it, is an argument towards the underlying methods or parameters of which that display is an instance: a display is a normative statement. The normative status of visualization can be understood not only in terms of Drucker's humanist methodology, but also in a more general sense as the visual foundations of western law. As seen above, Legendre's study of the foundation of images examines the primal performance of the limits of visibility, which stages the division between what is visible and that which cannot be represented.[78] But the primal formation of an image, for Legendre, can never properly represent the ultimately invisible source or referent, but instead only 'reveals' it. Etymologically, Legendre notes, 'reveal' is a compound of 'res' (thing) and 'velare' (to veil or hide), and thus to reveal is not to move the invisible or immaterial into the realm of perception, unchanged, but to cover it in the manifestations of form.[79] The 'thing' perceived is the 'veil', the matter of form; or, alternatively, the invisible 'thing' becomes 'veiled' by matter in order to be perceived. As Legendre explains, to 'reveal is to grant sight of what must be hidden . . . it is a veil cast over the world; it grants transparency to what slips away from [the individual] in [their] condition of speaking.'[80] To reveal is to make manifest, but in doing so the invisible 'source' that the revelation seeks to show is replaced by that which is perceptible. We see this same movement in Goodrich's idea of the 'costume' required for concepts to enter the social stage,[81] or Deleuze's disguised form of repetition,[82] discussed in Chapter 3. For Legendre, at the foundation of law is a mythic image that stages a normative claim about what it is possible or permissible to show, thus coinciding the grounds of law with the grounds of visibility.

Such mythic images, as discussed above, function as the source code of culture that handles its own emergence out of nothing,[83] and this is done through the application of its own techniques.[84] In digital display, this becomes a normative claim about how otherwise unseen data should be rendered legible to a user. A visible form on a screen is a concrete effect of, in Vismann's terms, a transfer process, or, in Drucker's, specific parameters of data processing. The resulting form, then, articulates a conclusion derived from these adopted assumptions about how to manifest data for perception. Like images in general, a digital display is a normative claim about how things should appear.

In terms of their techniques of display, font files do not store the outline shapes of letters. Instead, they hold mathematical coordinates for a minimal set of points in the imagined space of a grid. The coordinates – when parsed by the correct formula – give rise to a series of mathematically expressed curves that trace the outline of the letterform. The formula that enables the glyph data to be rendered as expected is the Bézier function, constructed by Pierre Bézier in the 1960s to model the bodywork of Renault cars.[85] Bézier curves have widespread application in many areas of design, due to 'their many geometric and analytical properties.'[86] As explained in more detail in Appendix 2, the Bézier function is a mathematical technique used to plot a discrete section of curve whose trajectory is determined by selected control points.[87] The coordinates of these points are chosen or manipulated to vary the start and end points of the line and its particular trajectory when plotted.[88] These mathematical techniques thus enable font files to store only basic coordinate data, with the actual shape of letterforms resolving into material space only in the moment of display.

Significantly, a Bézier curve has no material form in itself. It is an ideal, mathematical shape; a discrete, continuous line that can be positioned anywhere in the imagined coordinate grid of mathematical space, and manipulated into a desired shape via its control points. The line itself is immaterial, indicated only by the material techniques of mathematical representation (for example, the Bézier function, the noted coordinates of the control points). A series of these simple Bézier curves can be used to map complex imaginary shapes, using only limited coordinate data. In font files, lettershapes are encoded into a series of numerical coordinates, as can be seen in the code examples above (see Figure 5.3), where the numerical coordinate data of the letterform's various control points is evident within the programming language.[89] Such curves are known as 'vectors', and essentially contain a number of discrete points coupled with information about the direction a line should take in relation to them, but not its visual or material form as such. Distinct from a face held on a cast metal bodies, digital font files indicate a series of anticipated gestures in lieu of substantiated letterforms.

Display systems take these gestures, construct a plot of them using the Bézier function, and render them visible for a subject-user as a material image on screen. In graphic design, the transfer from a continuous vector curve to perceptible expression is known as rasterizing. A rasterized curve is one that is instantiated or plotted in a discontinuous grid – such as pixels on a screen or dots on a printed page. Figure 5.4 shows a model of this, using the lowercase a of this book's typeface (Warnock Pro). The high-resolution outline (although in this example a rasterized curve produced in a digital system and remediated here) is intended to represent the perfect immaterial line of the lettershape's series of Bézier curves, as compared to the pixelated shape that seeks to approximate it in the material grid of a display.[90] This figure uses a very low resolution in order to more clearly demonstrate the process; in a higher resolution, there are more and smaller pixels that accordingly approach a closer approximation of the ideal curve towards which its rasterized form aspires.[91]

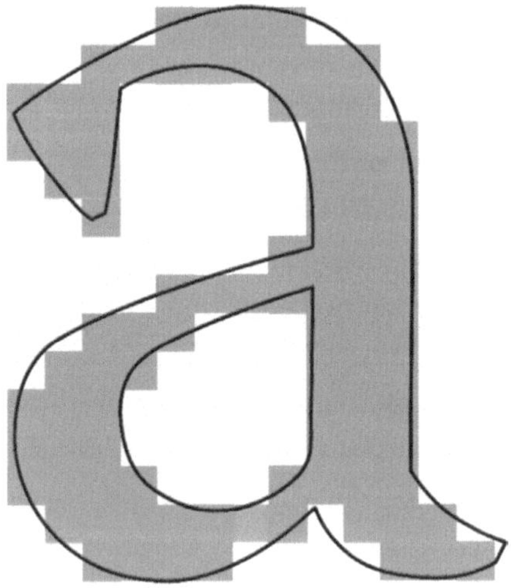

Figure 5.4: Rasterizing a Warnock a. Image credit: Thomas Giddens (reproduced with permission).

In digital typography, this process of rasterizing involves the reading of a font file by a suitable program, such as a PDF viewer, word processor, or web browser. The data points are converted into the mathematically expressed curve which is subsequently resolved into a discontinuous form made up of individual points in a digital grid. This grid is then displayed by the relevant hardware, such as a pixellated screen. Despite their continuous quality as imagined forms, contingency is imposed upon the curves of legal texts through the rasterizing process – in the moment of display itself. If, as Drucker claims, an instance of display is an argument towards the parameters that condition that display – a 'what if' claim about how data should be visualized – digital law reports argue towards the rasterization of law's otherwise immaterial form. Appearing on screen, the text of the law becomes a pixelated expression of an imaginary ideal. In this way, each instance of display of a digital law report argues for the materialization of its immaterial source.

Appearing as a material image as it is rasterized on the screen, the visible text of law overwrites the unseen conditions of its manifestation. And it is in this process of materialization that law stages its own authority as the 'cancelling' of a precedent and inaccessible source.[92] The updating of a previous source, says Vismann, is a general structure of modern legal authority.[93] She demonstrates this by tracing the evolution of written Roman law from the structures of military command: orders that initially took an oral form retained this primal quality when written, and the order became 'present in writing'.[94] As law moved towards its increasingly written form in the unfolding of the modern state, written commands were modelled on their preceding oral imperative, such that a legal text was 'nothing but a transmittable order'.[95] The authority of a written legal statement rests upon a precedent power to command, of which the distributed text is a materialized copy or, as discussed in Chapter 3, a 'media translation'.[96] In this way, says Vismann, 'the power of the written law . . . draws its authority from the act of cancelling'.[97]

> The writing process that gives law its force . . . can only do so by annulling a legal writing. Only then can it refer to a writing before . . . This unreadable, inaccessible writing belongs to the imaginary sphere which informs the symbolic order of law . . . [and is where] the force of law is produced. Cancellation results in, and moreover operates in . . . a blank sheet or the empty foundation of law.[98]

The material forms of legality – its institutional and typographic artefacts and modes of practice – stage the existence of some prior immaterial referent that provides law with authority. Prior to materialization is where (and when) we find 'the dream-command of law': here, 'law and dream coincide, since legal limits, that is to say definite orders, do not yet exist, but are somehow anticipated or dreamed of'.[99] The realm before the appearance of the text is a dream world, an imagined space or moment of legal desire where the anticipated ordering effects of right dwell *in potentia*. Like the imagined Bézier curves of the common law's digital display, this immaterial space anticipates the manifestation of law in perceptible form. The function of the cancel, which Vismann etymologically derives from *cancellus* ('barrier'),[100] is in part to limit entry to this sea of legal fantasy: 'to bar an inner space . . . and to regulate access to the secret, the *arcanum iuris*'.[101] Put in Legendre's terms, the cancel is the primal staging of both the authorizing referent and the subject's immersion in the institutional imaginary. Allaying any fears that publishing the law would enable the general population to enter the space of legal authority,[102] the material text, as cancel, actually functions both to limit entry and to instantiate law's claim to authority.

Taken as a general structure of authority, cancelling can be framed in multiple ways. It is the structure that underpins the jurisdictional theatre of referencing the divine authority that underpins and sanctions sovereign authority from which legal pronouncements derive, or of invoking a precedent source in the archive in a present text that updates and replaces it with an exposition or citation, as much as the jurisdictional compression of *nomos* or *jus* into the material forms of inscribed *lex*, or the replacement of the imagined or conceptualized principle or norm with the legible rule. Put in its most general terms, cancelling is the staging of the existence of an invisible or in any case inaccessible space of power behind the text that provides that text with authority. In multifarious ways, cancelling is the process that manifests the authority of law, authorizing as it inscribes law's institutional form.

Law rests on its practices of cancelling, which in the phenomenon of law reporting is a distinctly typographic practice and can be seen throughout the process of rasterization in which ideational forms are reduced to materiality. The typographic techniques of digital display embed the overwriting characteristic of the cancel in the very matter of common law text. Law's mythic discourse founds itself by erecting a screen to protect humanity from 'the *void without word*.'[103] In the primordial blankness without form, on the blank screen or page, there is no differentiation. It is by elaborating a line, by performing a radical division of the visual field, that form is opened and truth, knowledge, and law can be made perceptible. The line, in its unfolding, expresses a desire 'to make contact with the formless.'[104] The opening of form 'tames the formless and makes it visible, but . . . does not do so without touching its own limit, and thus opening onto the invisible itself.'[105] Inscription, in this way, is the drawing of form upon a limit: it is the screen between the visible and the invisible, the radical foundation of visibility where the unseen shrinks into material space. In jurisdictional terms, the staging of authority 'obliquely encounters the impossibility of grounding the juridical norm.'[106] At its expressive limit, legal discourse thus authorizes itself by covering the blankness of the page with text. In its matter, it expressively performs a foundational myth about the translation of life into institutional forms as the means by which the divine manifests itself in authorized forms and thereby protects us from the unstructured beyond.[107] The myth of our separation from absolute alterity provides an authorizing foundation for the subject in its encounters with the entire discourse system,[108] and in digital reports this is repeated in the very moment of display and encounter.

The cancel is the rasterizing point of legal appearance. In the rasterization of digital law reports is found an expression of the cancelling from which modern law derives its authority. The cancel, for Vismann, is the threshold at which the 'imaginary' of legal authority is transposed 'into a symbolic order'[109] of authorized legality. As in the display of digital law reports, the visible face of the law claims its authority by overwriting its unseen conditions of emergence: it derives its authority to command from the structural relationship between its network of transmissions (*fundere*) and the imagined or staged origin (*fons*) taken to condition these materially distributed expressions. Law appears to thrust forth its jurisdictional assertion as if out of the abyss, its form emerging out of immateriality as the law holds itself up and supports its own juridical weight by staging its own lack of material foundations, thereby rendering itself as powerful, absolute, singular, and without contingency.[110] While its technologies of display – like those of print – are radically distributed and plural, we nevertheless see this staging expressed in law's digital performance, signalling a normative claim about how the law should be rendered legible. In its display, the common law's assumed set of parameters consist of the rasterizing of otherwise immaterial forms of legal expression, a practice that expresses the general structure of modern legal authority described by the concept of the cancel. Such display thereby repeatedly expresses a normative claim about law's authoritative status, continually (re)performing its authorizing derivation from an inaccessible origin or divine beyond, and thereby (re)affirming its authority, in the distributed moments and matterings of appearance.

The vanishing face

The digital display of a law report is a vanishing sign, whose material basis is a complex of digital systems. Like the strike of the press, the trace on a digital display is unique, with this uniqueness enabling each trace to generate meaning. 'Graphical marks do not rely on difference for their value, but on specificity – the fact of each line or mark's unique identity and quality'.[111] What is encountered on the screen in the moment the text of a judicial decision is displayed is not a virtual copy of some (imagined) physical report,[112] but a direct expression of legal form:

> That which appears on a monitor . . . results from mathematical relations and calculations and is thus not the representation of something that preexists in the coordinates of actual space and time.[113]

Like printed copies, the appearance of a digital report is a unique repetition of the law, one of many artefacts in the distributed network of materials that constitutes legal expression. As part of this jurisdictional theatre, digital typographic legality repeatedly stages the authoritative moment of juridical appearance for subject-readers wherever there is a screen. Yet, unlike the unique texts created by the mechanical press, digital texts of law have a radical instability embedded in the techniques of their display that undercuts the idea that they are in any sense unique objects. Understood as vanishing signs, the argument their display expresses is not simply towards the materialization of an immaterial law, but also encompasses a constantly repeating gesture toward the impossible appearance of its formless form.

Digital display relies upon a constant flow of changing physical conditions. A computer screen's display is a process: it is an on-going event that unfolds over time. Mechanical print is also a process, which over time gives rise to printed documents. The temporal span of digital display compared to mechanical print, however, is hugely compressed. The process of display is enabled by both the computational cycles of software code and the hardware cycles of an output screen. The computational cycles consist of the rasterizing processes of resolving the Bézier curves from the document and font data and allocating the rasterized image to the array of pixels to be displayed. The hardware process consists of manipulating the light emitted from the screen in order to present the image to the subject-user. Both of these processes take time to happen, both are fleetingly brief, and both are repeated constantly to maintain an apparently stable image on the screen, and to enable that image to be manipulated and updated by a user.

In terms of hardware, the speed of a screen's refresh rate generates the illusion of a stable image, but is in fact flickering faster than the unaided human eye can detect. What is seen on a display monitor is 'not continuous' but is instead 'continuously refreshed': 'The rate at which the image is refreshed plays a crucial role in making the image appear continuous, even though the actual luminance of a point on the screen is intermittent.'[114] Research in human perception defines a threshold critical frequency where the human subject can no longer detect any flicker in the image, and instead perceives it as constant. While this critical frequency varies by luminosity of the display, a refresh rate above about 60Hz means flicker is not perceptible, even at higher light levels that increase the threshold frequency.[115] As an individual sits before the digitally displayed text, the flickering of the letters is not detected by their neurological and anatomical system of visual perception and processing,[116] resulting in the illusion of a static text available for reading.

A mechanically printed page, of course, is refreshed only once, and circulates as a relatively stable material object from which the fabulations of 'content' can be derived. The content of print versus digital documents is ostensibly staged in the same way (by static typographic figures), but the material substrate of a digital text is in a state of constant flux, of constant updating or of repeatedly being redrawn or traced upon the screen. Where the press unfolds as a process that produces a particular state of matter from which meaning can be made, computer systems have a dynamic quality that unfolds on a smaller timescale. The mechanical press only interacts slowly with its users (typesetters, compositors, press operators, annotators, and so forth), permitting minimal opportunities for updating or refreshing its material state and the (imagined) state of what it displays. The process of digital display results in a repeated generation of a constantly variable material state, with any perceived 'stability' having an enhanced dynamism as documents are moved, scrolled, and resized on screen – or, indeed, edited or redressed with a different face.

The material conditions that support the face are different from those of mechanical press, although the structure of body and face (that is, that of the face cancelling the unseen body) is fundamentally the same. We thus move from the material of metal type, of the forged piece of matter upon which the contours of the face are physically held and present in material space, to the imagined gestures output by mathematical formulae that become present only in their processing over time in the iterative resolution of a computer's coded system on a display output.

The simulated stability of the text will collapse out of perceptible space when not sustained by the system's processes. To host a display, a device is constantly processing and refreshing the image – CPU activity and screen refresh rates are measured in Hz, a unit denoting 'per second'. Digital devices are constantly maintaining a flow of unique material reconfigurations, the visual display is constantly vanishing and reappearing, being always cleared and redrawn at speeds faster than human perception can detect. What is encountered on the screen is not a simply present image – but a repeatedly vanishing sign.

For Peter Goodrich, a vanishing sign is the quintessential means of articulating power.[117] Drawing on Reformation discourses related to the control and fear of images, he observes that all signs are ultimately temporary. The repeated outputs of the press will eventually degrade and disappear in one way or another. But vanishing signs, such as the sign of the cross made in the air or on the forehead, have a transient materiality that almost immediately vanishes, and by virtue of this ephemerality the sign of the cross, for example, was 'much closer to the model it replicated' than one wrought in wood or iron.[118] The vanishing sign replicates the structure of power, observed by Vismann, as reliant upon a lost referent: 'the power of the image and in consequence the authority of the word is dependent upon an unrepresentable origin or source'.[119] The visible image cancels the invisible space of potential, deriving its power from that cancellation. But with a vanishing sign, the visible cancel almost immediately disappears, and in this transient revelation it gestures towards the invisibility it could not represent. And the quicker the vanishing, the quicker is the passage 'from the image to the thing signified'.[120]

In the rapidly refreshed display of legal texts on the screen, this process of drawing and vanishing legal signs – in the form of letters and words – unfolds at an intense rate. The blank space of the empty screen – the space of potential – is cancelled, filled with the images of the text, which in turn vanish and gesture back to the blank screen. This process of appearance and disappearance is repeated at least sixty times per second. On the screen is the constant oscillation between presence and absence of the words of law, the constant re-drawing or reopening of the law's letterforms, the constant restaging of the separation of legal images from the void, of the foundation of normative order – the repetitive cancelling of the invisible referent. This oscillation is so quick, the human subject cannot perceive it unaided, bringing the transmitting image closer and closer to its imperceptible source beyond images. The sign vanishes, the invisible almost manifests itself. The divine or mystical 'source' of sovereign power, the space of power behind the cancel to which the subject is denied access, appears on the screen – as an absence, then replaced again, updated and cancelled, by the rasterized letterform. This vanishing and cancelling repeats at the speed of the screen's refresh-rate, staging the illusion of a stabilized or materially constant text or source, itself in turn staging the ideational 'content' of the law as an invisible, rational structure of normative principle. But at all moments, in all displays, the words of the law are in a state of disappearance, making way for the invisible referent they cannot show.

The jurisdictional theatre of the archive – the staging of authority in law's moment of display – thus becomes a flicker of the (im)material, binding law's presumed audience of subjects through the constantly denied access to the prefigural space of power. The quality of this 'binding,' however, is not a simple application of force, but the setting up of a resonance within the subject through the repeated appearances and disappearances of the face of the law. The vanishing quality of the law, as a cancellation of an invisible source and the disappearance of that cancel to make way for the invisible, has historically taken place over the extend time periods available to the technologies of legal communication found in manuscripts and mechanical press. The rhythm of the press, however, has been replaced – cancelled – at least in part, by the increasingly fast-paced repetitions of digital display technologies. And in this increased speed is expressed an increasingly evident desire for the law to manifest itself in the impossibility of its formless form.

Conclusion

The study in this book has sought to demonstrate how the crafted matter or font (*fundere*) of typographic legality functions as a jurisdictional technology that stages the authorizing presence of the imagined source (the *fons*) of the law. While this staging takes on variable qualities with different instantiations of common law type, examples of which we have examined across this book's chapters, the shift in the common law's body to the materiality of digital inscription brings a more general shift in law's rhetorical and jurisdictional theatre. The style of performance becomes mutable, and the material and temporal location at which legal power is claimed is pushed away from the centre, into the radically distributed relays and interfaces of the digital infrastructure and the techniques of rasterization by which legal texts appear and are constantly refreshed in the very moment of viewing itself. Yet, as with the printed matter of law reports and transcripts examined earlier, in the context of digital display it remains the mundane matter of the text that generates the powerful fabulations of legality.

The law's display is crafted not only in the hallowed halls of the courts or the sanctioned offices of common law printers and law reporters – but in the very moment its texts appear to the eye of an implied audience on the medial screen, conditioned and controlled by the structures of typographic display and the user's own interventions. In repeatedly overwriting and cancelling the perfect, rationalist, mathematical form – unfettered by the contingency or discontinuity of the material world – law repeatedly claims its authority by performatively deriving its material agency from a precedent and pure rationality. It repeats on an infinitesimal scale the more general process of appearance that characterizes the common law's typographic techniques of cancellation by which its jurisdictional performances claim authority. In this way, jurisdiction is increasingly staged, and authority concomitantly claimed, in the continuous rasterizing processes of the common law's digital media technology.

By constantly vanishing, embedded in this distributed performance is a repeated gesture towards the unmediated source of legal power. This gesture is not unique to the digital. In each of the examples studied across this book, the matter of the typographic text (*fundere*) stages the imagined existence of legal authority derived from a precedent immaterial source (*fons*). The theatre of the archive does its work across the textual manifestations of the common law's practices of typographic legality. In the case of digital reports, in each cycle of the screen, in each plotting and rasterization and disappearance of the material texts of the common law, this same archival performance takes place at a rapid pace. The material performance of the founding myth of institutional order is enhanced, and the desire for authority to manifest itself without contingency or form is made increasingly overt.

Notes

1. See Johanna Drucker, *Visualization and Interpretation: Humanistic Approaches to Display* (The MIT Press, 2020). We will discuss her work in more detail across this chapter.
2. See Chapter 2.
3. See Frances Robertson, *Print Culture: From Steam Press to Ebook* (Routledge, 2013), 128.
4. Mak, *How the Page Matters*, 63.
5. Mak, *How the Page Matters*, 66.
6. See Mak, *How the Page Matters*, 67.
7. Mak, *How the Page Matters*, 66.
8. Mak, *How the Page Matters*, 9.
9. Drucker, *Visualization and Interpretation*, 64.
10. Drucker, *Visualization and Interpretation*, 11. As she puts it, 'graphical work *is* intellectual work': Drucker, *Visualization and Interpretation*, 12.
11. Drucker, *Visualization and Interpretation*, 15. Emphasis in original.
12. Drucker, *Visualization and Interpretation*, 19.
13. Drucker, *Visualization and Interpretation*, 26. Nancy frames *mathesis* as the 'it's that!' of mimetic representation: see Jean-Luc Nancy, *The Pleasure in Drawing*, trans. Philip Armstrong (Fordham University Press, 2013), 63.
14. Drucker, *Visualization and Interpretation*, 54–56.
15. Drucker, *Visualization and Interpretation*, 56.
16. Kieran Tranter, *Living in Technical Legality: Science Fiction and Law as Technology* (Edinburgh University Press, 2017), 27–33.
17. Tranter, *Living in Technical Legality*, 32.
18. Tranter, *Living in Technical Legality*, 31. Other features of Frankenstein's monstrosity include, says Tranter, his 'bourgeois irresponsibility' and his 'petty revulsion' to the creature he creates.
19. For an exemplary rendition of this critical point, oriented against the insular history of the English common law, see Peter Goodrich, 'Critical Legal Studies in England: Prospective Histories', *Oxford Journal of Legal Studies* 12, no. 2 (1992): 195–236.
20. Drucker, *Visualization and Interpretation*, 59.
21. Drucker, *Visualization and Interpretation*, 43–68.
22. Tranter, *Living in Technical Legality*, 32–33.
23. Jeanne Gaakeer, *Judging from Experience: Law, Praxis, Humanities* (Edinburgh University Press, 2019), 28–63. See also, on the humanities-based methods of the common law, Giddens, 'A Series of Unfortunate Events'. Humanism and the common law are discussed more fully in Chapter 2.
24. See Gaakeer, *Judging from Experience*, 26.
25. See, for example, Mary Poovey, *A History of the Modern Fact: Problems of Knowledge in the Sciences of Wealth and Society* (University of Chicago Press, 1998).

26. See Chapter 2.
27. See Chapter 3.
28. See Chapter 4.
29. [1935] AC 462. See n 32.
30. See note 22 in Chapter 4.
31. Web browsers display text under orders from a page's HTML code, using available system fonts. If a font is not available in the local system, the browser uses a suitable alternative. The ICLR's online reports are encoded with a hierarchy of preferred fonts: first Georgia, then Times, then Times New Roman, with the generic 'serif' as a back-up default (Paul Magrath, Head of Product Development and Online Content at the ICLR, email correspondence with author, 23 April 2025).
32. The case of *Woolmington* famously affirms the 'golden thread' running through the English common law that the criminal burden of proof must always rest on the prosecution (subject, of course, to certain exceptions). The DOC file from which this figure was derived was sourced from WestLaw, whose default download font for its DOC files is 13-point Times New Roman. To generate the remediations in the figure, the font of the downloaded report was changed but size and layout settings were left unaltered. The headnote appears, from top to bottom respectively, in Impact, Chiller, and Aptos. Each resonates with the text and its institutional context in different ways. Impact is a bold and modernist display face (typically used for titles and signs), perhaps generating a sense of the court's performative power and augmenting the rational fairness of the modern legal procedures it affirms. Chiller is designed to invoke an aesthetics of horror and dread, arguably suitable for both a murder case and being subject to the awesome power of the state. Aptos is Microsoft's current default for Word documents – arguably a conventional choice for professional legal texts with up-to-date legibility. These are just off-hand examples, and relatively pithy interpretations. Readers of this endnote, if there are any, can no doubt undertake their own alternative renditions and generate alternative analyses – thereby securing the point currently being made in the main text.
33. Legendre, *God in the Mirror*, 226.
34. Legendre, *God in the Mirror*, 51.
35. Goodrich, *Languages of Law*, 290.
36. Legendre, *God in the Mirror*, 49.
37. Legendre, *God in the Mirror*, 35.
38. Legendre, *God in the Mirror*, 50.
39. Goodrich, *Languages of Law*, 290.
40. Goodrich, *Languages of Law*, 278.
41. See Goodrich, 'Specters'.
42. Nancy, *The Pleasure in Drawing*, 21.
43. Nancy, *The Pleasure in Drawing*, 73. Inserted original-language text in original.
44. Nancy, *The Pleasure in Drawing*, 5–9.
45. Nancy, *The Pleasure in Drawing*, 1.
46. Nancy, *The Pleasure in Drawing*, 60.

47. Nancy, *The Pleasure in Drawing*, 13. Emphasis and inserted original-language text in the original.
48. Mak, *How the Page Matters*, 68.
49. Mak, *How the Page Matters*, 69.
50. Mak, *How the Page Matters*, 69.
51. Mak, *How the Page Matters*, 72.
52. TrueType (TTF) has become the dominant standard (it is the one used by Apple and Microsoft), alongside the standardized OpenType (OTF) format that houses TrueType alongside the format originally used by Adobe PDFs ('Type 1' or Compact Font Format, CFF). The TrueType font format was originally designed by Apple, and later adopted by Microsoft, and provides the font data used across Apple and Windows systems. More widely compatible, however, is OpenType, which was collaboratively produced in 1996 by Adobe and Microsoft to develop a standardized format to replace the conflicting ones between TrueType and the system developed by Adobe, for instance to display commonly used PDFs. Both Adobe's 'Type1' Format (now referred to as Compact Font Format, or CFF) and TrueType had become common, and the OpenType file format was designed to integrate these into a unified architecture that houses both CFF and TrueType encoding (alongside other available formats), rendering both of them legible to display systems. Adobe, since 2021, no longer uses its 'Type1' format, and has converted its font library to OpenType. See https://www.prepressure.com/fonts/basics/history (accessed 7 May 2025).
53. All OpenType files contain the 'Offset' table and the 'Table Record', which indicate the specific set of tables used in the current file. Alongside these are other compulsory tables that administer various practical necessities, such as the 'head' table, containing the size of the grid for individual characters and the measurement scale used (see https://learn.microsoft.com/en-us/typography/opentype/spec/head (accessed 1 May 2025)) and the 'OS/2' table, containing core layout data required by Apple and Windows platforms (see https://learn.microsoft.com/en-us/typography/opentype/spec/os2 (accessed 1 May 2025)), among others. In case you are interested, Microsoft's open specifications and guide for working with OpenType is very informative. The full list includes: 'cmap', 'head', 'hhea', 'hmtx', 'maxp', 'name', 'OS/2', and 'post'. See https://learn.microsoft.com/en-us/typography/opentype/spec/otff#font-tables (accessed 1 May 2025) for basic descriptors of each, and specific tables for TrueType and other formats within OpenType, as well as links to pages with further details.
54. See https://learn.microsoft.com/en-us/typography/opentype/spec/cmap (accessed 1 May 2025). Glyph data itself is held in a separate, dedicated table (the 'glyf' table). The cmap table maps the shape data for specific glyphs (e.g. for A) to their respective Unicode character (for the Latin uppercase A, this is U+0041). Most computer and phone operating systems use the standardized Unicode system of 'character codes' to index abstract alphabetic letters independently of their visual form by allocating to each one a unique numerical code. It is an expanding project that encompasses punctuation and other symbols, as well as non-Latin writing systems and emoji: see https://home.unicode.org/ (accessed 7 May 2025).

55. Linux uses the open source FreeType to display OpenType fonts.
56. Whilst this particular coding engagement is not formally published, GitHub provides a wide variety of open-source coding and reference materials for software developers. Cozens himself has produced authoritative texts on coding. See, for example, Simon Cozens, *Advanced Perl Programming*, 2nd ed. (O'Reilly Media, 2005). The font described in this example is the A from Adobe's open-source font, Source Sans, in which the code example is also set.
57. Goodrich, *Languages of Law*, 263.
58. Goodrich, *Languages of Law*, 289.
59. Goodrich, *Languages of Law*, 288.
60. Legendre, *God in the Mirror*, 117.
61. Legendre, *God in the Mirror*, 101.
62. See Chapter 4.
63. Goodrich, *Languages of Law*, 279.
64. Goodrich, *Languages of Law*, 270.
65. Goodrich, *Languages of Law*, 282.
66. Legendre, *God in the Mirror*, 88. Emphasis in original.
67. See Nancy, *The Pleasure in Drawing*, 93–94.
68. See Chapter 4.
69. On the technology of the 'person' as part of law's expressive apparatus, see discussion on Mussawir in Chapter 1.
70. As Goodrich has it, the creativity of literary expression is required to avoid the terrorism of dictatorship or the 'tyranny of rules' based only on reason: see Goodrich, *Advanced Introduction*, 12.
71. Julia Chryssostalis, '*Nomos* Is an Air: Hearing as a Juridical Faculty', in *HEAR*, ed. Danilo Mandic et al. (University of Westminster Press, 2023), 44. See also discussion of Adam Gearey's poetics of practical reason in Chapter 1.
72. The image is the costume that enables speech 'to enter to social and juridical stage': see Goodrich, 'Imago Decidendi', 28. On the staging that enters the mind in order to bind from within, see Goodrich, *Languages of Law*, 260–96. And, more thoroughly, Legendre, *God in the Mirror*.
73. Drucker, *Visualization and Interpretation*, 31.
74. For fuller discussion on the entangled materiality of juridical texts, see Giddens, 'Sentences Matter'.
75. Drucker, *Visualization and Interpretation*, 31.
76. Gaakeer, *Judging from Experience*, 23.
77. Cornelia Vismann, 'Jurisprudence: A Transfer Science', *Law and Critique* 10 (1999): 284.
78. See Legendre, *God in the Mirror*.
79. See Legendre, *God in the Mirror*, 101.
80. Legendre, *God in the Mirror*, 101.
81. Goodrich, 'Imago Decidendi', 28.
82. Deleuze, *Difference and Repetition*, 27.
83. Legendre, *God in the Mirror*, 226.
84. Vismann articulates the way cultural techniques are their own condition of expression. See Vismann, 'Cultural Techniques and Sovereignty', 89.

85. See P. Barry, 'Bézier Curve', in *Encyclopaedia of Mathematics*, ed. Michael E. Mortensen (Springer, 1997), 119.
86. Barry, 'Bézier Curve', 119.
87. In TrueType, the curves use three control points, while in CFF the curves use four. For more detailed comparison between CFF and TrueType, see https://learn.microsoft.com/en-us/typography/opentype/spec/glyphformatcomparison (accessed 1 May 2025).
88. Appendix 2 also has some example plots.
89. The coordinates are particularly visible in the TrueType example, where absolute x and y values are clearly indicated. In the CFF code, the lists of numbers indicate transpositions across the imagined coordinate grid from one point to the next.
90. Note that rasterization is never so simple. Due to the vagaries of material resolutions and their varying scales, this process is more complex than a direct plotting of the curve. Font files contain additional instructional data and tweaks to help font display systems manifest letterforms with maximum apparent adherence to their typographic models. For a detailed technical guide, see https://learn.microsoft.com/en-us/typography/opentype/spec/tt_instructing_glyphs (accessed 1 May 2025). And an introductory guide to the use of typographic grids in TrueType can be found here: https://learn.microsoft.com/en-us/typography/opentype/otspec160/ttch01 (accessed 9 May 2025).
91. Unlike a standard image file (e.g. a JPG or PNG), which captures size, shape, and other data in an unchanging resolution of pixels, mathematically modelled vector curves can be decoded and plotted at any size with no loss of detail. The continuous and immaterial quality of their mathematical description means that their resolution is infinitely variable until they enter material space and are reduced to a pixelated grid.
92. See, notably, Vismann, 'Cancels'.
93. See, notably, Vismann, 'Cancels'.
94. Vismann, *Files*, 49.
95. Vismann, *Files*, 49.
96. Piper, *Dreaming*, 145.
97. Vismann, *Files*, 53.
98. Vismann, 'Cancels', 137.
99. Vismann, 'Cancels', 134.
100. Vismann, 'Cancels', 134.
101. Vismann, 'Cancels', 135.
102. See Chapter 2.
103. Legendre, *God in the Mirror*, 58. Emphasis in original.
104. Nancy, *The Pleasure in Drawing*, 78.
105. Nancy, *The Pleasure in Drawing*, 75.
106. Cormack, *A Power to Do Justice*, 8.
107. It is the 'hum' of discourse that protects the subject from the abyss: see Thomas Giddens, 'Legal Aesthetics as Visual Method', in *Routledge Handbook of Socio-Legal Theory and Methods*, ed. Naomi Creutzfeldt et al. (Routledge, 2019), 320–25.

108. Legendre, *God in the Mirror*, 96.
109. Vismann, 'Cancels', 135.
110. On the staging of law's mythic derivation from beyond form, see Thomas Giddens, 'Institution and Abyss', *Law, Technology and Humans* 2, no. 2 (2020): 150–71.
111. Drucker, *Visualization and Interpretation*, 26.
112. On the historical development of digital documents, as new and different material configurations of the handwritten manuscripts they seek to emulate, see Mak, *How the Page Matters*.
113. Cornelia Vismann and Markus Krajewski, 'Computer Juridisms', *Grey Room* 29 (2007): 92.
114. Mahalakshmi Ramamurthy and Vasudevan Lakshminarayanan, 'Human Vision and Perception', in *Handbook of Advanced Lighting Technology*, ed. Robert Karlicek et al. (Springer, 2015), 14.
115. See Ramamurthy and Lakshminarayanan, 'Human Vision and Perception', 14–15. Display monitors come in a range of refresh rates, but 60Hz is the common standard, with faster rates available. Although anything faster than 60Hz will not necessarily increase the stability of a perceived image, it may be important in certain contexts – such as gaming, which requires accurate display of motion. On the importance of refresh rates for different contexts of use, and how it interacts with other elements of a computer system (e.g. the speed of the graphics processor, which might update the image slower than the screen) see https://www.intel.com/content/www/us/en/gaming/resources/highest-refresh-rate-gaming.html (accessed 21 May 2025).
116. For an overview of the complex anatomical and neurological features of visual perception, see Ramamurthy and Lakshminarayanan, 'Human Vision and Perception', 1–6.
117. See, generally, Peter Goodrich, 'The Iconography of Nothing: Blank Spaces and the Representation of Law in *Edward VI and the Pope*', in *Law and the Image: The Authority of Art and the Aesthetics of Law*, ed. Costas Douzinas and Lynda Nead (University of Chicago Press, 1999).
118. Goodrich, 'Iconography of Nothing', 107.
119. Goodrich, 'Iconography of Nothing', 112.
120. Goodrich, 'Iconography of Nothing', 107.

Conclusion

It is in the suppression and forgetting of the common law's typographic form that its invisible source, its ideational structures of reason and principle, are made available: to look for the *fons* we must overlook the *fundere*. Yet the study in this book has sought to demonstrate how the material images of typographic legality, far from being immaterial, provide the necessary conditions for law's invisible power. While its materiality is pressed into the background, it is precisely by means of its elaborate theatrical performance that the common law is staged as authoritative: legal authority is unavoidably entangled with its typographic expression. And this typographic expression, moreover, involves additional meanings and interventions within legal understanding that tend to be suppressed along with its medial form. As this book has sought to demonstrate, the meaningful heritage of the textual forms by which the common law is transmitted embed a range of interpretative trajectories and material significance into the common law's institutional texts. Insofar as the idea of modern law persists – as a rational structure of principle – it does so by the suppression of the necessary matter that supports it.

It may be the case, if law is generated simply by the performances of its material images, that to manipulate those images is to manipulate the law. Where the typography of the common law is varied by readers and subjects, such interventions have the potential to vary the quality of the jurisdictional performance itself. As the studies in this book have sought to demonstrate, to render a judicial text in a particular face does something to the quality of authority expressed by that rendition of the common law. Critical typographic intervention in common law discourse may be a fertile ground for engagement in law's veridiction practices, yet there is a persistence to law's immateriality that has the potential to disarms such critical work. In the repeated performance of the structure of the cancel in the manifestation of the law's typographic face, the quality of legality is embedded into the very appearance of text. This becomes emphatically evident in digital environments, where the common law appears on screen by means of the highly rationalist techniques of mathematical display. Moreover, like the function of repetition that supports the idea of an immaterial version instantiated by the suppression of the difference between its copies, the apparent mutability of typographic form in digital environments enhances the ease with which it can be suppressed as irrelevant – and concomitantly the sense that a text somehow exists independently from its material appearance. The font might change, but the words of judgment remain the same.

Such an impression, however, is precisely the product of the enduring practice of reading for what is not on the page: the immateriality of law is generated by reading law as if it was immaterial. This is a practice that remains particularly overt in law, permitting law to persist as an immaterial form at the expense of paying attention to its material conditions. In all instances, whether print or digital, the typographic legality of the common law is a material performance not only of the presence of legal authority, but of the insistent myth that it exists as an unassailable power beyond perception. We may change the face of the law, but insofar as we continue to treat it as law, and continue to suppress the critical potential of its medium, it still carries the modern western myth of its invisible source and authority. It is only by attending to the forms by means of which that myth is performed, in the most central part of its production in the primary texts of judgment, that we can encounter and work with it. To study typographic legality is not to become distracted from the meaningful reading of law, but to study the techniques, contingencies, and possibilities, that run throughout the generation of law's mythic power.

Appendix 1: A typographic primer

While the analyses in this book aim to introduce their typographic aspects in non-technical language, this appendix contains a consolidated overview of some basic typographic features and terminology that some readers may find useful as a general primer. It is included in part to help streamline the main text, but also in the anticipation that the main audience of this study may well be legal rather than typographic scholars – although it is hoped the volume will be of value to both. Figure A1.1 presents a diagram to orient this brief introductory guide, and in itself demonstrates some key features of typographic form.

When approaching a typeface, some features are more overtly determinative of its stylistic impression than others. Perhaps the two most influential features are the presence of 'serifs' and the 'x-height'. Serifs are the lines or slabs found at the end of various lines of a type (such as the tail of the q in Figure A1.1). Familiar font families like Garamond, Times New Roman, and Georgia have these serifs, which derive primarily from calligraphic writing practices in the renaissance (we discuss this in more detail Chapter 2). Fonts without serifs, known as 'sans serifs', omit these features at the ends of their major lines: familiar examples include Calibri, Arial, and Verdana. (See Figure A1.2 for samples of these faces.)

A font's x-height, meanwhile, describes the height of its lower-case or 'miniscule' letters relative to the overall height of the face. The x-height is the measurement from the baseline (upon which the letters sit) to the top of the x.[1] A larger x-height gives the impression of a larger typeface, even at the same point size: compare Garamond and Times New Roman at the same size. The samples in Figure A1.2 are also all set

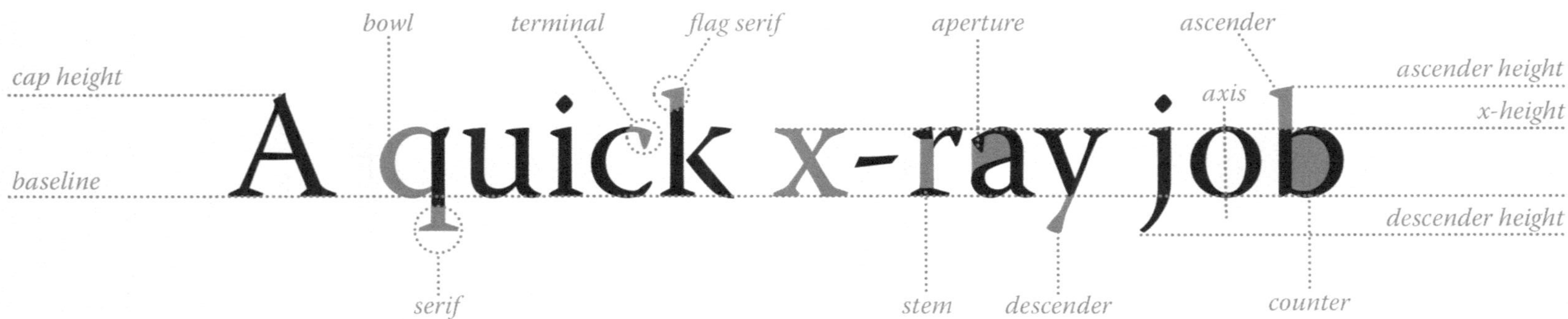

Figure A1.1: A quick x-ray job to map some key typographic terms, using this book's typeface (Warnock Pro). Image credit: Thomas Giddens (reproduced with permission)

Garamond	A quick x-ray job to map the King's civilized law font
Times New Roman	A quick x-ray job to map the King's civilized law font
Georgia	A quick x-ray job to map the King's civilized law font
Calibri	A quick x-ray job to map the King's civilized law font
Arial	A quick x-ray job to map the King's civilized law font
Verdana	A quick x-ray job to map the King's civilized law font

Figure A1.2: A comparison of common types, all set at the same size. Image credit: Thomas Giddens (reproduced with permission).

at the same point size, demonstrating further the different apparent sizes of each face. Larger x-heights are often used in faces intended for smaller dispaly, such as captions and footnotes, as they retain more legibility at smaller sizes (Times New Roman, for example, was designed for the small print of *The Times* newspaper, as discussed in Chapter 4).

The x-height interacts with the 'cap height' to produce its effects: the cap height describes the height of upper case or 'majiscule' letters. It is to be distinguished from the 'ascender height', which describes the length of the ascenders that protrude above the top of the lowercase letters (for example, the vertical stem of the b in Figure A1.1), and are often taller than the cap height. Conversely, the 'descender' is the part of the letter that droops below the baseline, such as the tail on the y in Figure A1.1.

Another high-level feature worth noting is line width variation. This is significant because it can significantly change the feel of a face, and stems largely from the history and heritage of both handwriting and type design. Early typefaces, such as Garamond, sought to emulate in a regularized manner the lines of familiar handwritten texts, primarily those from the renaissance (see Chapter 2). Later styles involved greater or lesser degrees of variation, producing different effects or signalling different lines of heritage. Some modernist sans serif styles even omit or minimize variation in their quest for a perfect geometric letter. The samples in Figure A1.2 show a variety of different line width variations, from Garamond's and Times New Roman's shifting lines, to the more regular line widths of Calibri and Arial.

The final major feature included in this brief guide, and connected with line width variation, is typographic axis. Axis describes the orientation of the letters, as indicated by the variation in line width or the shape of a letter. This variation is derived, initially, from the writing implement: a broadnib pen or quill produces different line widths depending on the orietnation of the hand and the direction of the line. Hence a 'humanist' axis most closely emulates the 'human' origin of letterforms. Later styles play with or omit this derviation, and use a vertical or 'rationalist' axis. Many modern or postmodern faces may vary their axis wildly between letters. You can see in Figure A1.3 an indication of how an axis is identified for the letter o, which is probably the easiest letter to see what is happening. Warnock Pro has a subtle humanist axis compared to Times New Roman's more pronounced orientation. More rational or modern letters might omit line-width variation, but can still have an axis derived from the shape of the letter: see the Calibri o. The o in Century Gothic is a circle, thus has no clear axis.

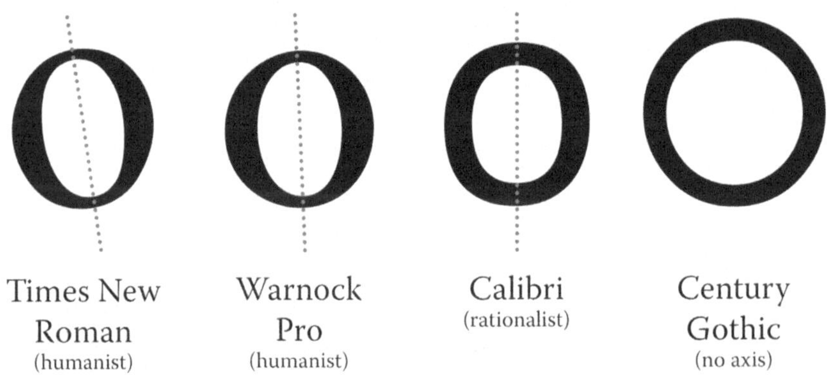

Figure A1.3: Typographic axis. Image credit: Thomas Giddens (reproduced with permission).

This primer is intended to be very introductory, and omits a huge amount of detail, discussion, nuance, and possibility in understanding and working with type as a discursive, aesthetic, or pragmatic form. The discussions in the main text hopefully demonstrate some of this greater depth, as it intersects with legal concerns. Below you will also find a very brief list of texts for further reading, from which (*inter alia*) the above guide has been variously derived, and which you may find useful if you desire further details or exploration of typographic form, style, anatomy, and discursive potential.

Further reading

Robert Bringhurst, *The Elements of Typographic Style* (Vancouver: Hartley and Marks, 2002).
– Both practical and poetic, applied and theoretical, contemporary and historical, Bringhurst's guide is invaluable.
Matthew Butterick, *Typography for Lawyers*, 2nd ed., 2018, https://typographyforlawyers.com/.
– A lawyer and type designer, Butterick has crafted an insightful and practical guide to the use and relevance of type in legal practice.
Derek H. Kiernan-Johnson, 'Telling Through Type: Typography and Narrative in Legal Briefs,' *Journal of the Association of Legal Writing Directors* 7 (2010): 87–122.
– The first part of this article, pp. 87–112, provides a useful overview, and is written for lawyers.
Robin Kinross, *Modern Typography: An Essay in Critical History* (Paris: Éditions B42, 2019).
– A detailed and thorough overview of the history of modern typography, tracing numerous stylistic developments and their wider cultural contexts.
Ellen Lupton, *Thinking With Type: A Critical Guide for Designers, Writers, Editors, and Students*, 2nd ed. (New York: Princeton Architectural Press, 2010).
– An excellent and thoughtful overview and introduction to type and page design and use.
Christopher Scott Wyatt, 'On Type and Typographic Anatomy,' in *Type Matters: The Rhetoricity of Letterforms*, ed. Christopher Scott Wyatt and Dànielle Nicole DeVoss (Anderson: Parlour Press, 2018), 2–31.
– A useful, brief critical and rhetorically oriented run-down of major typographic features and contexts, including some details of type history and digital typography.

Notes

1. The x is used to determine this standard, since other letters (notably more rounded ones like o or s) are often actually slightly taller, as well as dropping below the baseline. This visual trick helps preserve the impression of them being in line with the other letters: note how the top of the a in Figure A1.1 pokes up above the x-height line, and the bottom of the c and o, for example, dip below the baseline.

Appendix 2: On Bézier curves

This appendix contains a brief explanation of the mathematics behind the Bézier function and how it can be used to manipulate the curves used in type design and display. It is included in order to provide a fuller account of the techniques of digital display, and removed from the main text to an appendix due to its particularly technical nature that is not necessarily required in order to follow the main argument – but may nevertheless be of potential interest or usefulness to some readers.

A Bézier curve takes a parametric form, and is conventionally represented using the following general formula:

$$\boldsymbol{B}(x) = \sum_{i=0}^{n} \mathrm{C}_i^n (1-x)^{n-i} x^i \boldsymbol{P}_i$$

In this formula, $\boldsymbol{B}$ stands for the Bézier function itself, with x being the input parameter. The Bézier curve works only for values of x between 0 and 1. As these values of x are input, the formula outputs y values. These corresponding x and y values can be plotted as co-ordinates points on (imagined) mathematical axes. The output from the formula can thus be visually plotted to display a discrete section of curve. See Figure A2.1 and Figure A2.2 for examples.

With this formula, one is thus able to model a continuous, idealized curve whose specific expression and shape is determined by a series of anchor and control points that control the curve's specific shape. In the formula, these variable points are denoted by $\boldsymbol{P}$ and numbered using

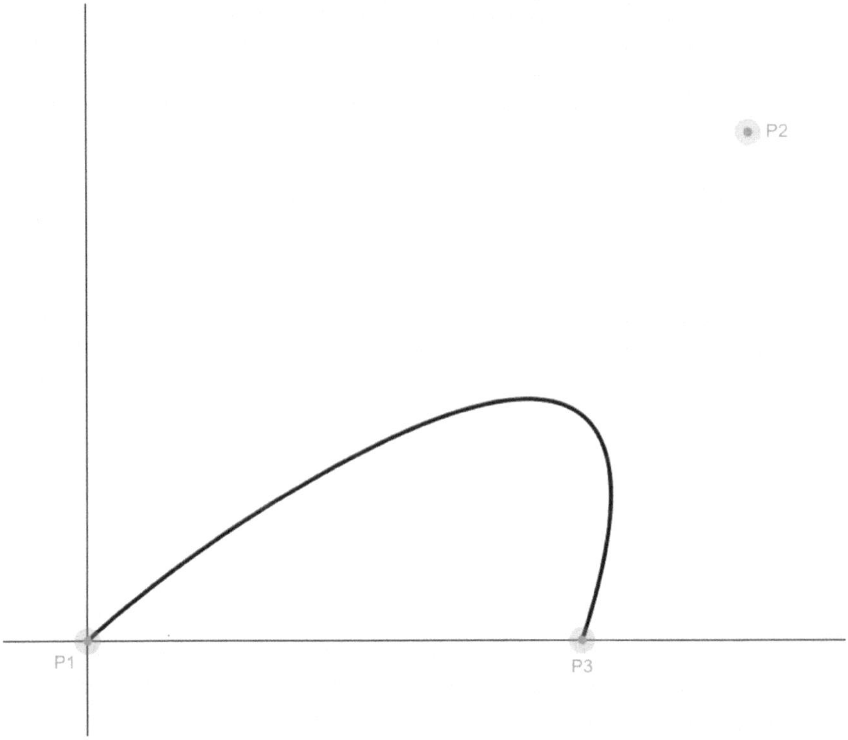

Figure A2.1: Example second order Bézier curve. Image credit: Thomas Giddens (generated using the Desmos graphic calculator available at https://www.desmos.com/calculator/cahqdxeshd; reproduced with permission).

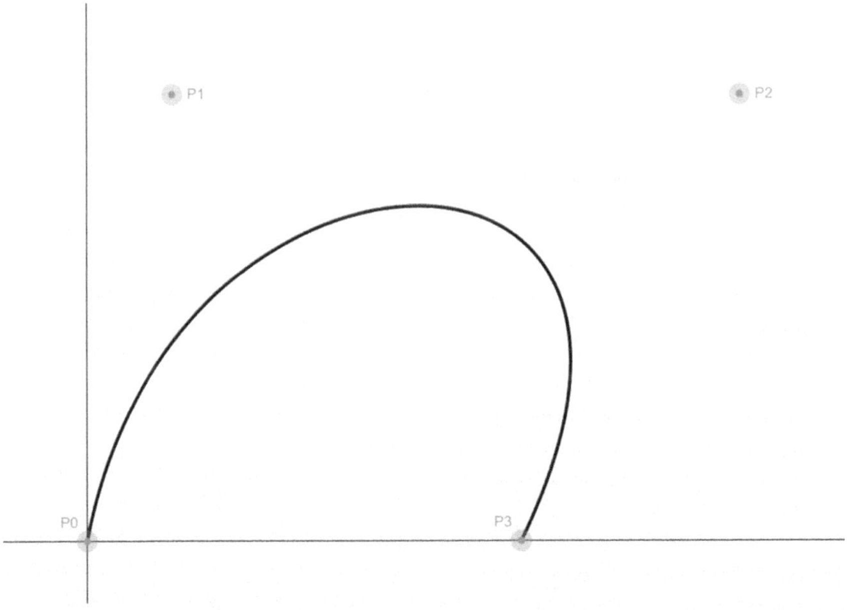

Figure A2.2: Example third order Bézier curve. Image credit: Thomas Giddens (generated using the Desmos graphic calculator available at https://www.desmos.com/calculator/cahqdxeshd; reproduced with permission).

subscript (i.e. $\boldsymbol{P}_0$ to $\boldsymbol{P}_n$). More complex curves require more control points, and in the general equation n denotes the order of the curve, implying the total number of anchor and control points. Font outlines are not stored as a single complex curve, as this would require either loss of detail or an unwieldy amount of control point data. For TrueType $n = 2$, so in a TrueType curve there are three points ($\boldsymbol{P}_0$, $\boldsymbol{P}_1$, and $\boldsymbol{P}_2$; see example curve in Figure A2.1) and four for a CFF curve (see example curve in Figure A2.2). The 'glyf' table in an OpenType font file contains the data for an ordered series of separate curves[1] that, when combined, construct the complex shape required for a letterform out of a number of shorter, simpler curves. This enables complex shapes to be stored within minimal coordinate data.

Back to the formula. For each value of x that is plugged into it, the summation function (Σ) adds up the results of the formula for each integer (whole number) value of i, from 0 up to the designated order of the curve, n.[2] The following shows the working for resolving the formula for $n = 3$ (which is the order used in CFF files). It shows each individual term that the summation function would compile, and then resolves these to it most basic form.

$$\boldsymbol{B}(x) = \sum_{i=0}^{3} \mathrm{C}_i^3 (1-x)^{3-i} x^i \boldsymbol{P}_i$$

$$\boldsymbol{B}(x) = \mathrm{C}_0^3 (1-x)^{3-0} x^0 \boldsymbol{P}_0 + \mathrm{C}_1^3 (1-x)^{3-1} x^1 \boldsymbol{P}_1 + \mathrm{C}_2^3 (1-x)^{3-2} x^2 \boldsymbol{P}_2 + \mathrm{C}_3^3 (1-x)^{3-3} x^3 \boldsymbol{P}_3$$

$$\boldsymbol{B}(x) = 1(1-x)^3 1\boldsymbol{P}_0 + 3(1-x)^2 x\boldsymbol{P}_1 + 3(1-x)^1 x^2 \boldsymbol{P}_2 + 1(1-x)^0 x^3 \boldsymbol{P}_3$$

$$\boldsymbol{B}(x) = (1-x)^3 \boldsymbol{P}_0 + 3(1-x)^2 x\boldsymbol{P}_1 + 3(1-x) x^2 \boldsymbol{P}_2 + x^3 \boldsymbol{P}_3$$

The anchor and control points ($\boldsymbol{P}_{0\text{-}3}$) are in play and affecting the shape of the curve at every moment along its resolution. The effect of adding another control point on the shape of the curve can be seen by comparing Figure A2.1 and Figure A2.2. We can also see the influence of control points algebraically, if we follow the process by which a curve would be plotted for varying values of x input into the formula. As noted, Bézier curves are designed to work only for values of x from 0 and 1. The curve follows x's journey along the real number line from 0 to 1.[3]

When $x = 0$, in the first term P_0 is multiplied by $(1 - 0)^3$, which equals 1, so the first term is just the value of $1{\cdot}P_0$, (i.e. P_0). Each of the other terms involve the control points being multiplied in one way or another by x, and since $x = 0$ the value of each of those terms becomes 0. This means the result when $x = 0$ is simply the value of P_0 (i.e. the starting point, or first anchor point, of the curve). Here is the resolution in algebraic form:

$$\boldsymbol{B}(x) = (1 - x)^3\boldsymbol{P}_0 + 3(1 - x)^2x\boldsymbol{P}_1 + 3(1 - x)x^2\boldsymbol{P}_2 + x^3\boldsymbol{P}_3$$

$$\boldsymbol{B}(x) = (1 - 0)^3\boldsymbol{P}_0 + 3(1 - 0)^2 0\boldsymbol{P}_1 + 3(1 - 0)0^2\boldsymbol{P}_2 + 0^3\boldsymbol{P}_3$$

$$\boldsymbol{B}(x) = 1 \cdot \boldsymbol{P}_0 + 0 \cdot \boldsymbol{P}_1 + 0 \cdot \boldsymbol{P}_2 + 0 \cdot \boldsymbol{P}_3$$

$$\boldsymbol{B}(x) = \boldsymbol{P}_0$$

When $x = 1$, all but the final term is multiplied in one way or another by $(1 - 1)$, which equals 0, so the value of each of those terms becomes 0. Meanwhile, P_n is only multiplied by x (i.e. is $1{\cdot}P_n$). This means the result when $x = 1$ is simply the value of P_n (i.e. the ending point, or final anchor point, of the curve). Again, here is the algebraic version:

$$\boldsymbol{B}(x) = (1 - x)^3\boldsymbol{P}_0 + 3(1 - x)^2x\boldsymbol{P}_1 + 3(1 - x)x^2\boldsymbol{P}_2 + x^3\boldsymbol{P}_3$$

$$\boldsymbol{B}(x) = (1 - 1)^3\boldsymbol{P}_0 + 3(1 - 1)^2 1\boldsymbol{P}_1 + 3(1 - 1)1^2\boldsymbol{P}_2 + 1^3\boldsymbol{P}_3$$

$$\boldsymbol{B}(x) = (0)^3\boldsymbol{P}_0 + 3(0)^2 1\boldsymbol{P}_1 + 3(0)1^2\boldsymbol{P}_2 + 1^3\boldsymbol{P}_3$$

$$\boldsymbol{B}(x) = 0 \cdot \boldsymbol{P}_0 + 0 \cdot \boldsymbol{P}_1 + 0 \cdot \boldsymbol{P}_2 + 1 \cdot \boldsymbol{P}_3$$

$$\boldsymbol{B}(x) = \boldsymbol{P}_3$$

To summarize, in the Bézier function, as the numerical value of x journeys along the real number line between 0 and 1, a curve is generated in mathematical space that begins with a value equal to the first point, moves in a continuous gesture through the values determined by the subsequent control point(s), and ends with a value equal to the final point. A series of these curves can then be assembled to describe the outline of a complex shape, such as a letterform or a Renault car, that can be scaled infinitely for digital display while requiring only minimal coordinate data.

Notes

1. See https://learn.microsoft.com/en-us/typography/opentype/spec/glyf (accessed 8 May 2025).
2. For more details on how various elements of the function operate and resolve (for example, the combination function C), see this introductory guide: https://medium.freecodecamp.org/nerding-out-with-bezier-curves-6e3c0bc48e2f (accessed 2 May 2025).
3. The real number line is a concept in pure mathematics denoting an imagined continuity of numerical value, as opposed to e.g. the discontinuous sequence of integers (1, 2, 3, . . .) or decimals (1.1, 1.2, 1.3, . . .).

References

Aamodt, Athelstane. 'Legal Typeface: The Letter of the Law'. *New Law Journal* 166, no. 7703 (2016): 22.

Anderson, Benedict. *Imagined Communities: Reflections on the Origin and Spread of Nationalism*. Revised edn. Verso, 2016.

Arditi, Aries, and Jianna Cho. 'Serifs and Font Legibility'. *Vision Research* 45 (2005): 2926–33.

Augsberg, Ino. 'Reading Law: On Law as a Textual Phenomenon'. *Law and Literature* 22, no. 3 (2010): 26.

Baker, John. 'Law Reporting in England 1550–1650'. *International Journal of Legal Information* 45, no. 3 (2017): 209–18.

Barad, Karen, and Daniela Gandorfer. 'Political Desirings: Yearnings for Mattering (,) Differently'. *Theory and Event* 24, no. 1 (2021): 14–66.

Barr, Olivia. 'A Jurisprudential Tale of a Road, an Office, and a Triangle'. *Law and Literature* 27 (2015): 199–216.

Barry, P. 'Bézier Curve'. In *Encyclopaedia of Mathematics,* edited by Michael E. Mortensen. Springer, 1997.

Bell, John. 'Sources of Law'. *The Cambridge Law Journal* 77, no. 1 (2018): 40–71.

Bewell, Alan. *Natures in Translation: Romanticism and Colonial Natural History*. Johns Hopkins University Press, 2017.

Bewell, Alan. 'Romanticism and Colonial Natural History'. *Studies in Romanticism* 43, no. 1 (2004): 5.

Biber, Katherine, Trish Luker, and Priya Vaughan, eds. *Law's Documents: Authority, Materiality, Aesthetics*. Routledge, 2022.

Biber, Katherine, Trish Luker, and Priya Vaughan. 'Law's Documents: Authority, Materiality, Aesthetics'. In *Law's Documents: Authority, Materiality, Aesthetics,* edited by Katherine Biber, Trish Luker, and Priya Vaughan. Routledge, 2022.

Bland, Mark. 'The Appearance of the Text in Early Modern England.' *Text* 11 (1998): 91–154.

Breckman, Warren. 'Marx and Romanticism.' *Critical Review* 34, no. 1 (2022): 28–52.

Bringhurst, Robert. *The Elements of Typographic Style.* Hartley and Marks, 2002.

Brown, Dan. *The Da Vinci Code.* Doubleday, 2003.

Brown, Marshall. 'Romanticism and Enlightenment.' In *The Cambridge Companion to British Romanticism*, 2nd ed., edited by Stuart Curran. Cambridge University Press, 2010.

Brumberger, Eva R. 'The Rhetoric of Typography: The Persona of Typeface and Text.' *Technical Communication* 50, no. 2 (2003): 206–23.

Butterick, Matthew. 'A Brief History of Times New Roman.' In *Typography for Lawyers*, 2nd ed. 2018. https://typographyforlawyers.com/a-brief-history-of-times-new-roman.html.

Butterick, Matthew. *Typography for Lawyers.* 2nd ed. 2018. https://typographyforlawyers.com/.

Butterick, Matthew. 'What Is Good Typography?' In *Typography for Lawyers*, 2nd ed. 2018. https://typographyforlawyers.com/what-is-good-typography.html.

Campbell, Kurt. 'The Sociogenic Imperative of Typography: A "Face" for the New South Africa.' *European Journal of English Studies* 17, no. 1 (2013): 72–91.

Carter, Harry. *A View of Early Typography up to about 1600.* Hyphen Press, 2002.

Chryssostalis, Julia. '*Nomos* Is an Air: Hearing as a Juridical Faculty.' In *HEAR*, edited by Danilo Mandic, Caterina Nirta, and Andreas Philippopoulos-Mihalopoulos. University of Westminster Press, 2023.

Cormack, Bradin. *A Power to Do Justice: Justice, Jurisdiction, English Literature, and the Rise of Common Law, 1509–1625.* University of Chicago Press, 2008.

Cover, Robert M. 'Foreword: Nomos and Narrative.' *Harvard Law Review* 97 (1983): 4–68; 4.

Cowan, Jake. 'Typographic Nationalism and the Banal Uniformity of Imagined Communities.' In *Type Matters: The Rhetoricity of Letterforms*, edited by Christopher Scott Wyatt and Dànielle Nicole DeVoss. Parlour Press, 2018.

Cozens, Simon. *Advanced Perl Programming.* 2nd ed. O'Reilly Media, 2005.

Daniel, WTS. *The History and Origin of the Law Reports.* William Clowes and Sons, 1884.

Dawson, John P. *The Oracles of the Law*. University Press of Michigan, 1968.

De Robertis, Teresa. 'Humanistic Script: Origins.' In *The Oxford Handbook of Latin Paleography*, edited by Frank T. Coulson and Robert G. Babcock. Oxford University Press, 2020.

Deleuze, Gilles. *Difference and Repetition*. Continuum, 1994.

Derrida, Jacques. 'Archive Fever: A Freudian Impression.' *Diacritics* 25, no. 2 (1995): 9.

Derrida, Jacques. 'Force of Law: The "Mystical Foundation of Authority".' *Cardozo Law Review* 11 (1990): 920–1045.

Donachuk, Aaron. 'After the Letter: Typographical Distraction and the Surface of Morris's Kelmscott Romances.' *Victorian Studies* 59, no. 2 (2017): 260–87.

Dorsett, Shaunnagh. '"Since Time Immemorial": A Story of Common Law Jurisdiction, Native Title and the Case of Tanistry.' *Melbourne University Law Review* 26 (2002): 32–59.

Dorsett, Shaunnagh, and Shaun McVeigh. *Jurisdiction*. Routledge, 2012.

Dreyfus, John, ed. *Type Specimen Facsimiles [1–15]: Reproduction of Fifteen Type Specimen Sheets Issued Between the Sixteenth and Eighteenth Centuries*. Bowes, 1963.

Dreyfus, John, ed. *Type Specimen Facsimiles [16–18]: Reproductions of Christopher Plantin's 'Idex Sive Specimen Characterum' 1567 and Folio Specimens of c. 1585, Together with the Le Bé-Moretus Specimen, c. 1599*. Bodley Head, 1972.

Drucker, Johanna. *Visualization and Interpretation: Humanistic Approaches to Display*. The MIT Press, 2020.

Duncan, Rhys. 'Battle of the Fonts: What's the Best Typeface for Lawyers?' *Legal Cheek*, 23 December 2024. https://www.legalcheek.com/2024/12/battle-of-the-fonts-whats-the-best-typeface-for-lawyers/.

Eisenstein, Elizabeth. *The Printing Press as an Agent of Change*. Cambridge University Press, 1980.

Eliason, Craig. 'A History of the "Humanist" Type Classification.' *Printing History* 18 (2015): 3–26.

Engholm, Ida, and Karen Lisa Salamon. 'Design Thinking Between Rationalism and Romanticism.' *Artifact* 4, no. 1 (2017): E1.1–E1.18.

Febvre, Lucien, and Henri-Jean Martin. *The Coming of the Book*. Verso, 1997.

Gaakeer, Jeanne. *Judging from Experience: Law, Praxis, Humanities*. Edinburgh University Press, 2019.

Gandorfer, Daniela. *Matterphorics: On the Laws of Theory*. Duke University Press, forthcoming.

Gearey, Adam. 'The Poetics of Practical Reason: Joseph Raz and Philip Larkin'. *Law and Literature* 19, no. 3 (2007): 377–99.

Gibson, Hayley. 'Reopening the Archive: From Hypomnesis to the Ontology of Law'. In *Law and Philosophical Theory: Critical Intersections*, edited by Thanos Zartaloudis. Rowman and Littlefield, 2018.

Giddens, Thomas. 'A Series of Unfortunate Events *or* The Common Law'. *Law and Literature* 33, no. 1 (2021): 23–48.

Giddens, Thomas. 'Institution and Abyss'. *Law, Technology and Humans* 2, no. 2 (2020): 150–71.

Giddens, Thomas. *Judgment: New Trajectories in Law*. Routledge, 2022.

Giddens, Thomas. 'Keeping up Textual Appearances: The UK Road Vehicles (Display of Registration Marks) Regulations 2001'. *Law, Technology and Humans*, 2020.

Giddens, Thomas. 'Legal Aesthetics as Visual Method'. In *Routledge Handbook of Socio-Legal Theory and Methods*, edited by Naomi Creutzfeldt, Marc Mason, and Kirsten McConnachie. Routledge, 2019.

Giddens, Thomas. 'Multiframe Fever: Comics as Archive'. *Studies in Comics* 14, no. 2 (2023): 263–79.

Giddens, Thomas. 'Sentences Matter: Law and the Typographic Imaginary'. *CounterText* 11, no. 1 (2025): 94–113.

Giddens, Thomas, Karen Crawley, and Timothy D. Peters. 'Cultural Legal Studies: Methodologies of Reflexive Attunement'. In *The Routledge Handbook of Cultural Legal Studies*, edited by Karen Crawley, Thomas Giddens, and Timothy D. Peters. Routledge, 2024.

Goh, Benjamin. 'Dream of the Legal Monograph'. *Law, Culture and the Humanities*, 2024, 1–17.

Goh, Benjamin. 'Two Ways of Looking at a Printed Book'. *Modern Law Review* 85, no. 3 (2022): 697–725.

Goodrich, Peter. *Advanced Introduction to Law and Literature*. Edward Elgar, 2021.

Goodrich, Peter. 'Critical Legal Studies in England: Prospective Histories'. *Oxford Journal of Legal Studies* 12, no. 2 (1992): 195–236.

Goodrich, Peter. '*Imago Decidendi*: On the Common Law of Images'. *Art and Law* 1, no. 1 (2017): 1–57.

Goodrich, Peter. 'Intellection and Indiscipline'. *Journal of Law and Society* 36 (2009): 460–80.

Goodrich, Peter. *Judicial Uses of Images: Vision in Decision*. Oxford University Press, 2023.

Goodrich, Peter. *Languages of Law: From Logics of Memory to Nomadic Masks.* Weidenfeld and Nicolson, 1990.

Goodrich, Peter. *Legal Emblems and the Art of Law:* Obiter Depicta *as the Vision of Governance.* Cambridge University Press, 2013.

Goodrich, Peter. 'Legal Enigmas – Antonio de Nebrija, *The Da Vinci Code* and the Emendation of Law'. *Oxford Journal of Legal Studies* 30, no. 1 (2010): 71–99.

Goodrich, Peter. *Oedipus Lex: Psychoanalysis, History, Law.* University of California Press, 1995.

Goodrich, Peter. 'Oedipus Lex: Slips in Interpretation and Law'. *Legal Studies* 13, no. 03 (1993): 381–95.

Goodrich, Peter. 'Specters of Law: Why the History of the Legal Spectacle Has Not Been Written'. *UC Irvine Law Review* 1 (2011): 773–812.

Goodrich, Peter. 'The Emblem Book and Common Law'. In *The Oxford Handbook of English Law and Literature, 1500–1700,* edited by Lorna Hutson. Oxford University Press, 2017.

Goodrich, Peter. 'The Example of Undressing: Obnubilations on the Empty Space of the Rule'. *Law and Literature* 30, no. 3 (2018): 409–22.

Goodrich, Peter. 'The Iconography of Nothing: Blank Spaces and the Representation of Law in *Edward VI and the Pope*'. In *Law and the Image: The Authority of Art and the Aesthetics of Law,* edited by Costas Douzinas and Lynda Nead. University of Chicago Press, 1999.

Goodrich, Peter. 'The Theatre of Emblems: On the Optical Apparatus and the Investiture of Persons'. *Law, Culture and the Humanities* 8 (2012): 47–67.

Goodrich, Peter. 'Visive Powers: Colours, Trees and Genres of Jurisdiction'. *Law and Humanities* 2 (2008): 213–31.

Granet, Elijah. 'Despair at the Supreme Court'. *Notes on the Style of the Law,* 27 December 2021. https://www.legalstyle.co.uk/2021/12/despair-at-supreme-court.html.

Harvey, David. *The Law Emprynted and Englysshed: The Printing Press as an Agent of Change in Law and Legal Culture 1475–1642.* Hart, 2017.

Hawkins, Ames. 'Why I Hate Times New Roman, and Other Confessions of a Creative-Critical Scholar'. In *Type Matters: The Rhetoricity of Letterforms.* Parlour Press, 2018.

Helgerson, Richard. *Forms of Nationhood: The Elizabethan Writing of England.* University of Chicago Press, 1992.

Herbert, Frank. *Dune.* New English Library, 1985.

Hurley, Suzanne Suarez. 'Advancing the Legal Profession with Typography'. *The Florida Bar Journal* 86, no. 9 (2012): 53–57.

Hussain, Aishah. '"Legal Font Wars": Supreme Court's Switch to Calibri Sparks Debate among Lawyers'. *Legal Cheek*, 22 December 2021. https://www.legalcheek.com/2021/12/legal-font-wars-supreme-courts-switch-to-calibri-sparks-debate-among-lawyers/.

Hyndman, Sarah. 'The Ultimate Font Face-off: Serif vs sans Serif in the Psychological Battle of Font Personalities'. *Type Tasting*, 16 February 2023. https://www.typetasting.com/blog-1/2023/2/16/the-ultimate-font-face-off-serif-vs-sans-serif-in-the-psychological-battle-of-font-personalities.

Illich, Ivan. *In the Vineyard of the Text: A Commentary of Hugh's* Didascalicon. University of Chicago Press, 1993.

Isaac, Frank. *English Printers' Types of the Sixteenth Century*. Oxford University Press, 1936.

Keedy, Mr. 'Zombie Modernism'. In *Texts on Type: Critical Writings on Typography*, edited by Steven Heller and Philip B. Meggs. Allworth, 2001.

Kiernan-Johnson, Derek H. 'Telling Through Type: Typography and Narrative in Legal Briefs'. *Journal of the Association of Legal Writing Directors* 7 (2010): 87–122.

Kinross, Robin. *Modern Typography: An Essay in Critical History*. Éditions B42, 2019.

Kostelnick, Charles, and Michael Hassett. *Shaping Information: The Rhetoric of Visual Conventions*. Southern Illinois University Press, 2003.

Lawson, Alexander. *Anatomy of a Typeface*. Hamish Hamilton, 1990.

Legal Geek. 'Legal Design WTF?' 2018. http://legalgeek.co/learn/legal-design-wtf.

Legendre, Pierre. *God in the Mirror: A Study of the Institution of Images (Lessons III)*. Translated by P. G. Young. Routledge, 2019.

Liddle, Dallas. 'The News Machine: Textual Form and Information Function in the London Times, 1785–1885'. *Book History* 19, no. 1 (2016): 132–68.

Lupton, Ellen. 'A Post-Mortem on Deconstruction?' In *Texts on Type: Critical Writings on Typography*, edited by Steven Heller and Philip B. Meggs. Allworth, 2001.

Lupton, Ellen. *Thinking With Type: A Critical Guide for Designers, Writers, Editors, and Students*. 2nd ed. Princeton Architectural Press, 2010.

Lyotard, Jean-François. *Discourse, Figure*. University of Minnesota Press, 2010.

MacCormick, Neil. *Rhetoric and the Rule of Law: A Theory of Legal Reasoning*. Oxford University Press, 2005.

MacDonald, Michael. 'Empire and Communication: The Media Wars of Marshall McLuhan'. *Media, Culture and Society* 28, no. 4 (2006): 505–20.

Mak, Bonnie. *How the Page Matters*. University of Toronto Press, 2011.

Manderson, Desmond. 'Bodies in the Water: On Reading Images More Sensibly'. *Law and Literature* 27, no. 2 (2015): 279–93.

Manderson, Desmond. *Songs without Music: Aesthetic Dimensions of Law and Justice*. University of California Press, 2000.

Mann, Meredith. 'Where Did Times New Roman Come From?' *The New York Public Library*, 9 December 2014. https://live-legacy-admin.nypl.org/blog/2014/12/09/times-new-roman.

Maroney, Terry A. 'The Persistent Cultural Script of Judicial Dispassion'. *California Law Review* 99 (2011a): 629–81.

Matthews, Daniel. 'From Jurisdiction to Juriswriting: At the Expressive Limits of the Law'. *Law, Culture and the Humanities* 13, no. 3 (2017): 425–45.

Matthews, Daniel. 'The Aesthetics of Sovereignty'. In *The Routledge Handbook of Cultural Legal Studies*, edited by Karen Crawley, Thomas Giddens, and Timothy D. Peters. Routledge, 2024.

Mawani, Renisa. 'Law's Archive'. *Annual Review of Law and Social Science* 8 (2012): 337–65.

Moran, Leslie J. 'Judicial Bodies as Sexual Bodies: A Tale of Two Portraits'. *The Australian Feminist Law Journal* 29 (2008): 91–108.

Morison, Stanley. *Printing The Times Since 1785*. Printing House Square, 1953.

Morison, Stanley. *The English Newspaper: An Account of the Physical Development of Journals Printed in London 1622–1932*. Cambridge University Press, 1932.

Morison, Stanley. *Type Designs of the Past and Present*. The Fleuron, 1926.

Mulcahy, Linda. 'Architects of Justice: The Politics of Courtroom Design'. *Social and Legal Studies* 16, no. 3 (2007): 383–403.

Mulcahy, Linda. *Legal Architecture: Justice, Due Process and the Place of Law*. London: Routledge, 2011.

Mussawir, Edward. *Jurisdiction in Deleuze: The Expression and Representation of Law*. Routledge, 2011.

Nancy, Jean-Luc. *The Pleasure in Drawing*. Translated by Philip Armstrong. Fordham University Press, 2013.

Nietzsche, Friedrich. 'On Truth and Lies in a Nonmoral Sense'. In *The Rhetorical Tradition: Readings from Classical Times to the Present*, edited by P. Bizzell and B. Herzberg. Bedford Books, 1990.

Nussbaum, Martha C. *Poetic Justice: The Literary Imagination in Public Life*. Beacon Press, 1995.

Ong, Walter J. *Orality and Literacy: The Technologizing of the Word*. Routledge, 1988.

Parker, Mike. 'W Starling Burgess, Type Designer?' *Printing History* 16, nos. 1–2 (1994): 52–108.

Parkes, M. B. *Pause and Effect: An Introduction to the History of Punctuation in the West*. Routledge, 2016.

Peters, Julie Stone. *Law as Performance: Theatricality, Spectatorship, and the Making of Law in Ancient, Medieval, and Early Modern Europe*. Oxford University Press, 2022.

Philippopoulos-Mihalopoulos, Andreas. *Spatial Justice: Body, Lawscape, Atmosphere*. Routledge, 2014.

Philippopoulos-Mihalopoulos, Andreas. 'The World Without Outside'. *Angelaki* 18, no. 4 (2013): 165–77.

Phillips, Anne. 'Gender and Modernity'. *Political Theory* 46, no. 6 (2018): 837–60.

Piper, Andrew. *Dreaming in Books: The Making of the Bibliographic Imagination in the Romantic Age*. University of Chicago Press, 2009.

Plucknett, Theodore F. T. *A Concise History of the Common Law*. Liberty Fund, 2010.

Poovey, Mary. *A History of the Modern Fact: Problems of Knowledge in the Sciences of Wealth and Society*. University of Chicago Press, 1998.

Ramamurthy, Mahalakshmi, and Vasudevan Lakshminarayanan. 'Human Vision and Perception'. In *Handbook of Advanced Lighting Technology*, edited by Robert Karlicek, Ching-Cherng Sun, Georges Zissis, and Ruiqing Ma. Springer, 2015.

Ridler, Victoria L. 'The Exercise of Jurisdiction and the Absent Author of Law's Speech'. *Law and Literature* 31, no. 1 (2019): 71–93.

Robertson, Frances. *Print Culture: From Steam Press to Ebook*. Routledge, 2013.

Rodgers, C. P. 'Humanism, History and the Common Law'. *The Journal of Legal History* 6, no. 2 (1985): 129–56.

Ross, Richard J. 'The Commoning of the Common Law: The Renaissance Debate over Printing English Law, 1520–1640'. *University of Pennsylvania Law Review* 146, no. 2 (1998): 323.

Rumsey, Jean P. 'Re-Visions of Agency in Kant's Moral Theory'. In *Feminist Interpretations of Immanuel Kant*, edited by Robin May Schott. Pennsylvania State University Press, 1997.

Rush, Peter. 'An Altered Jurisdiction: Corporeal Traces of Law'. *Griffith Law Review* 6 (1997): 144–68.

Samerski, Silja. 'Tools for Degrowth? Ivan Illich's Critique of Technology Revisited'. *Journal of Cleaner Production* 197 (2018): 1637–49.

Sarat, Austin. 'Editorial'. *Law, Culture and the Humanities* 9, no. 2 (2013): 205.

Savoie, Alice. 'The Women Behind Times New Roman: The Contribution of Type Drawing Offices to Twentieth Century Type-Making'. *Journal of Design History* 33, no. 3 (2020): 209–24.

Serafini, Frank, and Jennifer Clausen. 'Typography as Semiotic Resource'. *Journal of Visual Literacy* 31, no. 2 (2012): 1–16.

Shoemaker, Karl. '*The King's Two Bodies* as Lamentation'. *Law, Culture and the Humanities* 13, no. 1 (2017): 24–35.

Simpson, Gerry. '*Mabo*, International Law, *Terra Nullius* and the Stories of Settlement'. *Melbourne University Law Review* 19 (1993): 195.

Siskin, Clifford, and William Warner. 'If This Is Enlightenment Then What Is Romanticism?' *European Romantic Review* 22, no. 3 (2011): 281–91.

Smejkalová, Terezie. 'Legal Performance: Translating into Law and Subjectivity in Law'. *Tilburg Law Review* 22 (2017): 62–76.

Smiles, Samuel. *Men of Invention and Industry*. John Murray, 1884.

Steedman, Carolyn. *Dust*. Manchester University Press, 2001.

Stenner, Rachel. *The Typographic Imaginary in Early Modern English Literature*. Routledge, 2019.

Tans, Olaf. 'The Imaginary Foundation of Legal Systems: A Mimetic Perspective'. *Law and Literature* 26, no. 2 (2014): 127–43.

Tanselle, Thomas. 'The Concept of "Ideal Copy"'. *Studies in Bibliography* 33 (53): 18.

Tranter, Kieran. *Living in Technical Legality: Science Fiction and Law as Technology*. Edinburgh University Press, 2017.

Tschichold, Jan. 'The Principles of the New Typography'. In *Texts on Type: Critical Writings on Typography*. Allworth, 2001.

Ullman, B. L. *The Origin and Development of Humanistic Script*. Edizioni di Storia e Letteratura, 1960.

Vervliet, Hendrick D. L. 'Printing Types of Pierre Haultin (ca. 1510–87) Part I: Roman Types'. *Querendo* 30, no. 2 (2000): 87–129.

Vismann, Cornelia. 'Cancels: On the Making of Law in Chanceries'. *Law and Critique* 7, no. 2 (1996): 131–52.

Vismann, Cornelia. 'Cultural Techniques and Sovereignty'. *Theory, Culture and Society* 30, no. 6 (2013): 83–93.

Vismann, Cornelia. 'Derrida, Philosopher of the Law'. *German Law Journal* 6, no. 1 (2005).

Vismann, Cornelia. *Files: Law and Media Technology*. Translated by Geoffrey Winthrop-Young. Stanford University Press, 2008.

Vismann, Cornelia. 'Jurisprudence: A Transfer Science'. *Law and Critique* 10 (1999): 279–86.

Vismann, Cornelia. '*"Rejouer Les Crimes"* – Theater vs. Video'. *Law and Literature* 11, no. 2 (1999): 161–77.

Vismann, Cornelia. 'Tele-Tribunals: Anatomy of a Medium'. Translated by Sara Ogger. *Grey Room* 10 (January 2003): 5–21.

Vismann, Cornelia. 'Three Versions of a Defendant's Final Statement to the Court'. *Law and Literature* 23, no. 3 (2011): 297–308.

Vismann, Cornelia, and Markus Krajewski. 'Computer Juridisms'. *Grey Room* 29 (2007): 90–109.

Wall, Illan, and Daniel Matthews. 'Sovereignty and the Persistence of the Aesthetic'. *Modern Law Review* 87, no. 6 (2024): 1393–421.

Wall, Illan rua. 'The Ordinary Affects of Law'. *Law, Culture and the Humanities* 19, no. 2 (2019): 191–209.

Walters, Mark D. 'Legal Humanism and Law-as-Integrity'. *The Cambridge Law Journal* 67, no. 2 (2008): 352–75.

Warnock, John E., and Charles Geschke. 'Founding and Growing Adobe Systems, Inc'. *IEEE Annals of the History of Computing* 41, no. 3 (2019): 24–34.

Warnock Pro: A Multi-Faceted OpenType Family. Adobe Systems Incorporated, 2000.

Watson, Irene. 'Re-Centring First Nations Knowledge and Places in a Terra Nullius Space'. *AlterNative: An International Journal of Indigenous Peoples* 10, no. 5 (2014): 508–20.

Watt, Gary. *Dress, Law and Naked Truth: A Cultural Study of Fashion and Form*. London: Bloomsbury, 2013.

White, James Boyd. 'Imagining the Law'. In *The Rhetoric of Law*, edited by Austin Sarat and Thomas R. Kearns. University of Michigan Press, 1996.

White, James Boyd. 'Law as Rhetoric, Rhetoric as Law: The Arts of Cultural and Communal Life'. *The University of Chicago Law Review* 52, no. 3 (1985): 684–702.

Williams, Ian. 'Early-Modern Judges and the Practice of Precedent.' In *Judges and Judging in the History of the Common and Civil Law: From Antiquity to Modern Times*, edited by Joshua Getzler and Paul Brand. Cambridge University Press, 2012.

Williams, Ian. '"He Creditted More the Printed Booke": Common Lawyers' Receptivity to Print, c. 1550–1640.' *Law and History Review* 28, no. 1 (2010): 39–70.

Wyatt, Christopher Scott. 'On Type and Typographic Anatomy.' In *Type Matters: The Rhetoricity of Letterforms*, edited by Christopher Scott Wyatt and Dànielle Nicole DeVoss. Parlour Press, 2018.

Wyatt, Christopher Scott, and Dànielle Nicole DeVoss, eds. *Type Matters: The Rhetoricity of Letterforms*. Parlour Press, 2018.

Zurcher, Andrew. 'Spenser, Plowden, and the Hypallactic Instrument.' In *The Oxford Handbook of Law and Literature, 1500–1700*, edited by Lorna Hutson. Oxford University Press, 2017.

Index

EU Authorised Representative:
Easy Access System Europe Mustamäe tee 50, 10621 Tallinn, Estonia
gpsr.requests@easproject.com

Printed and bound by CPI Group (UK) Ltd, Croydon, CR0 4YY
18/06/2026
02142231-0001